ASPECTS OF TOURISM TEXTS
Series Editors: Chris Cooper (*Oxford Brookes University, UK*),
C. Michael Hall (*University of Canterbury, New Zealand*)
and Dallen J. Timothy (*Arizona State University, USA*)

Human Resources and Tourism
Skills, Culture and Industry

Darren Lee-Ross and Josephine Pryce

CHANNEL VIEW PUBLICATIONS
Bristol • Buffalo • Toronto

Library of Congress Cataloging in Publication Data
Lee-Ross, Darren.
Human Resources and Tourism: Skills, Culture and Industry/Darren Lee-Ross and
Josephine Pryce.
Aspects of Tourism Texts: v.2
Includes bibliographical references and index.
1. Tourism–Management. 2. Personnel management. I. Pryce, Josephine. II. Title. III. Series.
G155.A1L42 2010
910.68'3–dc22   2010005009

British Library Cataloguing in Publication Data
A catalogue entry for this book is available from the British Library.

ISBN-13: 978-1-84541-140-4 (hbk)
ISBN-13: 978-1-84541-139-8 (pbk)

Channel View Publications
UK: St Nicholas House, 31–34 High Street, Bristol BS1 2AW, UK.
USA: UTP, 2250 Military Road, Tonawanda, NY 14150, USA.
Canada: UTP, 5201 Dufferin Street, North York, Ontario M3H 5T8, Canada.

The policy of Multilingual Matters/Channel View Publications is to use papers that are natural,
renewable and recyclable products, made from wood grown in sustainable forests. In the
manufacturing process of our books, and to further support our policy, preference is given to
printers that have FSC and PEFC Chain of Custody certification. The FSC and/or PEFC logos
will appear on those books where full certification has been granted to the printer concerned.

Typeset by The Charlesworth Group.
Printed and bound in Great Britain by the MPG Books Group.

Human Resources and Tourism

ASPECTS OF TOURISM TEXTS
Series Editors: Professor Chris Cooper, *Oxford Brookes University, UK*
Dr C. Michael Hall, *University of Canterbury, Christchurch, New Zealand*
Dr Dallen J. Timothy, *Arizona State University, Tempe, USA*

This new series of textbooks aims to provide a comprehensive set of titles for higher level undergraduate and postgraduate students. The titles will be focused on identified areas of need and reflect a contemporary approach to tourism curriculum design. The books are specially written to focus on the needs, interests and skills of students and academics. They will have an easy-to-use format with clearly defined learning objectives at the beginning of each chapter, comprehensive summary material, end of chapter review questions and further reading and websites sections. The books will be international in scope with examples and cases drawn from all over the world.

Full details of all the books in this series and of all our other publications can be found on http://www.channelviewpublications.com, or by writing to Channel View Publications, St Nicholas House, 31–34 High Street, Bristol BS1 2AW, UK.

CONTENTS

PREFACE

There can be no doubting the key global economic role of the tourism sector. Some argue that it is the world's largest industry, some disagree. However, what cannot be denied are the many millions of people for whom it provides employment. Furthermore, despite global and national catastrophes, the industry has proved resilient – growing to unprecedented levels. This characteristic is unlikely to change in the future and will help ensure that tourism is a major employer and contributor to national and global wealth in both developed and increasingly emerging economies.

Despite technological advancements and their application to business procedures and operations, tourism remains a composite product, the key element being people. Indeed, so significant is the role employees play in service delivery that they too become a part of that product. From the authors' perspective, the input of tourism workers is that by which the product stands or falls. The role of human resource management in this context cannot therefore be overstated. Many employers are now beginning to understand this within an increasingly competitive and economically challenged environment.

The tourism workforce is heterogeneous with individuals having a wide variety of cultural differences and employment aspirations. This is due to complex and diverse structural characteristics of the industry, the employment relationship and the service product itself. This presents an intriguing canvas where human resource practice is often eclectic and, in some cases, atypical. Therefore, the study of human resource management in such a context becomes a fascinating look at a relatively deregulated industry. Understandably, it is necessary to adopt a perspective that is part prescriptive but, importantly, part enquiry or research-oriented. The authors believe this two-pronged approach is important as it accounts for the sometimes idiosyncratic nature of the tourism industry in human resource terms.

This book makes a conscious effort to combine theory and practice using a critical lens; thus, it is both descriptive and analytical. Moreover, our notion of human resource management is strategic. This reflects macro changes in business practices of sizeable firms and corporations but is also consistent with the traditional habits of small to medium-sized operators. In principle, the strategic approach is no different across sub-sectors although structural characteristics have a significant impact on practical human resource application.

Recent global developments have led to a reappraisal of human resource practice. In short, impacts of demography, global worker mobility, economic 'booms and busts', increasing workforce diversity and so on have all impacted on the employer/employee relationship. In some instances, employers have managed these changes proactively and positively, in others, the outcome has not been so enlightened. The aim of this book is to provide students with a sound theoretical and practical understanding of HRM. Furthermore, by using an inquisitive and probing style of narrative, we hope to instil a sense of enquiry in the reader, which is a necessary intellectual asset for the future. Therefore, a key feature of the book is its inclusion of learning outcomes at the beginning of each chapter and its use of 'critical notes' and 'reflective practice'. Furthermore, the text also presents a number of practical cases for further reflection and clarification of theoretical issues.

Chapter 1 reviews several notions of human resource management (HRM) and discusses the nature of services. It also grapples with the issue of defining tourism as an industry and introduces some characteristics of the sector which have been described by others as unique and challenging in an HRM context.

Chapter 2 considers human resources planning (HRP) within the broader context of strategic planning and discusses a number of HRP approaches. The issue of long standing job vacancies is identified together with a contingency approach in situations of labour shortage. The chapter concludes by noting the key impacts of 'downsizing' on both employers and workers.

Chapter 3 focuses on managing the employment process. It begins by discussing job analysis and job design, with a view to achieving high-performance and healthy workplaces. The chapter continues by exploring recruitment and selection. In particular, it considers the challenges faced by the tourism and hospitality industry. From there, managing the process progresses with an investigation of induction with consideration of its importance in orienting new employees and minimising problems associated with poor performance, reduced morale and labour turnover.

Chapter 4 begins by introducing performance management using a systems view to emphasise its essential strategic nature. It continues by highlighting some inherent difficulties of establishing performance management systems in the tourism and hospitality industry. Performance appraisals are then discussed together with an outline of key stages of the process. Perennial challenges based on subjectivity, perceptual distortion and context are also overviewed. The chapter concludes by identifying the phenomenon of self-appraisal and how it impacts on the performance appraisal together with a brief review of some common instruments used during performance interviews.

Chapter 5 sets out to explain the need and importance of training and development. It seeks to distinguish between the terms 'training' and 'development' and investigates various approaches to each. The chapter continues with consideration of 'education' and how it is linked to the process of employee training and development. It continues by discussing some issues relating to career development in the tourism and hospitality industry.

Chapter 6 examines the nature of 'work' and seeks to understand how employees and employers can work cooperatively toward achieving a balance between work and life. It discusses some of the benefits to both parties and within the process explores the role of occupational health and safety (OHS) in promoting safe and healthy workplaces. The chapter continues with an analysis of some current health issues affecting workplaces, especially tourism and hospitality organisations. In particular, it focuses on stress and describes ways of minimising the effects of stress.

Chapter 7 overviews the nature of industrial relations and how they relate to the tourism and hospitality industry. It explores understanding of the term 'industrial relations' and how it connects with human resource management and employee relations. From this platform the main theoretical approaches to industrial relations are investigated and the various stakeholders in industrial relations identified and discussed. The chapter concludes with an insight into the legal framework surrounding industrial relations.

Chapter 8 begins by contextualising diversity management in the broader category of migration and other demographic changes impacting on tourism firms. A generic understanding of culture is introduced prior to a brief discussion of global firms. Diversity management is defined and benefits accruing to the tourism firm identified. Perspectives of organisational diversity awareness are introduced followed by some major challenges to the overall notion of diversity management by category.

Chapter 9 begins with a discussion of generic ethical issues and developments in the business community. Using a tourism and hospitality focus, it then highlights some of the main ethical dilemmas therein. The chapter continues by discussing theoretical approaches to moral development and ethics. Human resources (HR) and the role of ethics in organisational contexts are then introduced together with a summary focus on codes of ethics/conduct and whistleblowing.

Chapter 10 considers the key issues which will affect the future of people and work in the tourism and hospitality sector. It debates the key role that HRM will play in the future of the industry. In so doing, the chapter touches on the talent shortage and discusses some of the implications for the industry. The chapter continues with a review of Generation Y and the ageing workforce and how related issues impact on the industry. Finally, the chapter considers the future of the tourism and hospitality professional.

CHAPTER 1

THE NATURE OF THE BEAST: HUMAN RESOURCES MANAGEMENT AND THE TOURISM CONTEXT

LEARNING OBJECTIVES

After working through this chapter you should be able to:

1. Understand the difficulties involved in attempting to define the tourism industry.

2. Identify the differences between personnel management and human resource management.

3. Understand the nature of services.

4. Identify the main challenges involved in establishing a human resource management strategy.

INTRODUCTION

The tourism industry is often described as complex, involving many dissimilar but related organisations along a supply chain (for example, consider the differences between an online travel agency and a luxury hotel). However, for those operating in the same sub-sector, strategic competitive advantage is becoming increasingly difficult to achieve. This is despite firms subscribing to any number of available quality accreditations and certification schemes (for example, see ISO 9001, Michelin, EHQ, AA and RAC, RACQ, Green Globe, Tourism Accreditation Australia Ltd, Sustainable Tourism Stewardship Council, UNWTO and so on). Seeking competitive advantage through accreditation may raise quality standards but also tends toward everyone offering a similar product, especially those participating in the same schemes. Points of differentiation or uniqueness become obscured, resulting in the delivery of a standardised service.

It has long been argued that people perform the most important role in tourism organisations. This is because, in an ever-frenetic marketplace, employees have the potential to provide a point of differentiation and thus competitive advantage within a sea of relative homogeneity (Kandampully, 2002). Indeed, the relationship between front-line

1

tourism workers and overall customer perceptions of service quality cannot be overstated. Maxwell *et al.* (2004) consider employees as 'service performers' and comment:

> [...] [staff] are central to service quality, so too is their management. (p. 162)

The implied link between effective staff management (or human resource management – HRM) and performance through service quality is acknowledged by a number of researchers. Notwithstanding the inherent challenges of establishing reliable metrics, many agree that a relationship exists between them. Gilbert and Guerrier (1997) consider this link to be positive along with Hoque (1999) and Mohinder (2004), who note that tourism firms using service quality-oriented HRM approaches tend to perform better than those that fail to make the association.

Garavan (1995) says much the same but emphasises the pursuit of service quality as a catalyst for engaging in HRM. Cheng and Brown (1998) consider the link between human resource management and organisational objectives to be a key enabler of effective recruitment, development, motivation and retention of staff in pursuit of competitive advantage. Chand and Katou's (2007) study of Indian hotels confirms the global currency of HRM upon organisational performance. Specifically they consider human resource management systems important catalysts for:

- multiskilling and experience;
- harmonised terms and conditions of employment;
- formal manpower planning;
- career planning;
- flexible jobs;
- cross cultural job design; and
- formal induction and training systems.

Others sharing this view include Grönroos (1994), Pitt *et al.* (1995) and Nolan (2002). Earlier, Guest (1987) argued that quality of staff, quality of performance and public image of the firm are key determinants of an effective HRM strategy.

It would therefore seem reasonable to argue that HRM, service quality and competitive advantage are inextricably linked. We can therefore begin to appreciate the central role played by HRM in tourism organisations. The aim of this chapter is to introduce some notions of HRM and overview the nature of services. It also considers the difficulty of defining the tourism industry and comments on some of its uniquely challenging characteristics in an HRM context.

Critical note
The relationship between front-line workers and service quality cannot be overstated; HRM service quality and competitive advantage are inextricably linked.

HRM: TOWARDS A DEFINITION

Most international HR practitioners and associated professional bodies, such as the UK's Chartered Institute of Personnel Development would no doubt agree with the assertion that organisational effectiveness is down to managing human resources. Indeed, there is a body of scientific evidence to support such a statement. However, what exactly is meant by the term human resource management (HRM)? More prescriptive ideas of HRM often use notions of 'personnel management' in order to make their point. Chronologically, the latter precedes the former and is often understood as 'operational' and exclusively managed and administered by a separate personnel department. Human resources management is commonly understood to have a broader and more integrated organisational remit. Synergistically, Thachappilly (2009) considers personnel management to concern employment contracts, disciplinary issues and compensation. Human resources management views workers as high-value business resources and essential in gaining strategic competitive advantage. In short, the main differences between the two are summarised in Table 1.1.

Table 1.1 A comparison of Personnel and HRM

Personnel	*HRM*
Administrative, traditional and routine tasks including dealing with employment law, payroll and other associated activities	Has a broad remit and considers workers as the primary resource contributing to organisational performance
Reactive in nature providing responses as demands and crises arise	Proactive in nature through continuous development strategies to manage and develop an organisation's workforce
Independent function of an organization through personnel department	Integral part of overall company function involving all managers
Holds that employee satisfaction motivates workers to improve performance through compensation schemes, bonuses, rewards, and the simplification of work responsibilities	Holds that improved performance leads to employee satisfaction through work groups/teams, 'challenge strategies' and job creativity

However, are these differences 'real'? Legge (1995) argues that differences only occur in the emphasis of particular aspects. She also asks whether HRM is a covert process of worker manipulation by management and notes rather cynically, after Fowler (1987), that: 'HRM represents the discovery of personnel management by chief executives' (p. 76).

3

Whether one sympathises with Legge's insightful commentary or not, there is no doubt that a universally appropriate definition of HRM is hard to come by. *Wikipedia*'s online definition of HRM is comprehensive:

> [...] the strategic and coherent approach to the management of an organisation's most valued assets – the people working there who individually and collectively contribute to the achievement of the objectives of the business. In simple sense, HRM means employing people, developing their resources, utilizing maintaining and compensating their services in tune with the job and organizational requirement. (http://en.wikipedia.org/wiki/Human_resource_management. Accessed February 2009)

However, it is non-specific and merely serves to reinforce the idea (Torrington, 1989; Timo & Davidson, 2005) that HRM can mean whatever the firm wants it to mean depending on context and purpose. Indeed, this perspective is illustrated, albeit 'tongue in cheek', in Box 1.1.

BOX 1.1 A tongue-in-cheek lexicon for the HR novice

- Conventional Wisdom – The mother of all oxymorons, neither conventional nor wise.
- Downsizing – The same thing as layoffs. If the company does have a Mortal Assets Department, the net result of downsizing is 'mortal remains'.
- RIFs – An acronym for 'Resources Infrastructure Flattening', it is really the same as 'downsizing'.
- Layoffs – What we called downsizing when we all knew what we were talking about.
- Statistics – The most valued HR science, which allows the HR Manager to prove his or her point when no one else will accept it – even when couched in plain English. Related to the 'fog index', it has also been said of statistics that it is like the drunk and the lamppost: it gives support, but not much illumination.
- Validity – When more than 50% of those you are trying to persuade believe what you say, your point has validity. When more than 90% believe, you have what's called a 'miracle'. When others swipe your ideas, it is termed, 'Second-hand Smoke'.
- Tests – What you use to test validity. If the test shows that your idea is not sound, change tests.
- Personality Test – A device used to ensure that the person you hire for your department will accept your ideas without validity or reality analysis. Usually given only to those who do not know the phrase 'invasion of privacy'.

- Budgeting – A game of unknown origin, budgets are pleas for money conducted in the following fashion: the Personnel Department needs $12 million for staffing and training, $11.99 million of which will go to staff salaries. It asks for $12 million, knowing that the company will only give a 10% increase in budget. This game can last 15 or more years, and is usually considered to be 'over' when HR foolishly proposes 'downsizing'.
- Training Department – The people with the whip and the chair.
- To Train – An intransitive verb meaning to educate intransigent people who disagree with or don't understand your system. It is intransitive since training often has no direct object.
- Work – Looking busy, or the amount of energy expended in trying to look busy. It has been estimated that work takes place during four to six hours of every eight-hour day.
- Loyalty – The formula for determining the degree of loyalty is: F=(W+B/O)R} where F=Faithfulness, W=Wages, B=Benefits, O=Opportunity, and R=Reality.
- Discretion – Swearing loyalty to your supervisor. In the textile industry, the better part of velour.

Source: Ethan (1994)

McGunnigle and Jameson (2000) prefer to consider HRM as a 'map', 'notion' or 'theory'. After reviewing the evidence, they conclude that there is much confusion and no comprehensively accepted definition. Additionally, HRM can be divided into 'hard' and 'soft' models'. The former is where workers are viewed in a 'rational' economic manner as an integrative resource in which the business invests to produce economic return. The 'soft' approach is where employees are considered assets and the main source of achieving competitve advantage. Employee commitment strategies are pursued in the belief that workers will regulate themselves towards achieving the organisation's goals. In reality, most firms operate between the two extremes. Consistent with Guest's (1987) normative model of HRM, McGunnigle and Jameson (2000) favour a focus on employee commitment as the common denominator of HRM into which feed other key associated areas of:

- culture;
- recruitment and selection;
- training and development;
- reward systems; and
- employee empowerment. (p. 405)

Accordingly, it is arguably more effective to consider HRM as a philosophy rather than a set of hard and fast practices and procedures. Clearly, administration linked to the personnel function of HRM falls into the latter category. However, it is worth considering the theory behind HRM, which is founded on the notion that workers are thinking, feeling and emotional. In short, they cannot be treated like other resources. As such, HRM seeks to engage holistically; recognising that achieving an appropriate 'fit' between employees' and organisational goals is paramount. Perhaps it is more effective here simply to acknowledge the inherent complexity and simply consider the goal of HRM in the tourism industry:

> To help tourism firms to meet their shared strategic goals by attracting, developing, maintaining and managing workers effectively and efficiently.

Critical note

Human resource management is best understood as a philosophy rather than a set of hard and fast procedures.

SERVICES AND THE TOURISM INDUSTRY

Services

It is often argued that service industries such as tourism have a number of important differences from their manufacturing counterparts: for example, the composite product is intangible. This means that the impacts of staff customer interactions cannot be defined and measured in material terms. Moreover, successful service encounters are based on the adeptness of employee performance at the interface and their ability to make customers feel welcome. It is also the case that every customer encounter has the potential to be overtly or subtly unique due to the abilities of each person and their ability to respond appropriately (or not) through the dialogue and encounter process. The third element unique to tourism services (especially hospitality) is that, with some minor exceptions, they have to be produced and consumed at the same point. Finally, the product has a limited shelf-life because tourism services are perishable. Whilst a tangible element of service such as a meal can be replaced, the accompanying welcome cannot be. According to Lashley and Lee-Ross (2003) '[...] service interactions are [...] time specific, it is not possible to rework [them] and [they] have to be right first time' (p. xviii).

These four characteristics help us to understand the nature of the tourism product and most firms operate between two extremes depending on the dominance of intangibles within the mix. This is an important issue and is linked directly to employment policy and overall HRM strategy. Essentially, the more intangibles a service has, the more important becomes the input and skill of the service deliverer. This 'service experience' is the main responsibility of the front-line employee and one which depends on the 'successful' interplay between the actors. Interestingly, the service encounter is the point at which management has little direct influence. Of course some tourism firms have attempted to minimise risk by developing 'scripts' which front-line workers are expected to follow. Unfortunately, if these instructions are followed too closely the encounter often comes over as contrived and non-flexible. Do you believe that McDonald's employees really mean for you to have a nice day? Perhaps 20 or so years ago customers felt that this was the case but no longer applies as customers are increasingly sophisticated and expect far more from the service encounter than their predecessors.

Working at the front-line

Indeed, one only has to consider the complex and demanding role of 'front-line' tourism workers to understand how behaviour at the customer interface cannot be left to chance; the role of HRM cannot be overstated here. In short, the perceived quality of the service relies on the 'success' of the ensuing dialogue between staff member and customer. The former must have the inherent or learned skills to react appropriately to any number of customer-generated stimuli. However, each encounter has the potential to be totally unique and is beyond the direct control of the supervisor or manager. Moreover, 'performing' at the customer interface for long periods can be stressful for the service deliverer, particularly if the emotions displayed are inconsistent with their true feelings. Workers must be able to display appropriate emotions consistent with the expectations of customers. These standardised company 'displays' can be observed in branded tourism organisations such as McDonald's, TGI Fridays and Shangri-La hotels; some are easier to 'script' than others; the more interactive the experience the more difficult the scripting process.

According to Mann (1999) there are two ways of managing emotions. The first requires workers to adjust their physical appearance to match the emotional display required and the second is a deeper approach where the employee imagines themselves in the customer's place. The first is simply a 'surface' reaction where the worker only affects the emotion. The second is deeper and requires empathy. Situations where the expected emotion is displayed by the worker but is at odds with their real emotion can produce negative outcomes particularly if the 'dissonance' is maintained over long periods. According to Lashley and Lee-Ross (2003) these could include 'burn out' through increased levels of mental strain, job alienation, increased absenteeism and labour turnover. In this context 'job fit', staff values, attitudes and competencies are key. Optimal recruitment, selection, training and development practices become of paramount importance reminding us of the important role played by human resource management in tourism organisations.

> **Critical note**
> Behaviour at the customer interface cannot be left to chance; the role of HRM is key here as each encounter has the potential to be unique and is beyond the direct control of the manager.

Reflections

Visit a local restaurant, travel agent or an organisation of your choice.

1. What did you think about the service received?
2. Was it of high quality?
3. What aspects of the service were most important to you?

The Tourism Industry

Tourism as an industry is not recognised by international governmental systems of industrial classification. Instead, it is usually represented by an amalgam of other industrial sectors. According to Riley *et al.* (2002) the best approximation of tourism (and employment therein) is to use statistics from various international classifications of restaurants, accommodation and cafes. In the UK the following sectors provide this information:

- hotels and other tourist accommodation (SIC 551, 552);
- restaurants, cafes etc. (SIC 553);
- bars, public houses and night-clubs (SIC 554);
- travel agencies and tour operators (SIC 633);
- libraries, museums and other cultural activities (SIC 925); and
- sports and other recreational activities (SIC 926, 927).

The international tourism industry is comprised of a fragmented and heterogeneous mix of organisations from both the private and public sectors. Some are directly concerned with customers and their satisfaction whilst others play a less direct and supportive role. Indeed, could suppliers of raw materials for tourism organisational refurbishment be considered as in the tourism business? Markets may be highly concentrated whereby supply is dominated by only a few large companies, for example, global accommodation – Accor (France), InterContinental Hotels (UK) and Marriot International (USA); Australian air travel – Qantas and Virgin Blue; international fast food – McDonald's and KFC, or diffuse where many smaller firms compete against each other. Immediately we can see a situation of complexity and thus one which is difficult to define. Riley *et al.* (2002: 10) would certainly agree and introduce other reasons hindering a universal definition of tourism.

- Informal economy ('unofficial' employment relationships between employer and worker).
- No universal agreement on what constitutes a 'tourist trip'.
- Paucity of reliable statistics.
- Multi-linkages to other sectors.

Another complexity is that tourism firms do not usually offer their product exclusively to tourists. Consider the potential customer profile of many resort-based firms. They undoubtedly have a mainstay of domestic and international tourists but they will also be used by members of the host community, particularly in the 'off season'. Indeed, many market their services to locals by offering discounted 'local specials'.

After reviewing various philosophies underpinning tourism and its definition, Leiper (1995) considers the practical key as establishing a common understanding and proposes that:

> Tourism can be defined as the theories and practices of travelling and visiting places for leisure-related purposes. (p. 20)

Leiper's pithy contribution is welcome but unnecessarily generic for our purposes. It also introduces the requirement for yet another definition; that of 'leisure' which is not entirely appropriate here unless we consider leisure to be subsumed within tourism without question. Bardgett (2000) points out that the defining feature of tourism is the tourist rather than the product and cites the internationally agreed definition:

> Tourism comprises the activities of persons travelling and staying places outside their usual environment for not more than one consecutive year for leisure, business and other purposes. (p. 7)

Unfortunately, this leaves us 'best guessing' when attempting to collect accurate statistical tourism data including employment figures. Due to difficulties of definition, Holloway (1989) concludes that the tourism industry should be thought of as a system. His simplified 'central chain of distribution' shown below provides a useful framework and at least allows an appreciation of most firms involved in the industry.

Following the more managerial/economic/functional perspective, the current chapter aligns its understanding of the tourism industry with that shown in Figure 1.1. While the content misses a number of alternative perspectives it provides initial guidance in identifying and establishing employment numbers in the tourism industry. Nonetheless, any collection of statistical tourism data is bound to be an estimate because of inherent challenges shown below:

- who to include – those businesses that deal exclusively with tourists or those that only serve tourists as part of their market, for example, retail outlets, petrol filling stations, taxi firms;
- organisational departments – only front-line workers or those who have no direct contact with tourists including accountants and maintenance; and
- definitions – neglect and poor administration at governmental levels (Szivas, 1999).

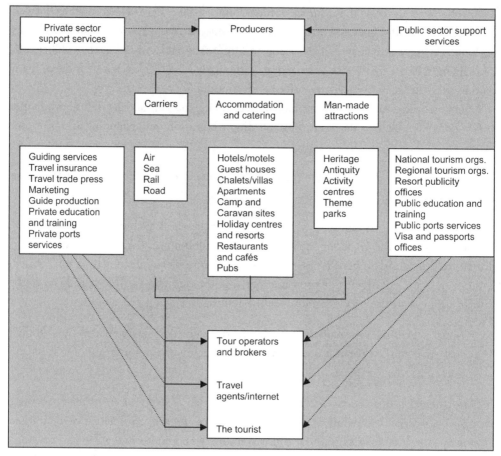

Figure 1.1 The tourism industry

Adapted from: Holloway (1989: 54)

Riley *et al.* (2002) recommend wisely that if tourism firms are used to approximate employment levels then certain assumptions must be made when interpreting data. The key here is that any definition of the industry must be flexible or 'working' due to its sheer diversity characterised by certain factors including:

- heterogeneous jobs across sectors by virtue of different business types and the impact of seasonality;
- differential skill requirements for jobs with the same title;
- unclear relationship between job, skills required and remuneration;
- variation in employment and occupational status;
- labour markets and high levels of mobility; and
- coexistence of multinational and small independent firms.

Adapted from: Riley *et al.* (2002: 13–15)

For the reasons outlined above we can conclude that a precise quantum of tourism employment figures will almost certainly always be elusive but we can assert that total tourism-related employment figures are significant. The World Travel and Tourism Council (WTTC) (2007) estimates that total employment is currently just under 250 million or 8.4% of total employment. This is predicted to rise to almost 300 million or one in every 10.8 jobs by 2018 which is around 9.2% of total global employment. However, these figures are likely to be conservative as a notable proportion of employment in the tourism sector operates in the black economy defined by 'unofficial' employment relationships characterised by undeclared financial transactions including 'cash in hand' and 'bartering' (Medlik, 2003; Partington *et al.*, 2003).

In part, the preponderance of an unofficial economy in the tourism sector helps us appreciate the challenges faced by both employers and workers. Such employment relationships at best are symbiotic and at worst exploitative and do little to address some of the common characteristics of the tourism labour market.

The short case below in Box 1.2 illustrates some of the perennial human resource challenges in the hospitality sector.

BOX 1.2 Case study – Hospitality staff are sick of gloomy working conditions

Miserable working conditions are taking their toll on hospitality workers, with staff in depressing environments taking more than double the number of sick days off a year as employees in other sectors.

A survey of more than 1000 UK workers, conducted by Lightspeed Research in March 2007, reveals that 38% of people working in the hospitality and service sector think that their working environments are 'gloomy' or 'depressing' and take 19 sick days off a year, compared with the typical surveyed worker's eight.

Six in ten of the hospitality workers questioned said a better working environment would make them more productive (by an average of 27%). This is the equivalent of businesses gaining one to two extra days each week from each member of staff.

Question

1. Discuss how employers/managers can create and maintain positive working environments.

Source: Duce (2007)

There are serious issues to be addressed here and any effective HR strategy must pay heed and manage them appropriately. The following section outlines some of the main characteristics of the tourism labour market and progress toward the implementation of HRM strategies in this sector.

> **Critical note**
> The tourism industry is best understood as an integrated system.

> **Reflections**
> Visit some firms in a tourism destination. Make sure they are not directly involved in tourism.
>
> **1.** Ask managers whether they believe their businesses are in the tourism industry and why.

THE LABOUR MARKET

It would be reasonable to argue that the tourism labour market is shaped by four key forces. The first and most powerful is the nature of tourism demand; simply, it is seasonal and characterised by periods of high and low activity. Second is the nature of employment where many jobs are temporary, part-time and low skilled. Third is management practice and working conditions, many of which could not be described as ideal. Finally, the nature of tourism workers has a key role to play. In some respects, these characteristics are difficult to deal with separately; for example, seasonality can be linked with poor levels of pay and impoverished working conditions. Truly, pay and working conditions are set by employers or managers but this, they would argue, is a direct response to periods of high and low demand for their product. In a sense, this is absolutely right so discussion of each issue in isolation is unrealistic. Whether you believe that poor pay and working conditions are appropriate strategic responses by managers is another story however!

Arguably, the main impact of seasonality on the hospitality and tourism labour market is its division into two categories of 'primary' and 'secondary' (also known as 'internal' and 'external' respectively). Workers in the primary/internal categories are known as 'core'; those in the secondary/external as 'peripheral'. Employees in the former enjoy relatively better working conditions than those in the alternative category. Typically, peripheral workers are generally low paid, undertake jobs of short tenure which have no clear opportunities for career progression with little chance of moving from the secondary to the primary segment (Piore, 1975). Additionally, these workers have fewer opportunities for training so skills may become outdated thus consolidating their secondary labour market position. Rooted in Atkinson's (1985) model of the 'flexible firm' developed at the Institute of Manpower Studies in the UK, workers in the secondary market should find less intrinsic satisfaction in their work because their jobs have less overall importance in the organisation. However, this notion of importance is very much a value judgement.

Some would argue that the job of a seasonal foodservice operative is of key importance as the incumbent is responsible for delighting customers. Its potential impact on service quality is therefore unquestionable.

Baum (2008) summarises the international labour market for hospitality and tourism as one which is diverse with different characteristics across organisations and sub-sectors. However, some common characteristics include: '[...] low productivity, [...] poor remuneration, demanding working conditions and limited opportunities for personal development [and ultimately high levels of labour turnover]' (p. 725). Similarly, Lee-Ross (1996), Lashley and Lee-Ross (2003) and Timo and Davidson (2005) cite the following which are divided into labour market and industry characteristics and shown in Table 1.2.

Table 1.2 Market and industry characteristics

Labour market characteristic	*Industry characteristic*
Unstable with high propensity to quit jobs	Majority of jobs are casual, temporary, part-time
Workers on average younger than other industries and paid less earning around 75% of the all industry average	Inclusion of customer in employment relationship (over reliance on tipping to augment income) and 'unofficial' rewards and other non-pecuniary benefits
Jobs attractive to younger people as 'working holiday' or stop gap until something better comes along or a chance for excitement and travel	Most jobs have few skill barriers
Weak internal labour market	Jobs in high demand so little pressure on employers to increase pay rates
Unskilled	Despotic management styles
Ethnically diverse	Lack of formal training
Some employees prefer undertaking temporary and part-time work only	Provision of on-site worker accommodation perpetuates paternalistic employment relationship and allows immediate access to labour
Increasingly workers retrenched from other more traditional (male) occupations – stigma attached to 'service' jobs dominated by females	Individual contract-making with employer

Received wisdom suggests that these characteristics contribute towards high levels of labour turnover, diminished service quality and low levels of customer satisfaction. For example, in Poulson's (2008) study of tourism and hospitality firms' HRM practices she concludes that questionable management approaches, inadequacies and training are to blame. The latter was identified as 'poor', 'misused' (p. 421) and situationally inappropriate. Significantly, she also notes that management were, in the main, unaware of these problems and that their willingness to engage a labour force below the age of 25 may also be associated with high turnover.

Poulston (2008) seeks to understand some commonly identified problems with the hospitality industry and links them with a number of outcomes. After reviewing the evidence four major areas of concern emerge and are shown in Figure 1.2.

Under-staffing: Poulston (2008) points out that under-staffing leading to stress has been well-documented and linked negatively with customer satisfaction. It has also been found to cause staff turnover but other antecedents include job alienation (Robinson & Barron, 2007), poor supervision and employment conditions. Other causes include poor pay, long hours, boring work and social stigma.

Training: Pratten (2003) considers that formal training is rare in the tourism and hospitality industry. There is a notion that operational skills required in housekeeping and food and beverage service are either simply extensions of domestic skills or generalisable (those which can be picked up and applied over a range of jobs in a number of establishments). Therefore no employee training is required. It is also the case that because of high levels of turnover, managers are reluctant to use resources for training because skills will be taken elsewhere soon after the event. Front-line employees who do not possess the required skills are under significant pressure as their mistakes will be observed by customers and will detract from delivering a high quality product. Pratten (2003) notes that a lack of training and development impacts on job satisfaction and attrition levels. Lashley and Best (2002) support this position adding that service quality will suffer as a result.

Theft and constructive dismissal: Anecdotally, employee theft is regarded as common in the tourism and hospitality industry. In an early study of restaurant workers, Mars and Nicod (1984) identified theft to be a composite element in a 'total rewards system'. The system comprised 'official' rewards such as wages and informal tipping with 'unofficial' 'fiddles' and 'knockoffs'. Indeed, workers were found to think nothing of stealing a range of items considered to be an 'acceptable' supplement to impoverished wages. This is alleged to cause staff turnover because theft squeezes profits which might otherwise be used for staff training thus stymieing staff development (Thoms *et al.*, 2001). Finally, Poulston (2008) notes that constructive dismissals are rife in the industry usually resulting from inept management and supervision. Poor and arbitrary management styles in the hospitality industry have been noted elsewhere including a lack of grievance and disciplinary procedures (Lucas, 2004).

She also draws to our attention the lack of trade union presence in the tourism and hospitality industry. However, unions are aware of the challenges faced by employees

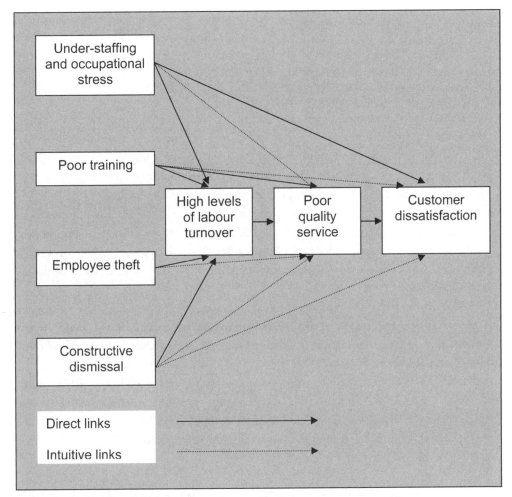

Figure 1.2 Identified problem areas and simplified *a priori* relationships

Adapted from: Poulston (2008)

as the case below illustrates. She classifies employment therein as 'vulnerable' for these reasons; Timo (1999) favours 'flexible' and 'precarious'. The situation with unions has been noted by others for the following reasons:

- highly fragmented workforce;
- tourism industry dominated by small firms which makes organisation and co-ordination of union activities difficult;
- traditionally hostile and union-busting management style; and
- high level of part time and temporary workers and high level of labour turnover. This also makes conditions less than ideal for organisation of union membership and activities.

BOX 1.3 Case study – TUC calls on tourism industry to audit supply-chain working conditions

The UK's Trades Union Congress has called on the UK tourism industry to audit working conditions in its supply chain.

The call follows an investigation by Tourism Concern showing that many of the 200 million workers employed in the global tourism industry, worth nearly $500 billion a year, suffer low and unpredictable pay, treacherous safety conditions, serious health risks, sexual harassment, long hours, and casual employment. Many have no contracts or training and are prevented from joining trade unions.

Assistant TUC general secretary Kay Carberry said, 'This is about companies treating working conditions as part of their social responsibility but also good business sense. Good treatment of all the workers your customers might meet will improve their performance. Customers will enjoy the holiday more and will want to travel with you again.'

Tourism Concern Programme Manager Guyonne James said, 'Every resort Tourism Concern researched can be found in the brochures of the major tour operators. The tourism industry has to start taking labour standards seriously if this abuse is to stop.'

The Tourism Concern report, entitled 'Labour Standards, Social Responsibility and Tourism', echoes the findings of a recent report from the International Labour Organisation. That report highlighted the long shifts, irregular hours, low and varied pay, and high alcohol consumption associated with holiday promotion, as well as the sometimes sexual nature of the work, all of which, it argued, create high-risk zones for the health and safety of staff.

Four companies account for 50% of the tourism business catering for UK residents holidaying abroad: First Choice Holidays, MyTravel Group, Thomas Cook and TUI. The TUC called for them to set the benchmark for auditing employment standards. First Choice Holidays declined the opportunity to comment on the subject and referred the enquiry to the Association of British Travel Agents (ABTA).

Ian Reynolds, Chief Executive of the Association of British Travel Agents, said that while tour operators have a responsibility to uphold labour standards where they can, in most countries labour regulations are the responsibility of national governments and tour operators do not have direct control over the employment practices of their suppliers.

He said some tour operators have signed statements of commitment. These recognise that tourism should generate benefits for the local community and improve the livelihood of local people.

He concluded, 'We believe our members are taking this responsibility seriously, but it does need to be seen in the context of everything they are doing to ensure sustainability in economic, cultural and environmental terms. We must not forget that tourism has already improved the quality of life for millions of people around the world.'

Questions
1. Discuss why working conditions in the tourism and hospitality industry are relatively poor.
2. Suggest how this situation might be improved.
3. What role should the unions play in addressing this perennial challenge?

Source: Anon (2009)

An additional industry characteristic is the ease with which anyone can begin trading. Barriers to entry are low and tourism attracts many entrepreneurs who often have no management expertise or any knowledge of the industry. Indeed, some may only enter the industry temporarily (Poulston, 2008), all of which may prohibit the delivery of high service standards. Reasons cited for starting one's own firm often centre around status, emotional attachment to a romantic ideal and being one's own boss. Interestingly, another reason for becoming an entrepreneur is an inability to work with or take orders from other people (Dalglish & Evans, 2000). These factors taken together would not describe an individual particularly predisposed to look after the well-being of workers nor have any systematic HRM strategy in place.

These characteristics of tourism and hospitality have long been acknowledged. Many right-thinking commentators suggest that the industry is overdue a more creative and strategic approach to its management of human resources. Indeed, the economic crisis in the first decade of the 21st century has acted as to reinforce the notion that tourism plays a key role in international economic development and employment. It is also arguably behind the recent UNWTO/ILO (United Nations World Tourism Organization/International Labour Organization) 'decent work' initiative designed to address some of the tourism industry's perennial employment-related challenges (see Chapter 9).

Critical note
The international labour market for tourism and hospitality is diverse with different characteristics across organizations and sub-sectors having common characteristics of high labour turnover, low productivity, poor remuneration and associated working conditions and limited opportunities for personal development.

> **Reflections**
>
> Interview the manager of a tourism organisation. Ask what major challenges they face running their business.

THE PARADOX

Despite the somewhat less than ideal working conditions and high labour turnover in tourism and hospitality, paradoxically, many workers do not report low levels of job satisfaction. There is some evidence to suggest that the negative connotations associated with temporary and part-time work may not altogether hold true for some employees. The often cited disadvantages of working part time include fewer opportunities for training and development (and promotion), less job security, fewer statutory employment protections and exclusion from contributory social security benefits (Dickens, 1992). Under 'normal' circumstances these conditions would be expected to have negative consequences for both the worker and organisation. However, Euzeby (1988) suggests the opposite to be true. He notes that the 'space' provided by this kind of employment could feasibly allow the incumbent to put other aspects of their life into some sort of order making their worklife balance more appropriate.

The other main reasons advanced for this apparent paradox centre around the entrepreneurial flair of some workers and the intrinsic nature of many tourism and hospitality jobs. Leinster (1985) suggests that front-line tourism workers are entrepreneurs in their own right seeking to maximise economic return by 'performing' at the customer interface. Of course this also plays into the hands of managers because they can effectively abdicate responsibility for setting reasonable levels of pay; preferring instead to let customers augment employee rewards. In this sense perhaps employees and managers share similar perspectives. The second notion posits that many tourism and hospitality jobs are perceived (initially at least) as glamorous allowing employees to meet and greet VIPs and (crucially) to satisfy a desire for social interaction in the workplace (Lucas, 2004). Sociologists have an explanation for the phenomenon known as the 'marginal worker' theory. This is where individuals perceive themselves as different from mainstream society in some way and are instrumental in setting their own unique pattern of personal and work preferences including strong bonding with other members of their group (Mars *et al.*, 1979).

Similarly, the 'occupational community' perspective argues that individuals become bonded to their work and work colleagues. This form of organisational culture is all encompassing and members fuse work and social activities so it is difficult to disentangle the two. Members derive their identity by strong association with work and related activities. Salaman (1974) defines them as:

People who are members of the same occupation, or who work together, have some sort of common life together, and are, to some extent, separate from the rest of society. (p. 19)

This perspective views the meaning of work to those that are doing it and can take two forms. The first is 'cosmopolitan' where members do the same work but in different geographical regions and the second is 'local' where individuals work in the same organisation. According to Lashley and Lee-Ross (2003) both of these forms are found in tourism organisations but they note that organisational cultures are not uniform. For example, in Lee-Ross's (1996) original study of hotel workers, four different types of communities were identified across dimensions of whether workers lived on or off the hotel properties and whether they described themselves as seasonal or year-round workers. Interestingly, these dimensions have little to do with whether jobs are full or part-time and are independent of department. Pryce (2007) favours the former cosmopolitan occupational community pointing out that the hospitality sector in particular has a 'pan-industry' sense of organisational culture. In a sense, this perspective resonates with the marginal workers thesis in that there appears to be a strong identification with the work group rather than the actual work itself. The characteristics of occupational communities are summarised in Table 1.3.

Table 1.3 Characteristics of occupational communities

Characteristic	Explanation
Job	Pervasive and sets norms for activities outside workplace
Tasks	Set limits over non-work activities influencing friendship patterns, non-work norms and values
Non-job activities	Organisation controls activities outside work like eating, sleeping, recreation etc.
Duration	Jobs of short duration may cause cultural norms and values to be set outside workplace
Skills – procedural and cognition – maintain 'mystery'	One thing having knowledge, facts and descriptions but another knowing how to apply
Self-control	Reliance on ill-defined procedures thus self control of community is maintained
Work-based friends, interests and hobbies	Members discuss jobs outside organisation, read work-related literature, have work-related hobbies, join work-related clubs and friends are also members of the occupational community

Adapted from: Lashley and Lee-Ross (2003: 158)

Similarly, there is other evidence which suggests that tourism employees have strong 'orientations' to work (Martin, 2004) where they have considerable control over the employment relationship thus maximising the incidence of job satisfaction. Rooted in the earlier work of Goldthorpe *et al.* (1968), the 'affluent worker' construct considers that orientations are identified based on the meaning work has to the individual via expectations they bring into the workplace. In short, orientations are classified as 'instrumental' whereby employees consider work as a means to an end. The 'bureaucratic' orientation views work as a means of social status and a means of long-term security. Finally, the 'solidaristic' perspective views the job more as a form of group activity where norms and values are more important than economic return for labour. Goldthorpe *et al.*'s (1968) original perspective has received some criticism. However, recent hospitality and tourism related research has identified additional categories of orientations including 'craft' and 'professional'. The key emergent issue however is partial support for the marginal worker theory inasmuch as a strong sense of individualism was identified amongst employees.

Overall, there is some evidence to suggest that tourism employees may in fact prefer not to engage directly with their manager. Instead, they either 'work for themselves' within the employing organisation or enter the industry to satisfy a personal need for social interaction. In this case the emotional side of the employment relationship appears to be bound with customers, issues of work life balance and other workmates. This situation may have been created unwittingly by an industry which historically has a poor record of employer/employee relationships. In other words, tourism and hospitality workers have gradually come to realise they must take personal responsibility for their own sense of well-being in the workplace as management are unlikely to do so.

Critical note

Despite the somewhat less than ideal working conditions and high labour turnover in tourism and hospitality, paradoxically, many workers do not report low levels of job satisfaction.

HRM STRATEGIES: THE CURRENT PICTURE

Although there has been much research on the topic of labour turnover in the tourism and hospitality industry, the exact relationship between the variables remains nebulous (as can be appreciated from the above discussion). Attempts to reduce labour turnover may therefore be patchy. Moreover, some issues may not strictly be under management control anyway. For example, dealing effectively with a labour market predisposed toward transience is difficult. Some may argue 'why bother' because labour turnover brings in new and fresh ideas to the workplace. Whilst this may sometimes be the case it is refuted here because (amongst other reasons):

- excessive labour turnover is detrimental to the consistent delivery of high quality service because incumbents are ever-changing, each of whom may have differing standards;
- retained trained workers will deliver a service based on agreed organisational standards;
- temporary worker shortages will increase the workload on others; and
- it is unlikely that a source of relatively low skilled employees brings anything novel to a firm nor would employers be likely to take notice.

Additionally, a *laissez-faire* approach based on employees working in their own interests is not acceptable. This mitigates the impact and importance of organisational values and norms, prevents the establishment of a formal organisational culture and creates a situation in which employees effectively control service quality. Thus, employers should target characteristics which are controllable including pay and associated working conditions, management styles, induction, training and employee development, motivation, retention, career planning and an awareness of the overarching role played by organisational culture on these elements including service quality. For example, Graham and Lennon (2002) recommend the aim of generating a relationship of mutual understanding between staff and the HR manager. This should motivate and influence workers to redirect their behaviour towards achieving organisational goals and instill a sense of pride through personal development and quality performance (p. 219). In short, managers should consider the adoption of appropriate HRM strategies. This is especially important given the foregoing discussion about front-line workers, their role at the customer interface and its impact on overall service quality.

Unfortunately, evidence suggests that the tourism industry is still languishing behind some other sectors in terms of HRM strategy. McGunnigle and Jameson (2000) point out that there is little agreement on what defines HRM in the hospitality industry. Also, many organisations consistently fail to adopt formal HRM models preferring to hire and manage workers informally. They note:

> Our research illustrates that it may still be the case that the willingness [of hotels] to adopt HR may be no more than 'an empty shell', or at least piecemeal and fragmented. (p. 416)

Sadly, almost ten years later Maxwell and MacLean (2008) draw a similar conclusion and state: '[...] the hospitality and tourism industry as a whole is not renowned for highly developed human resource practices' (p. 822). Internationally, the situation appears unchanged. According to Chand and Katou (2007) human resource departments in Indian tourism-related organisations are no more than cost centres. In a sense this is understandable as investment in employees is relatively easy to calculate. On the other hand, the benefits accruing from such investments are rather more difficult to observe and measure. Other researchers lamenting the industry-wide reticence to adopt formal strategic human resource management practices include Haynes and Fryer (2000) and Watson (1996). Baum (2008) considers that the tourism and hospitality industry merely seeks *ad hoc* solutions to these perennial HR challenges. This belies a sector-wide reticence to embrace a comprehensive and integrated approach to human resource management. Instead, tourism remains willing to increase its dependence on low and unskilled labour.

Hoque (1999) considers that only large hotels are likely to experiment with HRM practices. For example, HR can be seen in The Hilton group's drive for service quality through their HR policy initiative ('Esprit') as it builds on the four-pronged set of company values. The foci are on customers, service quality, employees (to enjoy being part of a cohesive team providing excellent service) and profit (Maxwell *et al.*, 2004: 170). Human resources management practices in the small to medium sized tourism sector are largely absent, or informal. According to Timo and Davidson (2005), cost minimisation strategies dominate HR strategies in most firms where low pay is the norm with tipping used to augment pay rates. They conclude that even multinational luxury hotel chains fail to pursue 'new' HR strategies in achieving competitive advantage. Instead they maintain a common low cost HRM strategy based on a flexible and low cost labour force. This is consistent with Lashley and Lee-Ross (2003) who divide employment practice in the tourism sector into two categories. One focuses on cost (and appears to be the most common) and the other on quality; both are shown in Table 1.4.

Table 1.4 Employment practice

The cost employment strategy	The quality employment strategy
Aims to create competitive advantage by cost management and low selling prices	Aims to create competitive advantage by building and delivering service quality which is difficult for competitors to copy
Labour costs viewed as key element of 'controllable' operating	Employees viewed as assets
Wages set at minimum rate set by government	Recognises front-line skills are essential and builds appropriate HRM strategies and practice around this core belief

Adapted from: Lashley and Lee-Ross (2003: 16–17)

The problem with the low costs approach is that it creates negative outcomes indirectly ranging from high levels of labour turnover and recruitment difficulties to lost customers and deliberate acts of sabotage by workers. Moreover, this strategy has a 'low-skill expectation' whereby positions and roles have been deskilled. This is compounded by prevailing practice which suggests managers abdicate responsibility from employees or take the 'easy' autocratic route. This is especially the case in seasonal destinations where 'hiring and firing' does not appear to be problematic due to the increased supply of unskilled workers (despite the inevitable negative impact on service quality and productivity). Earlier, Lee-Ross (1996) notes that the hospitality and tourism industry has long been accused of having managers who are autocratic, paternalistic and make decisions in an *ad hoc* manner and spend much of their time working alongside employees to minimise costs. Indeed, Witt and Witt (1989) trace this behaviour to the way managers are trained and developed. They coin this as the 'being there' style of management. Baum (1989) notes this characteristic and warns that the alleged uniqueness of an industry should not overshadow general principles of good management.

Critical note

The tourism and hospitality industry languishes behind some other sectors in terms of HRM strategy. There is little agreement on what defines HRM and many organisations consistently fail to adopt formal HRM models preferring to hire and manage workers informally.

Reflections

1. Undertake a web-based search of two national or multi-national tourism and hospitality corporations. Identify whether they have a formal HRM strategy and of what it is comprised.
2. Repeat the same exercise by interviewing the owner/manager of two small local tourism and hospitality firms.

SUMMARY

The tourism industry is heterogeneous and complex. It is comprised of firms which have obvious and direct links with the sector and those from associated industries which are not so clearly identifiable. This is the reason why both defining tourism and establishing its economic contribution in terms of contribution to GDP and job creation is challenging. However for the purposes of this chapter, we can assert that tourism is best represented as an integrated system (see Figure 1.1). We also acknowledge that it provides approximately 250 million jobs worldwide or 8.4% of total employment. This does not include those jobs existing in the 'unofficial' or 'black' economy and is therefore likely to be a conservative estimate.

Human resource management is a difficult 'concept' to define. Often it is juxtaposed against personnel management to emphasise the differences. A complicating factor is that HRM has also been divided into hard and soft models. Many elements of personnel can be identified in the former. Nonetheless, commentators agree that personnel practice is subsumed within HRM. Moreover, HRM is best conceptualised as a philosophy rather than a set of hard and fast policies and procedures.

Tourism has a number of differences from other manufacturing-oriented industries. For example, the product can often only be enjoyed at the point of delivery, is perishable, unique and intangible. Importantly, customer perception of service quality is bereft of direct management control and relies on the adeptness of front-line employees. More-over, this emotional labour can prove most stressful for the incumbent if they are expected to perform in a manner inconsistent with their deeply held values and beliefs. It is this very customer/employee encounter upon which hangs the reputation of the firm, the overall impression of service quality and ultimately its ability to compete successfully in the marketplace. The role of HRM in this context is intuitively paramount but over-whelming evidence suggests that service quality (and thus the ability to achieve com-petitive advantage) and sound HRM practice are inextricably linked.

Working conditions in the tourism industry have long been recognised as challeng-ing. Characteristics include seasonality which is held as the major cause of low pay and associated working conditions, low productivity, limited opportunities for personal devel-opment and high levels of labour turnover. The labour force can be divided into core and peripheral groups each having quite different working conditions. Core workers occupy positions in the firm's internal labour market whereas the latter group are firmly entrenched in the secondary labour market and have much degraded conditions of work. Despite this, evidence suggests that many tourism workers are not necessarily alienated from their jobs. Explanations for this apparent paradox centre around the individual's strong sense of affiliation to their work group (rather than the employer), an inherent entrepreneurial flair and a utilitarian attitude bound to the employee rather than the organisation. This worker orientation has significant implications for the success or failure of HRM practice. Indeed, currently researchers agree that formal HRM strategies are either non-existent or 'patchy' even in multinational tourism (and hospitality) corpor-ations. However, it would be a mistake to conclude that this position was solely due to the orientations of employees. Evidence suggests that tourism firms are owned and managed by under-qualified and ill-experienced individuals with a penchant for autocratic, 'hire and fire' and *ad hoc* management styles.

There can be no doubt that the inherent challenges discussed create barriers to the design and effective implementation of HRM strategies. However, a *laissez-faire* attitude is not acceptable. Furthermore, it is an abdication of managerial responsibility and only serves to perpetuate an array of problems, which with careful planning could be mitigated or resolved successfully.

CHAPTER QUESTIONS

1. Discuss the major challenges involved when designing and implementing a human resource strategy for:
- small to medium-sized tourism enterprises; and
- large tourism corporations.

2. Identify the major issues for both above sectors if there is no human resource strategy.

3. Explain how working conditions in some areas of the tourism industry may impact on establishing a coherent human resource strategy.

RECOMMENDED READING

Chand, M. and Katou, A.A. (2007) The impact of HRM practices on organisational performance in the Indian hotel industry. *Employee Relations* 29(6), 576–594.
A presentation of the extent and impact of human resource management practices upon organizational outcomes in India.

Baum, T. (2008) Implications of hospitality and tourism labour markets for talent management strategies. *International Journal of Contemporary Hospitality Management* 20(7), 720–729.
An assessment of talent management and its applicability to the tourism and hospitality industry.

Legge, K. (1995) *Human Resource Management: Rhetorics and Realities.* London: Macmillan.
Classic text discussing the myths and realties of human resources management.

Lucas, R. (2004) *Employment Relations in the Hospitality and Tourism Industries.* London: Routledge.
A thorough review of employment conditions in the tourism and hospitality industry.

Poulston, J. (2008) Hospitality workplace problems and poor training: a close relationship. *International Journal of Contemporary Hospitality Management* 20(4), 412–427.
A review of human resource challenges and outcomes for hospitality firms.

RECOMMENDED WEBSITES

International Labour Organization – http://www.ilo.org/global/lang–en/index.htm

International Organization for Standardization – http://www.iso.org/iso/home.htm

World Travel and Tourism Council – http://www.wttc.org/

Institute of Hospitality – http://www.instituteofhospitality.org/

Word Tourism Organization definition of tourism –
http://www.mta.com.mt/uploads/1675/WTO_definition_of_tourism.pdf

European Trade Union Confederation: 'Decent work' – http://www.etuc.org/a/2407

CHAPTER 2

CHANGE, WHAT CHANGE? HUMAN RESOURCES PLANNING IN A CONTEMPORARY ENVIRONMENT

LEARNING OBJECTIVES

After working through this chapter you should be able to:

1. Define human resources planning.

2. Understand human resources planning and its relationship with strategic planning.

3. Understand the concept of 'cultural fit' and discuss one related recruitment approach.

4. Identify basic HRM forecasting techniques.

5. Understand the implications of long-standing job vacancies and HRM policy responses to global economic recessions.

INTRODUCTION

Planning is an essential process not only in business but for most aspects of life. It allows individuals and groups to have some control over their destiny and informs responses to both expected and unexpected events. Some time ago tourism corporations typically had long-term plans often set for between five and ten years. The advent of information communications technology and recent world events such as the political polarisation of international regions, natural disasters, acts of terrorism and the global economic crisis has led organisations to rethink planning options. In particular, the ten-year strategic plan is no longer a viable option; instead, lead times have been notably reduced. Three to five years tends to be a maximum term (e.g. Shangri-La Hotels) with shorter one-year, six- and one-monthly intervening periods. Clearly, large corporations tend to work within longer timeframes but they have still been much reduced. The tourism industry is dominated by small to medium-sized firms, many of whom operate seasonally. Necessarily, plans would be formulated in accordance with the frequency and duration of the busy period. In some tourism destinations this may be for around six to eight months (e.g. USA – Sevierville,

Tennessee; and Switzerland – Arosa) whereas in others it could be for even shorter periods (e.g. UK – Great Yarmouth and Skegness).

Another development is an implicit acknowledgement by managers and planners that the business environment does not unfold in a neat, orderly and logical manner; as some items of apparel read: 'S*&te happens' and plans should be flexible enough to deal with contingencies. Butler, Ferris and Napier (1991) noted this emerging trend around twenty years ago. Thus, a contemporary view of strategic plans should incorporate an ability to deal with both intended and unintended aspects whilst still expressing corporate philosophy and a process of environmental scanning. An evaluation of the firm's strengths and weaknesses would remain important in order to develop aims and objectives and ultimately formulate strategies to achieve them. The key here is to appreciate that planning is not 'exact' and tourism firms should attempt to take advantage of unexpected developments. In a sense, the focus is shifted from planning as a 'science' to a process by which firms learn and build on opportunities including those which are serendipitous.

Human resources planning (HRP) is no different and relies on similar procedures as a foundation for the development of goals and human resources (HR) strategies. However, there is now a recognition by enlightened firms that knowledge is a key element of human resources. Moreover like modern strategy, knowledge and its acquisition is no longer regarded as purely 'scientific'. Operational expertise is now considered to be no more important than tacit, experiential and other less formally gathered and communicated information. Thus, HR planning needs to be more creative and flexible to account for the 'newer' forms of company knowledge.

Modern economies and thus service organisations within build their prosperity on 'intellectual capital' (knowledge-based economies) rather than through more traditional tangible resources. The future success of tourism firms depends on their ability to learn from their strategic and trading environments. This information needs to be communicated to workers who in turn share their experiential knowledge and skills to aid the design and implementation of new service innovations. In short, human resource planners need to use a holistic lens when addressing the issue of acquiring and managing knowledge as it is derived from a number of sources. According to Wood et al. (2006) these key areas include the firm's systems, processes and structures and the relationships they have with customers.

Firms practicing the above are engaged in the process of knowledge management and it is important to establish the appropriate systems and organisational culture to ensure the process is ongoing and iterative. A major challenge for most tourism firms is the unacceptable level of labour turnover. In terms of managing and augmenting knowledge for improved performance, this position unchecked, makes the acquisition and optimal use of a firm's intelligence very difficult. This is particularly so if 'core' workers regularly quit their jobs. Much expertise and an accumulation of company knowledge will be lost. The job of the human resource planner becomes vital in the modern economic context if this situation is to be minimised. In other words, 'learning capacity' must be built and managed effectively in tourism organisations for their long-term success and sustainability. Thus, the major source of competitive advantage is its intellectual capital.

Effective strategies for managing knowledge in tourism firms will only be realised by an employer's fundamental belief in the value of human resources. There are many approaches which encompass the above including planning procedures and embedded systems appearing in the present chapter. There is also an abundance of expertise available from various consultancy firms, government agencies and professional organisations. A list appears below in no particular order:

- The Chartered Institute of Personnel and Development (CIPD) – UK and international
  http://www.cipd.co.uk/about/intact
- The Society for Human Resource Management – USA and international
  http://www.shrm.org/Pages/default.aspx
- Asia-Pacific Human Resources Management Council – Asia Pacific
  http://www.conference-board.org/councils/councilsDetailUS.cfm?Council_ID=265
- Australian Human Resources Institute – Australasia
  http://www.ahri.com.au
- Investors in People – UK
  http://www.investorsinpeople.co.uk/Pages/Home.aspx
- United Nations World Tourism Organization – international
  http://www.unwto.org/index.php
- International Labour Organization – international
  http://www.ilo.org/global/lang–en/index.htm

This chapter begins by outlining the nature of strategic planning and continues by introducing human resources planning (HRP) within this context. Both areas are linked and some basic HRP approaches are overviewed. Job and 'culture' fit provide a focus for one specific recruitment and selection planning technique. The implications of long standing job vacancies are discussed, followed by a summary of several forecasting techniques. The chapter continues by outlining some contingencies in situations of labour shortage and surplus and summarily considers some important impacts of 'downsizing' on both employers and workers.

STRATEGIC PLANNING

As already noted strategic planning is not particularly scientific nor is it compulsory. Rather, it is a pragmatic choice in the hope of clarifying perceived external and internal complexity. Tools used for strategic planning purposes vary in their focus and complexity but differences matter less than usefulness. In other words, techniques must suit contexts, for example, small businesses would probably opt for simple ones whereas a large corporation's need for strategic information requires more complex procedures to be in place. However, all organisations require information to assist in the decision-making process. For example, consider the impending impact of a government directive to increase unemployment benefits above a national minimum wage. In a seasonal resort area this move would probably reduce the supply of temporary workers. Such legislation would force employers to act in a number of ways including:

- increasing hourly wages above the new imposed level to attract people into paid employment;
- automating or redesigning services to require less operational staff where possible;
- sourcing temporary employees from other regions; and
- exiting the tourism industry.

Of course, these responses are operationalised according to resources available. Typically, the small tourism firm relies on informal networks and government employment services to extend its search for labour beyond the boundary of regional 'travel to work area'. Conversely, large corporations have their own national or even global networks to source workers from further afield. Indeed, some may even be powerful enough to lobby governments to amend employment legislation in their favour. For example, enacted policies surrounding the mobility of potential labour between countries (e.g. European Union) would help increase the pool of potential workers.

Typically, firms need to understand both themselves, in terms of what they can offer stakeholders (or not) and the context in which they operate. Two approaches widely used for environmental scanning purposes are a PEST analysis (Political, Economic, Social and Technological) and a SWOT analysis (Strengths, Weaknesses, Opportunities, Threats). The former often precedes the latter because a PEST analysis has an external focus on the market from which the position, potential and direction for a business can be determined. A SWOT analysis measures a business unit or proposition from an internal perspective through internal factors (Strengths or Weaknesses). However, external factors are also considered (Opportunities and Threats) and in practice there is some overlap between the two techniques.

The process of scanning can be as detailed or scant as is appropriate for the tourism firm and the nature and complexity of both its external and internal environments. However, it should involve an assessment of the organisation's current position, how achieved and where it sees itself in the future. Table 2.1 provides a summary of issues worth considering when undertaking environmental analyses.

Table 2.1 Key environmental factors

External	*Internal*
Where is the tourism firm located geographically (location, location, location)?	Who owns the tourism firm – private or public sector, Pty, local, multinational, group etc.?
Level of infrastructure, communication and utilities available to the tourism firm.	Size and structure of the firm – complex, simple, bureaucratic, organic, mechanistic, divisionalised etc. Small firms depend more on informal directly communicated systems. Large firms usually have better developed formal HR systems although decision-making is more complex and less effective
What are the prevailing economic conditions for the organisation (interest rates, wage expectations etc.)?	How is the firm meeting its goals and objectives – what is its overall strategy and how does it impact on HR activities throughout the company?
What is the nature of the labour market? Diversity, unionised, management/ employee relations, negotiation, unemployment, over-supply, skilled, unskilled workers all impact on the policies pursued by the employer	Organisational history and culture. How do the founder's values and qualities impact on culture (basic assumptions and employee behaviour) of the firm?
What is the influence of political and legal factors on the tourism firm? Under what legal restrictions do businesses operate? How stable is the political landscape in an overseas tourism destination? How does the culture of the host nation impact on the firm?	What resources does the firm have at its disposal (financial, human, knowledge, raw materials etc.)?
How do demographic and diversity factors impact on the firm? How will age, population size, level of education etc. affect holiday entitlements, recruitment and training programmes? Also how will diversity impact on job attitudes, expectations and workplace behaviour?	

What are the overarching industry trends? How will the increasing use of on-line booking systems impact on some tourism organisations? How will increased website presence of tourism providers impact on traditional suppliers of this service?	
International factors such as economic cycles, competitiveness and entrepreneurial values will also need to be considered	

Adapted from: Härtel *et al.* (2007: 24-30)

These issues are crucial in establishing the tourism organisation's current situation and pertain to individuals, groups and or the organisation as a unit. Once accomplished, the firm's 'record' of, say, service quality may be benchmarked against that of a competitor to see if any gaps exist. There are a number of applications for the gap analysis procedure but all are based on the basic notion of a current situation or state and an intended future or end state. Typically, both are defined and the difference between the two is the gap. For example, a simple illustration of gap analysis for labour retention at unit (or organisational) level in tourism firms is shown below in Figure 2.1.

Additional appropriate benchmarking HR issues include; recruitment, selection, training and job design. There are also other issues to consider such as the overall quality grading of both establishments, quality of raw materials, nature of the service, ratio of staff to customers and so on. However, before direct valid comparisons can be made between organisations, planners must ensure they are comparing like with like. For example, would it necessarily be appropriate for a restaurant serving very basic menu items to benchmark against a fine-dining eatery? Probably not but this very much depends on the aspirations of the firm. If the answer is 'yes' and it has hopes of eventually achieving three Michelin stars, the journey would be difficult. Moreover, the implications for HR would be significant requiring a number of questions to be asked:

- What is the intensity and nature of competition in the restaurant sector for restaurants of high quality?
- Are there any barriers to entering this specific market segment?
- How many likely other restaurants are out there?
- How many are there likely to be over the next one to three years?
- If barriers are low and your restaurant becomes successful, will you attract more entrepreneurs into the region?
- Is your service likely to be imitated easily?
- If not, would consumers readily accept close substitutes instead?

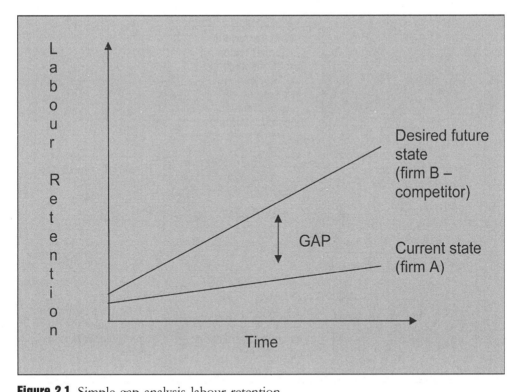

Figure 2.1 Simple gap analysis labour retention

Adapted from: http://www.marketingteacher.com/Lessons/lesson_gap_analysis.htm (accessed January 2009)

- What about suppliers, that is, are there many or only a few? If the latter, prices of supplies may become inflated. This applies in the sense of raw materials for menu items but also the supply of labour.
- How attractive are you as a potential provider of employment in terms of remuneration and associated working conditions?

The above are critical questions and similar were first posed by Michael Porter. His 'Five Forces' model proposes a rational procedure to assess environmental influences on a business. It was devised to help link a firm's strategy (market focus, differentiation, cost minimisation) to opportunities in the prevailing external environment and is shown in Figure 2.2.

The model has been criticised at a number of levels. For our purposes the most apposite is the assumption that all tourism organisations seek competitive advantage. This is clearly not the case as most firms are small and have 'lifestyle' aspirations rather than entrepreneurial growth. Whilst the term is vague it is commonly understood to be where owners are not motivated by classical entrepreneurial ambitions of growth (Lashley &

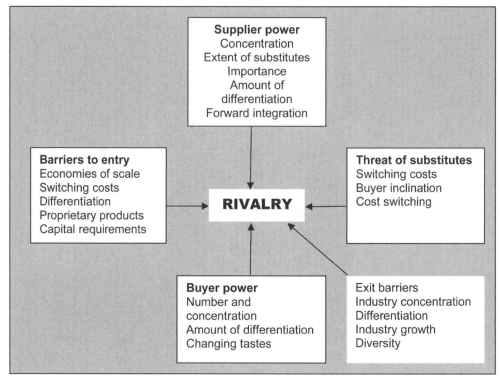

Figure 2.2 Porter's five forces

Source: Porter (1985: 6)

Rowson, 2007) but rather are happy for their tourism operation to simply support their lifestyle.

In short, all tourism businesses benefit from using strategic planning techniques. When, where and how they are applied depends on the company objectives. All vary and are designed to scrutinise different areas important to the business and thus planning process. Indeed, some owners may proceed using their own adapted versions specifically customised consistent with their business aspirations. Nonetheless, it would be inconceivable to begin a journey toward either an unknown destination or one that is known without a road map. This is the essential nature and importance of strategic planning and is also true of strategic human resources planning. However, the question remains: 'How are the two linked?'

Critical note

Strategic planning is a pragmatic approach used to clarify perceived external and internal complexity.

PLANNING FOR HUMAN RESOURCES

Human resources planning (HRP) may be explained in a number of ways, for example, according to Nankervis *et al.* (2008) it is an ongoing process with short, medium and long-term contingency options, in order to comprehensively reflect human resource (HR) strategies and to modify associated HR processes. Moreover, these plans are based on information provided by a human resource information management system (HRIS). Figure 2.3 shows a typical human resource information system used in larger firms.

All organisations need such a system but it is certainly not the case that one size fits all. Small firms often have a simple HRIS which, while unsophisticated, is appropriate usually consisting of a database, spreadsheet and word processing application; large firms have

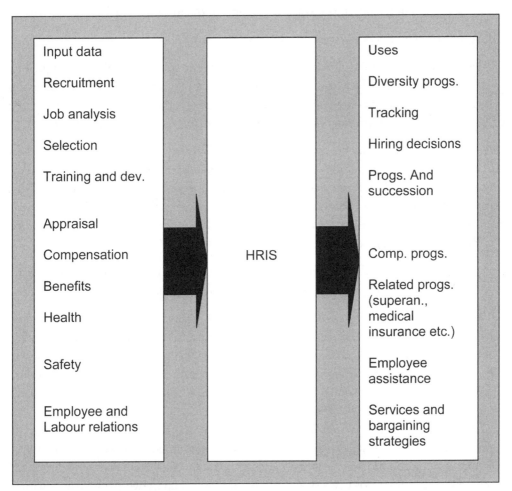

Input data	HRIS	Uses
Recruitment		Diversity progs.
Job analysis		Tracking
Selection		Hiring decisions
Training and dev.		Progs. And succession
Appraisal		
Compensation		Comp. progs.
Benefits		Related progs. (superan., medical insurance etc.)
Health		
Safety		Employee assistance
Employee and Labour relations		Services and bargaining strategies

Figure 2.3 Human resources information system

Adapted from: Mondy (2008: 114)

other dedicated applications. It matters little what systems are used so long as they are suitable for the organisations concerned. As with all information used for decision-making, it should be timely, contemporary, concise, understandable, relevant and complete. An appropriate HRIS is an essential part of the overall HRP process which seeks to inform effective utilisation of the human resources of the firm, taking into account changing internal and external circumstances. Whilst the process is ongoing with a long-term perspective, it must still maintain an awareness of current short and medium-term environmental movements.

Other definitions say much the same thing, for example, the Strategic and Business Planning Free Resource Center (BPFRC, 2009) considers HRP to be:

> The process by which management ensures that it has the right personnel, who are capable of completing those tasks that help the organization reach its objectives.

More strategically, HRP may be considered as the process of:

> Rigorous HR planning linking people management to the organization's mission, vision, goals and objectives, as well as its strategic plan and budgetary resources. A key goal of HR planning is to get the right number of people with the right skills, experience and competencies in the right jobs at the right time at the right cost.

Here we see an emphasis on linkage with overall business strategy. This point is key because failure to consider the process in a systemic manner would almost certainly ensure organisational inefficiencies. It would also be unrealistic as HR exists to serve the whole organisation. Thus, resonance between business objectives and HRP is essential and should be driven by the overall vision, mission and strategic goals of the organisation.

This emphasis is expressed very simply by the BPFRC (2009):

> Human resources planning needs to reference the details of the overall strategic plan of the organization. In effect, it serves the strategic plan.

In a practical sense HRP seeks to optimise the deployment of human resources strategically in response to changing business conditions and is viewed as inclusive involving more than just the HR department (Nankervis et al., 2008). In short, it matches labour demand and supply projections within the internal and external contexts of organisations. The strategic alignment of HRP is shown in Figure 2.4. The three overall stages of the planning process are also illustrated.

Essentially, the HRP process is similar to that of strategic planning. Both seek to understand positions relative to the broad business environment and use the same underpinning logic in the process. Strategic planning carefully considers external and internal forces likely to impact positively or negatively on the firm and HRP does likewise within the overall organisation-wide planning process. However, this scenario is an ideal and whether the two are truly in concert very much depends on the commitment and

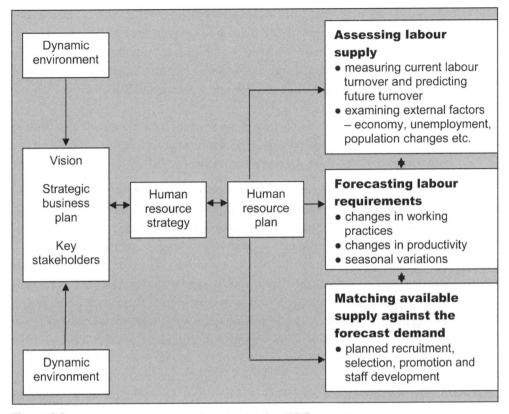

Figure 2.4 Strategic alignment and stages in the HRP process

Adapted from: Nankervis *et al.* (2008) and Advisory, Conciliation and Arbitration Service (ACAS, 2009)

management philosophy of organisational seniors. To be effective, HRP involves general and line management, human resources department and workers. Dessler *et al.* (2004: 131) summarise the role of each below:

- *General managers* – advise on long-term goals and strategies of the firm including a demand for systematic HRP including environmental scanning when developing goals. They also secure commitment from line managers in developing and implementing HRP and provide input to the succession planning of senior members of the firm.
- *Line managers* – consider systematically the factors likely to impact their part of the firm in the future and how these may affect achievement of business objectives (number and skills of workers; training and development needs, creating employee awareness of acceptable performance standards and how they relate to the business). Also to implement and monitor the HRP.

- *Human resources department* – develop and integrate HRP and to advise line managers in their HR preparations. They must also ensure that HR policies and programmes are appropriate to the firm including advising line managers when developing and implementing training. It is also important that human resources stimulate awareness of the value of HRP and associated policies for the future of the firm.

- *Employees* – responsible for identifying own needs and communicating this to management in order to facilitate their development and future career. Also act as a source of practical feedback regarding the impact of HRP procedures and policies.

Nankervis *et al.* (2008) underscore the importance of integration between key decision makers, sections and departments through a '[...] strategic HRM planning group' (p. 116). This links all HRM functions together and allows modifications based on environmental feedback to ensure that results are integrated with organisational functions and strategies. However on a cautionary note, these authors point out that only a few firms adopt a truly strategic HR perspective. Indeed, the nature and form of integration will depend on the context, for example, a truly entrepreneurial firm may focus on training, development and establishing long-term careers. On the other hand, a small seasonal tourism operation will often only be concerned with attracting sufficient numbers of employees with the right skill and cultural fit for positions of short-duration with limited career options. If this firm does not seek to grow, as many tourism 'lifestyle' operations do not, this may be one of only very few objectives. Nonetheless, hiring appropriate people is a key concern for all organisations whether large, small, lifestyle or entrepreneurial. The following section highlights the importance of 'cultural fit' in the recruitment context.

Critical note

HRP and strategic planning both seek to understand the broad business environment and use the same underpinning logic in the process. Strategic planning carefully considers external and internal forces likely to impact positively or negatively on the firm and HRP does likewise within the overall organisation-wide planning process.

Reflections

Interview a local tourism employer.

1. Ask whether they have a human resource plan. If so, what aspects does it include beyond recruitment, selection and payroll.
2. Ask how the HRIS system informs the planning procedure.
3. Undertake desk research of one large tourism organisation.
4. Compare the human resource plans and HRIS of both firms.

HIRING CULTURALLY APPROPRIATE PEOPLE

Tourism firms invest hundreds of thousands of dollars each year recruiting key staff based on a carefully considered set of criteria. Usually these are skills/experience/ability-based and some companies will make use of a personnel requisition form (or equivalent) on which are listed job details including various requirements such as education, experience, knowledge, desired abilities and physical requirements. Understandably, these tend to be based around the job as the organisation is seeking to achieve 'job fit'. After all, if someone has an appropriate skill set and worked in a similar field, they would be expected to perform adequately in a new related role. However, there is another key area which some argue is more important. Recently, this has come to be known as 'cultural fit' or the degree to which the candidate's values are compatible with those of the firm. According to human resources consultant Bruce Whatt (2005) 90% of hiring managers believe that cultural fit is important (although only 36% assess for it). He notes that workplace knowledge and skill sets have a limited shelf-life whereas organisational culture tends to be enduring. Importantly, aspects of culture such as values and attitudes are very difficult to change. Individuals should therefore be hired who already possess those compatible with those of the firm.

In the tourism industry, workers tend to be employed on a temporary, part-time, short-term basis or some configuration thereof. Seasonality is cited as the industry characteristic responsible for these working arrangements (see Chapter 1). Correspondingly, many employers rely on 'informal' systems of training and some offer little or none whatsoever. This is an unfortunate consequence of using a reactive 'least cost' HR approach and can lead to several negative outcomes. Putting aside the pros and cons of this philosophy for the time being, the importance of achieving cultural fit via the selection process becomes most appropriate. There is an argument that suggests many tourism and hospitality operational competencies may be picked up on the job especially where procedures have been codified and deskilled. If we accept the argument that cultural skills cannot be taught, the importance of achieving immediate cultural fit through appropriate recruitment and selection procedures seems obvious. Indeed, Whatt's (2005) assertion that selecting culturally appropriate workers is more important than achieving job fit generically would appear to have some currency for the tourism industry. This is especially the case for those operating at the customer interface.

Differentiation

As discussed in Chapter 1, tourism organisations are now focusing on their employees as an important potential source of product differentiation. This goes beyond simply having the required operational skills but includes intangibles which are arguably culturally-oriented and the most important elements of the tourism product. The service interface is the key area where overall impressions of quality are formed by customers. It is therefore important that employees are able to 'perform' in an appropriate manner. Many organisations are insightful enough to know that, paradoxically, the interface is an area where direct control becomes impossible (unless the employee is shadowed – which is not recommended!). As such, 'scripting' has emerged as an indirect technique to manage the service encounter.

Whilst this goes some way in dealing with the matter, there are often challenges. For example, if the employee sticks rigidly to the script it may become awkward and insincere. Indeed, if the service is complex and highly customised, simple scripting becomes ineffective and may even impact negatively on perceived quality. Clearly, the liberty front-line employees enjoy during the encounter depends on the degree of empowerment bestowed by management. The other issue is where staff affect sympathetic and appropriate responses during the encounter over long periods. If they do not possess the required cultural service values and attitudes situations of high internal stress usually result (to say nothing of the impact this has on service delivery). Ultimately, workers become alienated from their jobs and leave the organisation.

Gale (2009) observes that hiring people who are already culturally predisposed to the firm is now quite common in the hospitality industry as the article below in Box 2.1 shows.

BOX 2.1 Case study – Hire For attitude, train For skill

Recognising a valuable candidate for work in the hospitality industry is 'not just about intellectual abilities or problem-solving skills – it's also customer orientation,' says Dr Fred Mayo, clinical professor at the Preston Robert Tisch Center for Hospitality, Tourism and Sports Management at New York University.

'In a hotel you need people who are positive, friendly, cordial and encouraging,' he says. 'The last thing you want when you've traveled a distance to a hotel is someone frowning at you at the front desk. Despite what's going on in a staff member's life, you have to welcome people with open arms. To find people with that outlook on life isn't easy.'

Capella Singapore General Manager Michael Luible agrees. 'It is always a challenge to find the most exceptional talent,' he says. 'While there are many people with hotel and service industry experience, we are seeking dedicated and talented staff who possess something special – a unique combination of personality, attitude and aptitude.'

Hiring for personality and attitude is commonplace in hospitality, and many consider it a best practice across the industry.

'When it comes to the hiring process, as a third step, we look at "Does the personality match?" and "Do we have a good gut feeling about the individual?"' says

Henrik Mansson, senior vice president of human resources for Movenpick Hotels & Resorts. 'People come from different industries but are hired for the right attitude.'

Ellen Dubois du Bellay, vice president of learning and development for Four Seasons Hotels and Resorts, says the same is true at her company. 'The thing that is nice about hospitality is you don't need to be attracting people who have experience in the industry always. You can take people from retail (or other industries) if they have an attitude that allows them to serve guests.'

What does that entail? 'Personal service, for our guests, depends on spontaneous and unscripted acts of kindness,' Dubois du Bellay says. 'We need people to be able to deliver that. Attitude is really important, so we spend time looking for it in interviews, because it is hard to train people to be nice. We want to try to stack the deck in our favor in that regard.'

Fairmont Hotels & Resorts also finds it critical to its success to 'hire for talent and train for technical,' says Carolyn Clark, senior vice president of human resources. 'The Fairmont selection interview helps us identify candidates who have a natural passion to provide great guest service,' she notes. 'We believe if we put time and effort into hiring the right people with the right talents to work in the right environment with the right leadership, training and recognition, we will see higher engagement and retention.'

Further, such engagement can lead to a healthier bottom line, as Fairmont finds that its hotels with the highest employee engagement scores also have the highest guest service scores (this finding is noted in author Joe Wheeler's recent article entitled 'Forging the Next Generation of the Service Profit Chain'). 'Talented and engaged colleagues provide memorable service and create guest loyalty, which in turn drives profitability and long-term sustainability,' Clark says.

Questions

1. Explain how you would approach the challenge of hiring the 'right' frontline employee using 'cultural' fit as a main criterion.
2. Discuss how to address the issue of managing existing employees who fail to meet the firm's cultural criteria?
3. If new employees are culturally appropriate is there a need to train them further?

Source: Gale (2009)

In essence, the process of hiring for cultural fit is not that different to job/skills focused approaches and may be achieved through the existing recruitment and selection process. Obviously, managers must understand the cultural tools which are being used and how to apply them. These could include behavioural questions, pre-employment dinners and events, realistic job previews and so on. However, there are a number of behavioural/attitudinal questionnaires which may also be used to assess cultural fit. Some are designed by the employing firm whilst others can be used or adapted from standard instruments.

Reflections

Visit three local tourism employers.

1. Ask about their recruitment and selection procedures.
2. Ask whether they choose workers based on skills, work attitudes or a combination of both.

The Service Predisposition Instrument

An example of an attitudinal questionnaire designed to address cultural fit is the Service Predisposition Instrument (SPI) (Lee-Ross, 2000 – see Appendix 1 at the end of this chapter). This tool is specific to service industries and identifies a candidate's values and attitudes towards service delivery. The SPI is easy to adapt depending on context and has been used in a number of sectors including, tourism and hospitality, healthcare, and local and international government. It is currently available on the Testgrid website (http://www.testgrid.com/viewfile?docNo=3944) and appears as 'A service attitudes predictor'. It may also be used as an organisational diagnostic tool to assess the cultural attitudes of workers already employed in the organisation.

Essentially, the SPI is a 33-item questionnaire designed to assess the attitudes of potential front-line service industry workers. Questions are based on the 'three-component' view of attitudes (for example, see Ajzen & Fishbein, 1980):

- Cognitive – perceptual responses and verbal statements of belief;
- Affective – sympathetic nervous responses and statements of affect/emotion; and
- Conative – overt actions and statements concerning behaviour.

The model on which the SPI is based proposes that the affective outcome 'Personal satisfaction with service provided' is maximised when three cognitive expressions are satisfied by the existence of six service dimensions. Furthermore, the relationship between the service dimensions and the cognitive expressions and the cognitive expressions and affective outcome is moderated by the degree of 'deference' present internally in the service provider. Figure 2.5 shows how these relationships are mapped through the Service predispositions model.

The six service dimensions are explained as:

- competence – considers comprehensive job and skill-based knowledge to have a positive impact on service provision;

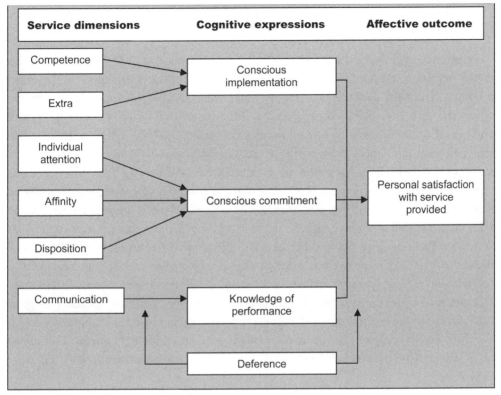

Figure 2.5 Service predisposition model showing the relationships between service dimensions, cognitive expressions and the personal outcome moderated by deference

- extra – understanding that customers may require additional services to those expected;
- individual attention – considers that all customers may have individual requirements that need to be addressed;
- affinity – understanding that establishing a close initial relationship with customers helps in explaining unintended service delays;
- disposition – willingness to go beyond normal job responsibilities to satisfy customers; and
- communication – considers clear and open communication with customers important.

Cognitive expressions are explained as:

- the degree to which the service provider feels they have fulfilled their service tasks;
- the degree to which the service provider feels obligated toward their customers; and

43

- the degree to which the service provider considers important knowledge about their work accomplishments.

Stage three of the model accounts for personal satisfaction with service provided, that is, the reactions and impressions employees feel as a result of working at the customer interface. The final variable of deference acknowledges that customers drive the encounter even if they prove to be awkward. It is understood as an amalgam of cultural and personal differences which manifest as a composite moderator. The model predicts that deference influences how positively employees respond to other model-specified variables. In short, employees who are highly deferential are more likely to believe that nothing is too much trouble when delivering a service. Therefore service dimensions, cognitive dimensions and the personal outcome will be scored higher than individuals who only rate deference as marginal (i.e. below '4' on the associated Likert-type scale). A Service Predisposition Score (SPS) may also be calculated as a summary index of candidates' overall service orientation. Output can be subjected to various statistical analyses (correlation, regression, mean testing, factor analysis etc.) but this is not usually necessary. In a practical sense, mean scores per dimension and an overall SPS are usually enough as they can be simply entered onto a computer spreadsheet via Excel for example. Managers are then able to compare them with a set of pre-established industry norms. This allows an assessment of their cultural suitability for the job. An example is shown below in Figure 2.6.

The above shows that the job applicant is not culturally suitable for the position of tour desk attendant. Clearly, the potential costs of failing to select the appropriate person are immense. The following section discusses the issue and introduces some simple formulae used to identify the organisational costs of failing to fill vacant job positions.

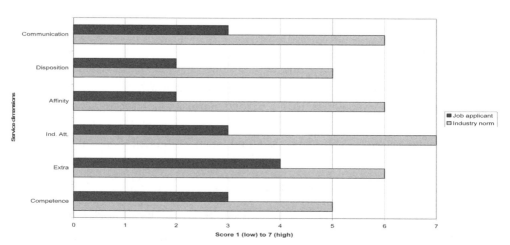

Figure 2.6 Hypothetical comparison of mean SPI scores with pre-established norms for the job of tour desk attendant

> **Critical note**
>
> In essence, the process of hiring for cultural fit is similar to job/skills focused approaches but managers must understand the cultural tools which are being used and how to apply them.

VACANT POSITIONS

Calculating the cost of vacancies is imprecise as it depends very much on the nature of the role and the industry in question but some simple approaches can help clarify the situation. Some argue that putting a dollar value on the cost of a vacancy is important as it allows managers to understand the issue in terms they can understand easily. Most managers realise the intuitive costs of failing to appoint an appropriate person for a job first time and these include:

- demotivation;
- increased absenteeism and labour turnover;
- high stress levels in the workplace;
- inconsistent service delivery; and
- poor performance.

Thus, a focus on cost places an appropriate lens on the recruitment situation. Calculating the cost of vacancies shows the commercial impact of not having appropriate employees in key positions. However, it is important to remember that formulae used can only provide cost estimates. Sullivan (2005) provides some guidance for those which are simple and easy to calculate. He considers five to be key and they are shown in Table 2.2.

Table 2.2 Simple cost of vacancy formulae

Average revenue per lost employee	Tourism firm's revenue per worker divided by number of working days in a year. This gives average daily revenue per worker. Thus, if there is a vacant position, the revenue generating potential can be assessed (or rather the 'missing' revenue of an unfilled position can be appreciated)
Salary 'multiplier' of revenue that is lost – based on the idea that all employees generate an amount of money above their salary	Total dollar amount the tourism firm spends via payroll for one year divided by the number of employees. This gives an average employee salary which can then be divided into the revenue per employee.

	This calculates a number known as the salary multiplier (usually between two and seven). Next multiply the multiplier by the worker's daily salary to get the revenue each worker is expected to generate. Similar to the 'average revenue per lost employee', if a worker is not placed on a job on that day, they cannot generate the average daily salary multiplier
Revenue lost	This is the average yearly revenue generated by a worker divided by the working days in a year. If there is an unfilled vacancy revenue will be foregone
Budget expenditure per employee that is lost (for positions where direct measures are impossible)	Tourism firm's annual budget divided by number of workers. This gives the average budget expenditure per worker. This can be divided by the number of working days per year to give the budget value of each individual

Adapted from: Sullivan (2005)

The values of such formulae depend on context, assumptions and attention to financial detail. For example, if vacancies are filled by temporary workers, employers would normally have to factor in the potential for lower productivity. If someone else covers the position for a short while there will be cost implications such as overtime pay and possibly poorer performance outcomes. Sullivan (2005) draws attention to other issues arising from long-standing job vacancies which need to be considered when calculating costs; they are summarised in Figure 2.7.

Inappropriate employee selection is likely to cause increased voluntary and involuntary labour turnover which, in turn, leads to long-standing job vacancies. As Figure 2.4 shows, implications of this situation extend throughout the organisation beyond costs which can be identified directly. However, prior to appointing anyone, the tourism firm must first establish staffing requirements through careful internal and external environmental scanning and data scrutiny; the following section discusses some of these issues.

STAFFING REQUIREMENTS AND FORECASTING

Any determination of staffing requirements will necessarily account for the tourism firm's overall strategic objective of provision, type and flexibility/customisability of the service product. A hotel or tour operator must be able to secure workers with appropriate skills

On the team

Lower productivity, loss of experience, leadership and skills, disruption of team cohesion.

Lower team creativity as co-workers frustrated and overworked.

Increased accidents, error rates and lower service quality.

Increased 'negativity' amongst teams, higher levels of grievance and union activity.

Employers reluctant to terminate poor performing employees.

Increased management time and effort

Teams with vacancies need more management attention, decreasing time spent on more strategic management issues.

Managers often skip normal responsibilities to fill in for the vacant employee.

Opportunity costs for things managers and co-workers could have done if they didn't have to carry the extra load of filling in for a vacancy.

Vacancies caused by top management decisions can cause managers to lose hope and may lead to a high management turnover rate.

Out-of-pocket and other costs

High-cost consultants or agency staff 'fill in help' could mean higher costs or overtime for existing workers.

The new hire may be of lower quality (low performance) and unlikely to be immediately productive.

Where one employee leaves others may follow causing more vacancies.

Many new hires don't work out and must be replaced in the short-term this stretches the length of the vacancy.

Individual employee impacts

People doing unfamiliar jobs, decreasing productivity, frustrated and overworked employees, high quit rates, increased sickness, lateness, and absenteeism.

Vacancies may hold up vacation time for current employees which may lead to increase stress or frustration.

If temps or 'fill-ins' must be hired, they usually have a higher error rate than the average employee and they are unlikely to generate many new ideas.

Customer impacts, competitive advantage, culture, and value

Negative message to stakeholders about stability and vulnerability of company, they may go elsewhere, increased competitive pressures.

Errors resulting from vacancies may lower sales volume and occasionally result in lost customers.

'Panic' hiring of poor performers who may be difficult to retrench.

Top level vacancies can impact on sources of external financing and future partnerships or mergers and sends a negative message to analysts and the stock market.

Weakening of the corporate culture.

Your image and recruiting

'Message' to competitors that firm is 'weak', may become bolder in the product and employee poaching/headhunting markets.

Message to future recruits that the organisation is not easily able to recruit replacements.

Message to current employees that firm is in decline and high vacancy rates may over-stress recruiters and the recruitment process.

Figure 2.7 Impacts of long-standing job vacancies

Adapted from: Sullivan (2005)

for this purpose. After establishing the firm's labour needs, both internal and external labour markets must be scrutinised to see whether there is likely to be an over or under supply of workers. This is an ongoing process given the dynamic nature of both the external and internal environments. For example, what happens if another significant competitor secures most of the skilled external labour you require; potential shortages presumably? On the other hand after analysis, the tourism firm may have an over-supply internally. Similarly, how does the firm cope with key employees moving elsewhere or with a round of retirements? In a sense, the latter issue is more manageable because retirees should have been identified already and suitable succession planning procedures established.

Succession planning may be defined as:

> The process of making sure there is a suitable supply of appropriate successors for current and future positions in the tourism firm. Usually, these are key positions consistent with strategic planning to ensure the long term success of the company and to satisfy the development and career progression of incumbents.

The very basis of succession planning is based on a pluralistic notion that a balance needs to be achieved between the often competing demands of the firm and its workers. As such, the process deserves much attention as individual aspirations can differ between managers and between employer and employee. Dessler *et al.* (2004) explain succession planning through the following activities:

- analysis of the demand for key positions by level, function and skill;
- auditing existing executives and projecting likely future internal and external supply;
- planning career paths of individuals based on estimates of future requirements plus performance appraisals to find an appropriate match;
- career counseling based on a realistic assessment of the firm's potential to deliver and the individual's capacity to perform;
- fast-tracking careers targeted at future needs of the firm;
- strategic recruitment to satisfy short-term and long-term aspirations; and
- identify the processes by which vacancies are filled.

Adapted from: Dessler *et al.* (2004: 128)

Issues other than planned retirements, for example, are less predictable, this is why planning is of paramount importance as it better prepares managers for contingencies; expect the (partially) unexpected! Forecasting, like the HRP process, is not an exact science but careful planning can improve its accuracy. The process of forecasting involves first identifying demand for the tourism product and then interpreting in HR terms how many workers are required to deliver the product. Providing services is a little more difficult than producing manufactures in quantitative terms but can be achieved so long as there is a thorough understanding of what particular jobs entail. For example, assume a tourist resort contains three restaurants of dissimilar standards. One is pitched at the high end of the market (c) whilst the other two (a and b) provide more modest services as represented below in Figure 2.8.

Clearly, the fine-dining front-line employees deliver a more customised and complex service than the other two eateries. Thus at face value, the job of food service attendant would appear as a single category for the purpose of forecasting. On closer inspection the roles between restaurants differ quite considerably. More staff are needed for fine-dining service delivery (per *couvert*) than in the other operations where a simpler and less labour intensive mode is required. Additionally, the duration of meal consumption varies between customers. It is reasonable to argue that the modest meal will be consumed in less time than the complex service. However, the situation is complicated because restaurant 'c' does not cater exclusively for one type of client. Therefore differences will be apparent even within the same restaurant. For example, a romantic meal for two is likely to take longer than a business meeting but both may take place in the fine dining eatery. Forecasting therefore becomes even more difficult in these circumstances but the issues are not insurmountable so long as managers are aware of subtle differences per role and plan accordingly. It is therefore prudent to view forecasting techniques in tourism and hospitality as merely blueprints or guides given the above contextual factors.

Mondy (2008) outlines some of the more popular HR forecasting techniques and a summary is provided below:

- Zero-base – uses the firm's current level of employment as basis for determining future requirements. The process is repeated each year. If an incumbent leaves (for whatever reason), the position is not filled unless it can be justified after analysis. New positions are treated in a similar way.
- Bottom-up – an interactive approach between all levels of the organisation. Beginning at the 'bottom', managers are asked to forecast and justify HR requirements. This input is used as the process moves up the organisation resulting

a   b   c

Figure 2.8 One resort, three restaurants

in an aggregate forecast for the whole firm. Use of information from all levels forces debate amongst all mangers resulting in a more 'strategic' output than would otherwise be the case.

- Relationship between sales volume and HR requirements – often cited as the most useful metric. Sales are expressed along the '*x*' axis of a graph with number of employees required shown on the vertical axis. As sales increase so too does the need for staff. This technique allows managers to estimate the number of employees required at various levels of demand. There are various associated statistical techniques including correlation and regression analysis but the graphical approach is probably the most simple.
- Simulation models – using mathematical modeling techniques allows planners to input various contingencies or 'what ifs' thereby increasing the likely accuracy of forecasts. However, simulation models are only as good as the algorithms they use. In short, they are not a panacea but can be very powerful nonetheless (all things being equal).

Adapted from: Mondy (2008: 106–107)

Critical note

Forecasting involves identifying a demand for the tourism product and then deciding how many workers are required to deliver the product.

Reflections

Visit three local tourism employers.

1. Ask how long-standing vacancies impact on their organisations.
2. Identify the forecasting techniques they use.
3. Conduct desk-research to identify other ways of ascertaining the cost of long-standing job vacancies.

Internal and external sources of labour

Predicting HR needs accurately is one thing but gaining insight into the availability of workers is another. Organisations need to know the calibre of human resources they have at their disposal internally. Furthermore, if gaps in supply are forthcoming they need to know from where employees can be sourced. For example, does the planner look to the external labour market or can the internal market be trained and developed?

Where small firms are concerned, which is the most likely scenario for tourism, information about existing workers is often lodged in the head of the employer. While this is a perfectly reasonable and practical system for a small labour force whose relationship with the boss is probably familial and personal, a similar strategy is not appropriate as firms grow. Unless operations employing more than 15 or so workers use an HR database, matching talents, skills and aspirations with jobs becomes difficult. Many computerised databases are available and all should include information on employees including (but not limited to) experience, knowledge, skills, appraisal evaluations, developmental needs and aspirations (see discussion of HRIS, pp. 5–6). This allows the planner to see whether their internal labour market has the requisite knowledge, experience, skill etc. for immediate and future demand; if not, an external search may be necessary.

Appropriate individuals may be forthcoming locally but if not, the planner should consider other options such as extending searches into other geographical regions, offering superior remuneration packages. Some tourism firms may even consider the option of appealing to a more modest market. For example, a resort might decide to offer a three-star instead of an existing five star product. This would mean simplifying operations and employing individuals with fewer skills than their erstwhile colleagues possessed. Such a move would increase the external labour pool as marginally skilled workers would now be appropriate at a reduced wage cost. Action such as this is admittedly drastic and would only be appropriate if planners were confident such a demand was present. On the other hand, firms might decide to increase their pool of external labour by lowering hiring standards but provide subsequent training.

Seasonality

Conversely, analysis may reveal a surplus of labour. In this case, tourism firms may resort to a policy of reduced hours and a shorter working week, offering voluntary redundancies, early retirement opportunities and holding off replacing workers who leave the organisation. Typically, tourism organisations have an oversupply of employees during quiet trading periods known as the 'off-season'. This means laying off employees until the beginning of the following season. Usually, employees are well aware of these patterns of employment and are content to work on a seasonal basis. In any event, tourism firms always shed workers over some months of the year depending when their off-season occurs. Indeed, some operations close down altogether at this time so that the entrepreneurs can take annual holidays and refurbish for the next trading period. Others operate using a 'skeleton' labour force which is matched closely against the drastic reduction in demand for the service. Often the remaining workers will be allocated other duties such as maintenance and general upkeep of the property rather than continuing in their traditional service roles. These workers are known as 'core' (see Chapter 1) and occupy key positions in the tourism organisation. They also enjoy enhanced pay and working conditions relative to the 'flexible' peripheral workers employed on a seasonal basis. Their retention is important because loyalty to the employer is likely to be enhanced and they:

- allow the organisation to function appropriately during the quiet periods;
- are able to perpetuate (and train if necessary) consistent quality standards to incoming seasonal workers; and
- communicate the tenets of company culture (see earlier for a discussion of 'cultural fit').

Some employers in the tourism industry also use retention payments to key individuals if they cannot afford to offer continuing employment during the off-season. As an alternative to downsizing and if costs can be borne, managers may also consider providing extra training for employees to ensure they have a ready internal supply of skilled workers when demand for the service returns. This flexible approach by employers is now more important than ever and is not just restricted to the management of seasonality. Impacts of global recessions are far-reaching, affecting all businesses.

Under 'normal' circumstances, large tourism corporations tended to be insulated from unified seasonal impacts given their diversity and global focus. As such, seasonality effects were largely insignificant due to differences in global demand patters. Employees would heretofore have expected a relatively uninterrupted career with this kind of firm (notwithstanding the more increased mobility of workers generically and the expectation of more than one career). However, the economic financial crisis has put an end to this situation and firms adopting 'positive' strategies will become even more into the foreseeable future. Currently, a number of tourism organisations are being proactive as Crowell's (2009) article in Box 2.2 attests.

BOX 2.2 Case study – Staff management is key for smaller budgets

Much has been written about the recession – lending has halted, occupancy is down and rates are being cut. But what's going on at the actual hotels? Despite all the gloom and doom, hotels still need to operate and provide the optimum level of service on a smaller budget. For a hotel to stay alive in today's environment, it is up to its GM to take stock of every daily task and streamline operations. One of the most crucial areas of attention is staff. If handled properly, a good, hardworking staff can give a hotel the chance to see an economic upswing.

Allan L. Reagan, managing director of AR Hotels and owner of the Wyndham Austin (Texas), started to prepare for the recession in July 2008. Instead of making a few cost-saving staff cuts early on, he invested more in his employees by cross training them. 'So, we're reducing head count through attrition, but training the others to do multiple jobs, trying hard not to reduce their hours,' Reagan said. 'We don't want to reduce the quality of the guest experience.' Jobs that lend easily to cross training are laundry, shuttle van driving, maintenance in common areas, washing dishes and busing tables, he said. It may be prudent for smaller hotels to go without a concierge, according to David Prentiss, GM of Homewood Suites Chicago-Downtown. The front desk staff could be trained to serve that role – but Prentiss said to be sure the smaller, multi-tasking staff isn't spread too thin. 'You can't shoot yourself in the foot,' Prentiss said. 'If you're a hotel that has 15 desk clerks on, and you can go to 12 or 13, you've reduced significant dollars. If you have two and lose one, you just reduced 50 percent of your staff.' 'It requires our managers to manage,' Reagan said. 'If they just managed and deployed people in the same way, have one person stand here and there, this would absolutely fall apart.'

When taking a good look at her hotel's expenses, Angela Greer, GM of the Radisson Hotel Bloomington (MN) by Mall of America, noticed a few staff positions that were 'luxuries'. The cuts she made weren't due to the recession but came as a result of better planning. 'We're using our labor smarter,' she said. She moved several employees from hourly wages to salary wages, and those employees now work 50–55 hours a week. 'Don't be afraid of upfront costs and see what it saves you over a year,' Greer said. During this period of uncertainty, staff morale, too, becomes a concern. And to keep guest service at the proper level, that morale is important. 'You're hurting yourself if you don't have an appreciation of your staff, causing good staff to leave you.'

Question

1. Outline an 'emergency' staffing strategy for a tourism/hospitality operator with only ten staff.

Source: Crowell (2009)

In any event, planners should not assume that workers automatically understand the ramifications of reduced demand for the firm's product on their job prospects, that is, a labour surplus! If an oversupply has been identified does the firm operate a 'first in, last out' policy? Does it shed junior members first and/or are protocols contained within a formal union/management agreement?

Communicating 'bad news'

One thing of which we can be certain is that 'downsizing' is highly stressful for everyone including managers and has a raft of outcomes that may be more extreme for some than others. Worker responses will vary and include an initial knee-jerk reaction (which is often a true reflection of their feelings) and then a more considered response. Not all employees will react negatively; some may respond in the opposite way depending on their personal circumstances. However, the more common response is emotional and negative. Consequentially, the firm also experiences outcomes which may be potentially damaging. Mondy (2008) summarises them as:

- costs associated with low morale of those losing jobs and the 'guilt' of those remaining – the former will have a new focus on personal and family liabilities rather than those of the employer. Feelings of guilt may impact on productivity of remaining staff;
- workers seeking more secure employment elsewhere – it is common for the most productive employees to leave the firm thus reducing the skills and knowledge base of the remaining workforce;
- reduced employee loyalty through lack of perceived reciprocity;
- loss of acquired company knowledge and weakened corporate culture;
- increased workloads and stress of those remaining;
- loss of internal skills required when demand returns through 'over-retrenching' – may result in loss of market share and an inflated payroll due to use of consultants and other independent contractors; and
- layoffs may be liable to claims of discrimination claims particularly if workers share common characteristics such as age, gender and ethnic group.

Adapted from: Mondy (2008: 111–112)

A number of key issues must be observed when communicating news of imminent redundancies. No one likes telling or receiving this sort of information. The manager will feel awkward and nervous prior to communicating and distressed afterwards. This is an important consideration and counselling for both parties should be made available. Workers should be assured that managers are trying to make their passage from employment as smooth as possible by providing 'outplacement services' whereby they are helped to find employment elsewhere. Outplacement consultants may be used to provide a range of training options depending on the needs of individuals and career planning advice. Indeed, these consultants can also coach managers in how to convey redundancy communications. The 'success' of the process depends on whether employees feel they were treated with respect and dignity at all times.

Critical note

'Downsizing' is highly stressful for everyone including managers and has a raft of outcomes that may be more extreme for some than others.

Reflections

Visit three local tourism employers.

1. Ask how the global economic crisis has impacted on their organisation.
2. Identify how they have responded in HR terms.

SUMMARY

Strategic human resources planning is essential for all tourism firms if they are to maximise the opportunity of achieving their broader organisational objectives. Global developments over the last ten years and the more recent global financial crisis has led many tourism firms to reappraise the process. While a long-term perspective has been retained (to avoid the negative outcomes of 'short-termism'), plans now focus on shorter time frames. Additionally, strategy is no longer fixed but adaptable or 'living' to account for agreed targets and objectives but also to take advantage of unforeseen opportunities as they arise.

Human resources planning is an integral part of the broader strategic planning process and follows a similar set of procedures based upon internal and external scanning techniques. It is understood as an ongoing process with short, medium and longer term contingency options which reflect human resource strategies. In short, the human resource plan needs to be consistent with the overall strategic plan. Organisations must understand where they need to be over an agreed period; so too human resources and the integrated manner in which the aim will be achieved. The degree of sophistication involved depends on the complexity of the internal and external business environment and the aspirations of the organisation. Small seasonal tourism firms tend to operate simple planning procedures centred around ensuring enough capable staff are available during their busy trading period. Larger firms plan more comprehensively and encompass training, career development, succession planning and so on. Most organisations use a HRIS consistent with their needs for this purpose.

The three stages of the human resources planning process are assessing the labour supply, forecasting requirements and matching available supply against predicted demand. Forecasting demand for human resources is achieved indirectly through an appraisal of likely demand for the tourism product. Simple formulae may be used to indicate the firm's requirement for employees. However, it is important to remember that the calculations are used as a simple guide only as many contingencies impact on the provision of the tourism product. Once forecasts have been agreed, the planner needs to see whether enough staff are available and of appropriate calibre. If not, a decision needs to be taken whether to seek appointees externally or perhaps train those already employed. Appointing and/or training individuals for front-line positions in the tourism industry is challenging. Currently, some employers favour a 'cultural' approach whereby employees are selected based on pre-existing attitudes they have toward their work. It is argued, within reason, that 'skilling' people is relatively easy, changing attitudes is not. Therefore, attitudes held by candidates must resonate with the organisation in order to achieve a cultural match.

On the other hand if there is an over-supply of labour, the firm needs to consider downsizing or implementing some other form of arrangement whereby incumbents can retain their jobs. Given the current global economic crisis, many employers are currently taking a creative approach in planning their future human resource requirements. In other words, they are seeking to retain employees under changed working conditions. This helps ensure a ready supply of suitably skilled people once the crisis has been resolved.

Critical note

Behaviour at the customer interface cannot be left to chance; the role of HRM is key here as each encounter has the potential to be unique and is beyond the direct control of the manager.

Reflections

Visit a local restaurant, travel agent or an organisation of your choice.

1. What did you think about the service received?
2. Was it of high quality?
3. What aspects of the service were most important to you?

CHAPTER QUESTIONS

1. Discuss the key role of human resources planning for tourism organisations and comment on its relationship with more general strategic planning.

2. Explain the term 'cultural fit' and comment on its importance in terms of human resources planning.

3. Define the term 'knowledge economy' and discuss how contemporary tourism firms may benefit from organisational learning.

RECOMMENDED READING

Azjen, I. and Fishbein, M. (1980) *Understanding Attitudes and Predicting Social Behaviour.* New Jersey: Prentice Hall.

Classic text introducing the theory of reasoned action.

Härtel, C.E.J., Fujimoto, Y., Strybosch, V.E. and Fitzpatrick, K. (2007) *Human Resource Management: Transforming Theory into Innovative Practice.* Frenchs Forest: Pearson.

Comprehensive US-oriented human resources management text.

Lashley, C. and Rowson, B. (2007) Trials and tribulations of hotel ownership in Blackpool: Highlighting the skills gaps of owner-managers. *Tourism and Hospitality Research* 7, 122–130.
> Research exploring the nature and characteristics of entrepreneurs in the small to medium-sized tourism sector.

Lee-Ross, D. (2000) Development of the service predisposition instrument. *Journal of Managerial Psychology* 15(2), 148–157.
> Theoretical underpinning of the service predisposition instrument.

Porter, M. (1985) *Competitive Advantage: Creating and Sustaining Superior Performance*. New York: Free Press.
> Classic text which introduces the author's 'five forces' model essential for effective business planning.

RECOMMENDED WEBSITES

Strategic planning – http://managementhelp.org/plan_dec/str_plan/basics.htm

Strategic planning – http://www.planware.org/strategicplan.htm

Strategic human resources planning –
http://www.workinfo.com/free/Downloads/176.htm

Canadian Tourism Human Resource Council (strategic human resources planning) –
http://cthrc.ca/en/programs_services/hr_tools.aspx

European Commission: tourism and the knowledge economy –
http://www.opencityportal.net/NetGrowth/ICTWorkshop/Activity.asp?CategoryID=
STAa88&PartnerLong=Opencityportal&Language=English#STA717

APPENDIX 1

Service predispositions survey

This questionnaire is being used for a study of the predispositions of hotel workers toward providing services for customers. This survey will help determine your attitudes by obtaining information about how you react to this element of your work.

On the following pages you will find several different kinds of questions about your job. It should take you no longer than 15 minutes to complete the entire questionnaire.

The questions are designed to obtain your ideas. There are no trick questions. Your individual answers will be kept completely confidential. Please answer each item as honestly and frankly as you can.

Thank you for your cooperation.

SECTION ONE

Please circle the number which most represents your feelings towards the statement, for example, if you agree strongly with statement 1, you might circle number '7' on the scale. If you disagree strongly, you might prefer to circle number '1'.

1. It is my responsibility to satisfy clients, even if this means deviating from my job instructions.

1	2	3	4	5	6	7
I would never deviate from my job instructions			Sometimes, if there is only a moderate amount of deviation from my job instructions			Client satisfaction is important, I always do whatever I can to make them happy

2. I think it's important to show concern for my clients, I would always like to give them something extra.

1	2	3	4	5	6	7
Clients receive adequate care, there is no need to give anything extra			Moderately, some clients will always need more care than others			I always ensure clients are happy, even if it means giving them something extra

3. I would like to know whether or not I am doing a good or bad job.

1	2	3	4	5	6	7
Not at all important to know			Sometimes			Always like to know

4. It would be important to me to try and gain an understanding of my clients' needs quickly.

1	2	3	4	5	6	7

An understanding of clients' needs is not unimportant

Occasionally it is important

It is very important that clients needs are understood

5. I definitely want a career in this profession and am committed to clients and the work I would do in this job.

1	2	3	4	5	6	7

Barely committed

Moderately committed

Extremely committed

6. It would be important to me that I communicate effectively with all of my clients.

1	2	3	4	5	6	7

It's unimportant because everyone has the same requirements

Sometimes in special circumstances

It's very important that I communicate clearly with each individual client

7. Even if clients were difficult, I would always behave politely.

1	2	3	4	5	6	7

I never behave politely towards difficult clients

Sometimes

I always behave politely, even toward the most difficult clients

8. It would be important to me to I know how well I am doing my work in this job.

1	2	3	4	5	6	7

Not at all important

Moderately important

Extremely important

59

9. I would always like to offer clients individual attention to understand what they really need.

1	2	3	4	5	6	7
I never offer clients individual attention			Sometimes		I always give individual attention to each client when possible	

10. Extra demands from clients would always be difficult to meet.

1	2	3	4	5	6	7
I can usually cope with demanding clients			Sometimes I can meet with the extra demands of clients		I find it difficult to meet with extra demands from clients	

11. I feel confident that I would know how to do my job.

1	2	3	4	5	6	7
I have no confidence			I have a moderate amount of confidence		I am confident that I can carry out my job	

12. It would be important to me to share clients' expectations in this job.

1	2	3	4	5	6	7
Sharing expectations is not important			Occasionally sharing expectations is important		It is very important to share the expectations of clients	

13. If I had all the money I needed without working, I would still choose to work in this profession because a sense of commitment to clients is important to me.

1	2	3	4	5	6	7
Not an important part of my job			Moderately important		Extremely important part of my job	

14. I feel that I would carry out my job duties to the best of my ability.

1	2	3	4	5	6	7
Never			Sometimes			Always

15. If I were busy, I would make a point of always communicating to clients about the chance of delays.

1	2	3	4	5	6	7
I would never tell clients that there may be delays			Sometimes		I would always tell clients if delays were likely	

16. I think about looking for another job.

1	2	3	4	5	6	7
Never			Sometimes			Always

17. It would be important to me to have all the knowledge needed to provide clients with excellent service.

1	2	3	4	5	6	7
I do not have sufficient knowledge			I have a moderate amount of knowledge		I have enough knowledge to carry out my duties	

18. I would find it easy to be polite to awkward clients.

1	2	3	4	5	6	7
It's very difficult to be polite to awkward clients			Sometimes		I have no problem behaving politely	

19. I would be generally satisfied with the service I provided to clients.

1	2	3	4	5	6	7
Not at all satisfied			Moderately satisfied			Extremely satisfied

20. If a client asked for something outside my field of responsibility, it would be my duty to help where possible.

1	2	3	4	5	6	7
My duties are clearly defined, I do no more or less than my job instructions			Sometimes, if there is only a moderate amount of deviation from my field of responsibility			I always respond to requests even if it means doing something outside my field of responsibility

21. I consider that I would implement my work tasks in an appropriate and professional manner.

1	2	3	4	5	6	7
Not important			Moderately important			Extremely important

22. I would think about quitting this current job.

1	2	3	4	5	6	7
Never			Sometimes			Always

23. It would be important for me to try and understand individual client's precise needs.

1	2	3	4	5	6	7
It's not important to know each individual's precise needs			Occasionally			I always try and understand each client's needs and requirements

SECTION TWO

Listed below are a number of statements which could be used to describe a job. Please indicate whether each statement is an accurate or an inaccurate description of your job. Once again, please try to be as objective as you can in deciding how accurately each statement describes your job.

Write a number in the space beside each statement, based upon how accurate the statement describes your job.

1	2	3	4	5	6	7
Very inaccurate	Mostly inaccurate	Slightly inaccurate	Uncertain	Slightly accurate	Mostly accurate	Very accurate

1. My duties and responsibilities are clear, I would never deviate from what I am supposed to do even if it made the client unhappy ....

2. I would find it hard to be polite toward difficult clients ....

3. I would not think it's always necessary for me to carry out all of my job duties to the best of my ability ....

4. I enjoy my job and do not plan to quit it in the near future ....

5. A lack of understanding and sharing of clients' expectations would not affect my ability to satisfy them ....

6. Overall, I believe that the service I offered clients would be satisfactory ....

7. If clients asked me to do something extra and not within my remit, I would contact the appropriate person for help ....

8. It would impractical for me to try and understand each client's individual needs all of the time ....

9. In my job, it would not really matter whether I was committed to clients or not ....

10. It would be unimportant whether some gaps in my knowledge would cause me to make small mistakes in my job ....

11. I frequently think that the service I offered clients would be poor ………

12. It would not be really important to communicate effectively with clients all of the time ………

13. It would not be necessary for me to know how well I was performing in this job ………

SECTION THREE

Listed below are a number of basic demographic questions which will help us categorise your responses.

Sex (please tick): Male ……. Female …….

Age (please state): ………….

Nationality (please state): …………………….

Marital status (please state): …………………….

Highest qualification achieved (please tick or state): …………………………………………….

Job title (please state): …………………….

Thank you for your cooperation

CHAPTER 3

MANAGING THE PROCESS

LEARNING OBJECTIVES

After working through this chapter you should be able to:

1. Understand the human resource management process.

2. Explain 'strategy'.

3. Explain 'strategic human resource management'.

4. Identify and explain aspects of the HRM process and how it relates to organisational strategic intent.

5. Examine and discuss various HRM activities.

INTRODUCTION

Human resource management (HRM) is the aspect of management which deals with people. It is invariably linked to all other facets of management, e.g. accounting and finance, marketing, information technology, production and administration. The ultimate goal of HRM is to maximise productivity of people within the organisation. Primarily, the management of the organisation's people is a role and responsibility of frontline and operations managers. All managers are responsible for managing the organisation's people. HRM is as important to frontline and operations managers as are their other responsibilities, e.g. finance and budgeting. The extent to which managers are involved in the HRM process varies from organisation to organisation with some firms affording most of that responsibility to the human resource (HR) manager and the HR department rather than the frontline and operating managers. Teo (2002) reported that while there is a shift to devolve HRM responsibilities to line managers, these managers were reluctant to assume such duties.

Theoretically, HRM is viewed from two perspectives: hard (instrumental) HRM and soft (humanistic) HRM. The hard approach to HRM focuses on the quantitative and strategic aspects of managing people such that it highlights the economic value of 'human resources' and how such resources are instrumental in maximising organisational performance and can be utilised to provide a competitive advantage for the firm. Wilcox and Lowry (2000) point out that reframing and repositioning of HRM as a strategic partner within the business provides acceptance of employees as economic resources. Within this context HRM policies and practices are said to be aligned with business strategies of the organisation and the promotion of practices such as restructuring, downsizing and outsourcing are seen as strategic actions.

By contrast, the soft approach promotes an employee-centred focus. It takes into account the 'humanness' of employees and considers them as 'proactive contributors' to the firm. It emphasises the importance of commitment, job satisfaction, motivation, trust and knowledge and so accentuates employee engagement, autonomy, development, participation in decision-making and collaboration. The soft approach also aligns HRM policies and practices with the organisation's strategic intentions but it does so by recognising that its competitive advantage can be achieved through valuing its people and their contributions to the firm.

Hard and soft HRM can direct the organisation's approach to managing their HR. An organisation may vary their approaches depending on internal and external factors. Further, the HRM approach can be determined by the organisation type. Lashley and Taylor (1996) identified four archetypes which describe tourism and hospitality organisations. They reported styles of managing HR which best suited each of these archetypes. For example, in their discussion of Marriott, Lashley and Taylor (1996) point out that labour intensity is high and customisation limited but the role of staff as key players in the provision of service is a critical consideration for Marriott. Adopting a soft HRM approach suits Marriott because it enables frontline staff to participate in a quality culture of trust, engagement and empowerment. Lashley and Taylor (1996) contrast this style with that at McDonald's where they suggest it exemplifies 'a command and control style'. In this case, employees are afforded little discretion, restricted autonomy, and narrow responsibilities. Lashley and Taylor (1996: 161) emphasise that this approach suits McDonald's and that the organisation is able 'to develop and maintain a close fit between the key characteristics of the strategic drivers and actual service delivery through utilisation of an appropriate HRM style'. Amongst discussion of the various approaches to managing HR, it is important to consider the HRM processes and develop HRM practices which can best assist organisations in achieving their strategies.

> **Critical note**
> HRM is as important to frontline and operations managers as are their other responsibilities, e.g. finance and budgeting. It is generally viewed from two perspectives: hard (instrumental) HRM and soft (humanistic) HRM. Consideration of the HRM process is critical to either perspective on HRM

THE HRM PROCESS

The human resource process involves a number of aspects in its implementation: job analysis, job design, recruitment, selection, training, development, performance management and compensation. The organisation's mission, goals, and strategic choices underpin the entire process (See Figure 3.1). These are developed and responsive to external and internal influences, such as labour markets, industrial relations systems, competitive remuneration systems, ethical standards, national culture and global economic climate. D'Annunzio, Maxwell and Watson (2000: para 3) add that for the tourism and hospitality industry external factors also include 'career opportunities, the nature of educational outputs and the industry image'. Internally, workplace culture and relations guide the implementation of the HRM process and its associated activities toward organisational objectives. Culture and values which reflect commitment to the HRM process from all stakeholders (senior and middle managers, frontline managers and supervisors, and employees) will ensure integration of HRM best practices.

The strategic HRM objectives should be derived from and align with the organisation's objectives and strategies. Subsequently, HRM practices and activities should support the achievement of HRM objectives. For example, if a company is focusing on customer satisfaction as a strategic business objective, it will need strategic HRM action plans that focus on implementing training programmes for frontline staff; or plans that concentrate on attracting, developing and maintaining staff with a customer-oriented attitude; or plans that accentuate involving employees in improving processes and participating in decision-making. Without appropriate alignment, the work that people do can be totally removed from the goals and direction intended by the organisation. In addition, HRM objectives and practices need to be evaluated. Ideally, this will include involvement from key stakeholders, including employees.

It is argued that by adopting HRM best practices, organisations will be rewarded by engaged, committed and motivated staff who subsequently enhance organisational productivity and profitability. Redman and Matthews (1998) advocate a number of HRM practices which are considered to reflect best practice in assisting service organisations to achieve their quality strategies while being an 'employer of choice'. They have based their selection of HRM practices on Purcell's (1996 cited in Redman & Matthews, 1998) 'HRM bundle', which consists of: careful recruitment and selection; extensive communication systems; team working and flexible job design; training and learning; employee involvement; and performance appraisal with link to contingent reward systems. Redman and Matthews (1998) have extended the practices to include retention, job security and employee relations.

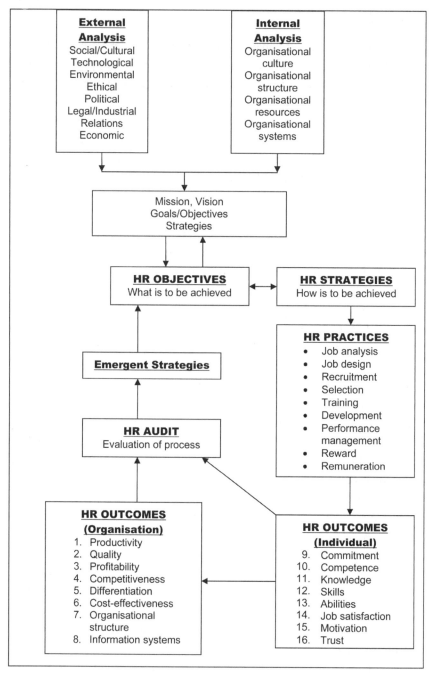

Figure 3.1 A model of Strategic HRM

Source: Compiled from De Cieri, R. and Kramar, R. (2005) *Human Resource Management in Australia: Strategy, People, Performance* (2nd edn). North Ryde: McGraw-Hill Australia Pty Ltd; Stone, R.J. (2008) *Managing Human* (2nd edn). Milton, Qld: John Wiley & Sons.

> **Critical note**
>
> The human resource process involves a number of aspects in its implementation: job analysis, job design, recruitment, selection, training, development, performance management, and compensation. It is driven by the organisation's mission, goals, and strategic choices.

THE HRM PROCESS IN TOURISM

While there are examples of good HRM practice in tourism and hospitality, generally the commentary indicates that HRM practices and employment conditions are poor for workers in the industry. HRM practices are represented by activities such as:

1. informal recruitment methods;
2. skills shortage;
3. low skills entry;
4. low wages;
5. lack of training;
6. lack of development and promotion of the profession;
7. limited recognition of succession opportunities; and
8. high levels of labour turnover.

The industry appears to be restricted by limited perspectives on development of HRM policies and practices and even the most prominent players in the industry (e.g. the large hotel chains) seem to present an *ad hoc* approach with little insight into the potential for the industry to develop people of high calibre and professionalism that will lead the industry into the future. For example, McGunnigle and Jameson (2000) conducted a study with the top 50 corporate UK hotel groups. These establishments were thought to engage with HRM best practice. Surprisingly, McGunnigle and Jameson (2000: 416) found that there was minimal adoption of HRM philosophies with the hotels examined and commented that the industry 'has a long way to go before it can claim that it is encouraging a "culture of commitment"'. In Australia, a similar picture is painted by Michelson and Kramar (2003) who found that the effective development and implementation of HRM processes in Australian organisations was progressing slowly and inconsistently.

Riley *et al.* (2000) advance the argument that there are economic reasons which determine HRM policies and practices in tourism and hospitality. Nickson (2007: 19) adds that the situation is compounded by issues relating to 'the predominance of SMEs, a low-skill base, employer antipathy to a more progressive approach to HRM, labour market characteristics, organisations ensuring best fit HRM practices to support a high volume, low-cost strategy'. These are reasonable perspectives; however, it is a short-term approach for organisations to adopt. In the long run the industry will continue to suffer with skills shortages, limited professionalism and a negative image. D'Annunzio *et al.* (2008: para 5) emphasise that 'educators, managers and industry leaders in the sector [...] take the initiative in managing their workforce [...] [and] strategic alliances between education, industry and government bodies are suggested as raising the awareness of talent management'. Nonetheless, there are some tourism and hospitality organisations which promote HRM best practices. For example, in their quest to manage for quality, the Ritz Carlton (a two-time Baldrige Award recipient) has exhibited creative practices which are reflective good HRM practices. The Gold Standards, which are the foundation of The Ritz Carlton quality philosophy, ensure engagement with employee orientation, developmental training, and rewards that mirror the organisation's mission, vision, values, and goals (Evans, 2008). The Ritz Carlton shows how the search for quality can improve HRM practices.

It is envisaged that through awareness of HRM practices, all tourism and hospitality providers can make an effort to develop HRM policies and practices that emulate good HRM practice. This chapter begins with an examination of the process of HRM planning and leads into a discussion of job analysis and job design as fundamental HRM activities. It continues with an exploration of recruitment, selection and induction and how these are applied in the tourism and hospitality industry.

Critical note

The tourism and hospitality industry is proliferated by a variety of HRM practices, ranging from hard to soft approaches and from non-existent to more complex practices. Organisations within the industry are challenged by the need to attract, maintain and develop a sustainable workforce. It is hoped that by creating awareness of best HRM practices, tourism and hospitality operators can engage more progressively and employ good HRM practices.

Reflection

Consider the organisation you work for or one with which you are familiar and reflect on the HRM policies and practices that are embraced and promoted by this organisation. Do you consider the organisation to be exhibiting HRM best practices?

HRM PLANNING

The tourism and hospitality industry is renowned for its poor image as an employer of choice. Many of the persistent issues are related to poor HRM practices. Hall's (1989 cited in Boella & Goss-Turner, 2005: 56) report highlighted a number of factors including that:

> [the] industry did not meet the aspirations of those seeking work and that the industry needed to improve its methods of management in a number of separate but inter-dependent areas including recruitment, induction, training and welfare, career structures, conditions of employment, industrial relations and management styles, pay and recruitment of women.

Clearly tourism and hospitality organisations are challenged with being recognised as 'employers of choice'. Some of the international tourism and hospitality organisations are beginning to employ strategies to shift perceptions. Such strategies include promoting tourism and hospitality work as a career opportunity and not just a job; the unusual working hours as an opportunity for flexibility and quality of life; and the full rewards package, e.g. meals, working with people, bonuses for travel and accommodation as industry members.

Implementation of HRM strategies begins with HRM planning. Stone (2008: 53) defines HRM planning as '[the] process of systematically reviewing human resource requirements to ensure that the required number of people, with the required knowledge, skills and abilities are available when needed'. Similarly, De Cieri and Kramar (2006: 207) point out that HRM planning 'is the process through which organisational goals are translated into HRM goals concerning staffing levels and allocation. Human resource planning involves forecasting HRM needs for an organisation and planning the necessary steps to meet these needs'. HRM planning will not be discussed further here as it was explored in Chapter 2 but only to say that it is important to the HRM process as it plays a critical role in determining subsequent strategic choices, e.g. recruitment and selection.

JOB ANALYSIS

The provision of products or services relies on the completion of a number of tasks. Collectively, these tasks form 'jobs'. **Job analysis** is the systematic process of examining jobs and obtaining detailed information about them. It involves evaluating the tasks, duties, and responsibilities associated with a job and assessing the knowledge, skills and abilities required to perform the job adequately. Stone (2008: 153) notes that job analysis 'focuses on the job content, the job requirements and the job context. It identifies what employees are expected to do'. The purpose of job analysis is to gather information for the other HRM activities such as development of job description and job specification, job design, HRM planning, recruitment, selection, training, appraisal and compensation. De Cieri and Kramar (2006) cite Cascio (1991) in saying that job analysis is the 'building block' of HRM. The type of information collected includes not only information on what job is performed but also how, why, where and when is it performed. Such information is also important to line managers in the organisation of their staff and work-flow processes; selection of suitable staff; and, in ensuring that employees are satis-factorily fulfilling the requirements of their jobs. In addition, the information gained from job analysis is important to the organisation as it provides a mechanism for matching people with job requirements and so achieving a high performance and competitive workplace.

The fundamental information gained from job analysis consists of two types: **job descriptions** and **job specifications**. De Cieri and Kramar (2006: 179) define a job de-scription as an inventory of 'the tasks, duties and responsibilities (TDRs) that a job entails'. Stone (2008: 156) extends this definition by noting that a **job description** is 'a written statement explaining the purpose of a job, what activities are performed, the conditions under which they are accomplished and the performance standards required'.

The definitive nature of job descriptions is questioned, especially in service organis-ations such as tourism and hospitality ones where staff are expected to be more respon-sive to customer needs and cross-training is encouraged. Kaye (1995, cited in Boella & Goss-Turner, 2005: 45) notes that 'rigid job descriptions [...] are becoming redundant. People increasingly do not have a "job" they have a "role"'. As Kay (1995) suggests, perhaps the way forward is for organisations, and HRM in particular, to focus on 'role analysis' instead of job analysis. In line with this approach, the job advertisement below, discusses the role of a 'Product Manager, Adventure' in the UK.

PRODUCT MANAGER, ADVENTURE

Industry Sector: Tourist Board
Job Term: Permanent
Country: England
County: London
Town: South West London
Location: Victoria
Home Based: No
Salary: £25000 to £30000 per annum
Posted: 18/08/2009

The role is responsible for the creation, planning, negotiation, development and com-mercial management of the travel products within Adventure which encompasses Ski Dream, Made to Measure and Ranch America.

MAIN RESPONSIBILTIES – several listed

KNOWLEDGE, SKILLS & EXPERIENCE – several listed

KEY MEASURES

- Revenue and profit targets met
- Delivery of product that meets the brand proposition
- Business growth
- Improving and introducing new supplier relationships
- Product brochure content

PERSONAL ATTRIBUTES

Willingness to work long hours as and when required and the ability to travel internationally as and when required is essential.

Source: travelindustryjobs.co.uk; Accessed on 12.09.09 at:http://www.travelindustryjobs.co.uk/jobboard/cands/jobView.asp?v=1007962&hidJobs=1007962,&c=1&ms=1&locallstJobSector=17788&locallstJobType=&locallstRegion=&locallstArea=&locallstSubArea=&localstrKeywords

This leads on to the reality that performing a job satisfactorily involves more than just fulfilling the requirements of a job description. Jobs require individuals to possess specific knowledge, skills, abilities and other personal characteristics. These are generally contained in job specifications. **Job specifications** are the human attributes or **human capital** of the job. They form an inventory of the knowledge, skills, abilities, personal characteristics and formal qualification, which an individual must possess in order to perform the job satisfactorily. This is particularly pertinent to the tourism and hospitality industry because the individual qualities of employees contribute to the success of an organisation (Goldsmith *et al.*, 1997; Lee-Ross & Pryce, 2004; Mahesh, 1988; Schneider & Bowen, 1995). Of interest is Mahesh's (1988: 10) comment:

> [...] the customer's perception of service quality is more directly linked to the morale, motivation, knowledge, skills and authority of front line staff who are in direct contact with customers, than in the case of a product selling organisation.

Hence, human capital is a key consideration for service industries. The information collated into job descriptions and job specifications is useful in the development of selection criteria, recruitment processes, selection techniques (e.g. personality tests), interview questions, and criteria for performance management and appraisal. Such benchmarks ensure adherence to equal employment opportunities (EEO) requirements.

Critical note

Job analysis is a basic HRM activity. It is a process through which jobs are examined to determine their associated tasks, duties and responsibilities; their relationship to other jobs; the conditions and resources necessary for the work to be performed;

and the personal qualities and competencies expected of individuals to perform satisfactorily. Job analysis results in the production of job descriptions and job specifications.

Reflection

Consider the job of the human resource manager of a tourist attraction that you are familiar with. Perform a job analysis on this job. In the process, consider:

1. What are the tasks that constitute the job?
2. What are the knowledge, skills and abilities needed to perform those tasks?
3. How would environmental factors (e.g. new industrial relations laws) impact on the job, especially with regard to skills and knowledge requirements?

JOB DESIGN

Job analysis examines existing jobs. By contrast, **job design** focuses on creation of new jobs or redesigning of existing jobs to be efficient in terms of maximising output of resources (including people) and effective in relation to satisfying expectations of the various stakeholders. It examines the way the job will be performed and considers what tasks should be grouped together for a particular job. Job design is generally considered to be a more proactive approach than job analysis and often aligned to motivating workers. Job design is key to linking jobs with the organisation's strategies. As De Cieri and Kramar (2006: 66) note 'the strategy may require new tasks, different tasks or different ways of performing the same tasks'.

The approach to job design is also dependent on the organisation's strategy. For example, Evans (2008) maintains that a strategic focus on quality management highlights factors such as teamwork, employee engagement, recognition of internal customers, reduction of hierarchy, attention to processes and use of steering committees. He also points out that designing effective services is dependent on the level of customisation, labour intensity and customer contact and interaction. In a fast-food outlet, customisation is low but labour intensity and customer contact and interaction are high. Such an establishment could still have a strategic focus on quality but the emphasis is on the physical facilities and procedures rather than variation on individuals' behaviour and professional judgement. In such a situation, job design is driven by speed of service rather than employee job satisfaction.

Traditionally, approaches to job design have centered on organisational structure to clarify responsibility, specialisation, standards and authority and to maintain stability. This can result in organisations which are highly structured and regimented with a 'corporate ladder' that can extend over five or more layers from frontline staff to CEO. These organisations can also be suffocated by the rigorous rules and regulations that envelope their bureaucracy. Typically hotels adopt a functional structure where the organisation is separated into functional areas such as food and beverage, front office, housekeeping, sales and marketing, maintenance, human resource management and accounts.

Similarly, tourist attractions are departmentalised into sales and marketing, administration, cleaning, retail, food and beverage, and maintenance. In either case, each department is topped by a manager and communication occurs vertically down the 'chain of command' rather than up and horizontally. The advantage of such a structure is that employees' responsibilities, duties and authority are clearly detailed. In addition, individuals can specialise in a particular job. This is evident in the organisational chart from Tourism Queensland (Figure 3.2).

Such structures have merit but contemporary organisations are encouraged to design work systems which are more agile, achieve high performance and enable them to maintain or gain competitive advantage. High-performance work systems are characterised by innovation, flexibility, knowledge and skill sharing, customer focus, dynamic response to changing business environments and market needs. In terms of achieving these goals, Evans (2008) points out several disadvantages of functional structures: separates employees from customers, inhibits process improvement, and segregates quality into compartments such as 'Quality Control' or 'Quality Assurance' departments. In reality, how work is organised, i.e. job design, is affected by several factors: management philosophy, management style, organisational culture, organisation's operational guidelines, company size, number of employees, labour markets, customer influences, financial stability, economic conditions, government regulations, union influence, and professional or industry standards and traditions.

Essentially, job design is best approached by thinking of the organisation as a three level system: the individual level (the workers), the operational level (supervisors and middle managers) and the organisational level (senior managers and executives). Evans (2008: 230–231) promotes this idea and says:

> At the individual level, work systems should enable effective accomplishment of work activities and promote flexibility and individual initiative in managing and improving work processes. Empowering employees and using work teams are ways to achieve these objectives. At the process [operational] level, work systems must promote cooperation, cross-functional teamwork, and communication. This often is done through project teams and other forms of cross-functional communication (such as product design teams). At the organizational level, senior managers must design a supportive work environment through compensation and recognition policies, and health, safety, and support services.

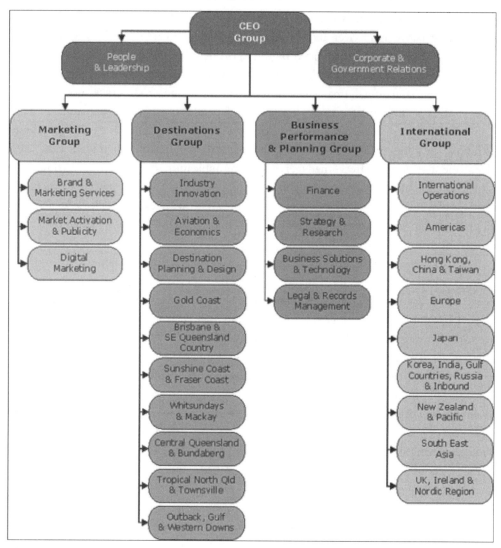

Figure 3.2 Tourism Queensland Organisational Chart

Source: Tourism Queensland accessed on 14.09.09 at: http://www.tq.com.au/tqcorp_06/fms/tq_corporate/images/organisation_chart/org-chart-final.gif

Job design affords a mechanism for tapping in on the inherent potential of employees and encouraging employee performance and productivity. Effective job design promotes the achievement of the organisation's strategic intent through employee satisfaction. Simons (2005) notes that in order to achieve such high performance, job design should enable employees to be informed of four fundamental elements: control, accountability, influence and support. Stone (2008: 176) adds that 'productivity, job stress and quality of work life are tied to job design'.

> **Critical note**
> Job design (i.e. design of work systems) is an important aspect of an organisation's strategy implementation. Efficient and effective job design is critical to achieving the goals and objectives of the work unit and integrating this with meeting employees' needs and ensuring their wellbeing.

METHODS OF JOB DESIGN

Methods of job design are varied but three which are renowned for promoting high performance workplaces are: **job enlargement, job rotation**, and **job enrichment**. At the basic level is **job specialisation** which involves employees performing standardised, routine and repetitive tasks. While this approach is efficient and is associated with low-skilled, low-cost labour and minimal training, it does have shortcomings such as: repetition, mechanical pacing, no end product, limited social interaction, no employee involvement, higher costs (due to absenteeism and turnover), and lack of flexibility (Stone, 2008). Many jobs in the tourism and hospitality industry fall into this category, e.g. housekeeping or cleaning tasks, food and beverage tasks, receptionists' tasks and sales tasks. Hulin and Blood (1968) compared employees with low growth needs to those with higher growth needs and reported that the former would be less satisfied in enlarged and more challenging jobs than the latter. This would suggest that not all staff want to be highly motivated. Nonetheless good job design is important as it can improve working conditions for all workers. It takes into account employees' mental and physical abilities and well-being, as is shown below in Figure 3.3. In so doing, it can alleviate workplace stress. The approaches below work toward achieving these goals.

Job enlargement refers to the horizontal expansion of workers' jobs to include several tasks of a similar nature and similar or slightly higher level of responsibilities. The purpose of job enlargement is to increase motivation, interest in work and self-esteem through increasing the complexity of work. In so doing it is expected to improve employee performance and increases job satisfaction. Exposure to a variety of tasks through job enlargement promotes multiskilling and aligns with flatter organisations. Evans (2008: 231) reports on the introduction of job enlargement at IBM and says 'This approach reduced fragmentation of jobs and generally resulted in lower production costs, greater worker satisfaction, and higher quality, but it required higher wage rates and the purchase of more inspection equipment.' Other issues related to job enlargement are the requirement for training to increase employees' knowledge, skills and capabilities.

In a similar vein, **job rotation** aims to increase employees' interests, motivation and skills set. However, in contrast to job enlargement where more tasks are added to the job, job rotation involves increasing task variety by shifting employees from one job to

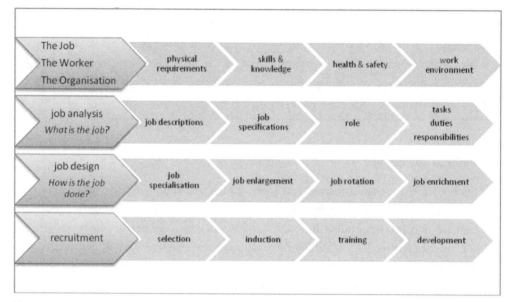

Figure 3.3 Aspects of job analysis and associated HR activities

another where the jobs have similar or more challenging levels of skill requirements. Job rotation can also refer to variety in working conditions, i.e. when or where the job is undertaken or completed. Interestingly, Hackman and Oldham (1980) found that while workers' skills increased, there was minimal increase in motivational levels.

Job enrichment also seeks to improve job performance and job satisfaction. It too involves changes in job content but it extends the job by increasing the range of tasks in terms of planning, decision-making, organising and control responsibilities, autonomy and challenges afforded to the employee. This approach is appealing to organisations seeking a flatter structure because it enables frontline workers to assume the role of supervisors and/or managers, albeit incrementally. The 'expansive loading' provides employees with opportunities for personal growth, responsibility, recognition, greater achievement and career advancement. It is sometimes referred to as 'vertical job loading' because of the added authority and responsibilities.

While there are many approaches to job design, it is a process which entails particular steps, including:

- assessing current work practices;
- undertaking a task analysis;
- designing the job;
- implementing the new job design; and
- evaluating the new job design.

The following checklist (Table 3.1) can assist in the process of job design.

Table 3.1 An example of a job design checklist

Job design		Yes	No
Task variety	Repetitive tasks – are the same muscle groups or mental tasks done over and over? Static positions – are there few or no opportunities to change position? Fast work pace – is there muscle tension and stress?		
Work/Rest schedules	Long work period(s) – is there potential for fatigue?		
Adjustment period	Are there allowances for adjustment periods or varying pace of work for new/returning employees?		
Training	Have employees had adequate training?		
Mental variety	Is there some variety or ability to choose what to do next?		

Source: Canadian Centre for Occupational Health and Safety (accessed 14.9.09 at: http://www.ccohs.ca/oshanswers/hsprograms/job_design.html#top)

Reflection

Think about a tourism and/or hospitality organisation with which you are familiar and describe how the organisation engages with job design. Does it utilise the approaches of job enlargement, job rotation or job enrichment? If so, how? If not, develop an action plan and discuss how you would introduce such approaches in the organisation.

RECRUITMENT AND SELECTION

In an age when organisations are seeking to gain the cutting competitive edge, recruiting and selecting the 'right' kind of individual is paramount. The questions is how do we determine who is the 'right' person. Do we consider the job, the organisation, the industry or the customer? It has already been noted (Chapter 2) that tourism and hospitality organisations spend a considerable amount of time, money and effort in hiring people who fit the job. A further consideration in Chapter 2 was to hire people who were 'culturally fit', i.e. whose values and attitudes matched those of the organisation.

While larger organisations may embrace best HRM practices, it seems that on a wider scale approaches to HRM are informal, *ad hoc*, simplistic, basic and reactive (Kelliher & Johnson, 1987; Nickson, 2007; Price, 1994). Additionally, it is noted that recruitment and selection in service sectors is generally conducted using unstructured approaches and conducted by untrained selectors (Poppleton, 1989; Lockyer & Scholaris, 2004). From their study of over 80 hotels, Lockyer and Scholarios (2004) reported that generally hotels lacked systematic procedures for recruitment and selection, especially the smaller hotels. This seems narrow-minded of organisations, especially when one considers the importance placed in the literature on HRM planning and the consequences, particularly financial, of poor HRM practices.

The associated costs of inadequate recruitment and selection include absenteeism, low morale; disciplinary problems; dismissals, high-labour turnover, and training. Hence, effective recruitment and selection are critical when it comes to business competitiveness. As Stone (2008: 197) notes, 'For many companies, talented people are the prime source of competitive advantage'. He defines **recruitment** as 'the process of seeking and attracting a pool of qualified applicants from which candidates for job vacancies can be selected' and **selection** as 'the process of choosing the candidate who best meets the selection criteria' (Stone, 2008: 197).

The process begins with the identification of the organisation's objectives which should be informed by external factors such as labour markets and internal aspects such as organisational culture. The resultant HRM planning will determine the number and types of jobs to be filled and inform the job analysis and subsequent development of job descriptions and job specifications. This information is used to initiate the recruitment process and informs selection of staff. Such a systematic approach ensures that EEO requirements are being satisfied.

Stone (2009: 270) notes that the 'selection process begins with a linking of organisational, human resources and employment objectives'. Essentially, the organisation's objectives and culture underlie the selection policies, criteria, and procedures. It is anticipated that these will guide the selection of the right person for the job at the time as an organisation's success is dependent on the selection of the most suitable candidate. A good match between the job and the person works positively toward ensuring employee satisfaction and organisational effectiveness. In light of the critical nature of careful selection, employers should seek to gain as much work-related information about the candidate as possible. Generally, information is sought from methods considered reliable and valid, such as application forms, interviews, employment tests, reference checks, and medical examinations (see Figure 3.4). Assessment centres can play a key role in the selection process. Equally important is the training and development of human resource managers and selectors.

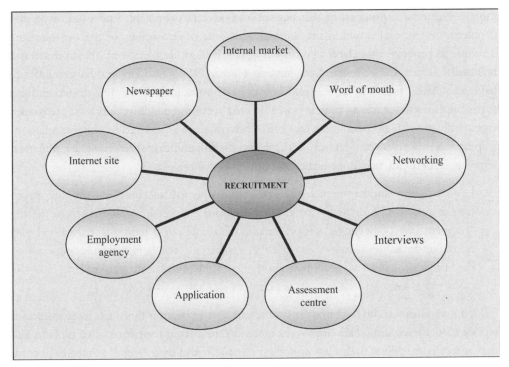

Figure 3.4 Examples of recruitment methods

De Cieri and Kramar (2006) acknowledge the difficulty in predicting precise numbers of new recruits that will be required at a particular time and for a particular job. This is further complicated by the contingent, dynamic nature of employment in organisations. People are constantly being promoted, transferred, on leave, resigning, retiring, or dismissed. Jobs are continually being redesigned, especially in response to technologies. Global economic climates are frequently shifting. All these factors and other external and internal influences impact on recruitment and selection. For tourism and hospitality this is exasperated by the challenge of portraying a positive image of the industry and for organisations seeking to be the 'employer of choice'. In addition, turnover is generally high and so, recruitment and selection is expected to accommodate shifting and immediate needs of organisations.

RECRUITMENT AND SELECTION IN TOURISM/HOSPITALITY

Further, there is some question as to whether traditional recruitment and selection methods and techniques suit the industry. For example, Lockyer and Scholarios (2005) recognised that an alternative approach to 'best practice' in HRM needs to be considered for the tourism and hospitality industry. They described an approach which highlights the 'social processes' of recruitment and selection. They argue that while the traditional more bureaucratic approach to recruitment and selection is reliable and valid, it created problems and struggled within the internal and external constraints of the organisation. The 'social process' model of recruitment and selection is not new to the tourism and hospitality sector. Other researchers, such as Herriot (1989) and Iles and Salaman (1995) have recognised the relevance and importance of non-traditional, unsophisticated and less formal approaches such as reliance on personal recommendations and local networks. Conventional strategies recognize that HRM activities are influenced by the interrelationship between business and labour markets, ownership, and management styles; however, what such 'best practice' approaches do not consider are:

> [...] the tenure and experience of those responsible for selection [...] the role played by the selectors' knowledge of the local labour market [...] [and] the use of the 'grapevine' [...] Selection decision makers who hold short tenure in their hotel may not have the same degree of knowledge, experience, contacts and influences within the hotel or the local community to understand the local labour market and make use of informal networks. (Lockyer & Scholarios, 2004: 125–127)

Dell and Hickey (2002: 7) add to this discussion by noting that 'most organisations will need to attract and retain employees quite different from the people they replace, and they will need to adjust their targeting, their channels, and their overall-strategies accordingly'. This includes recruiting people from such non-traditional sources such as from the pool of older workers and foreign workers. For the tourism and hospitality industry with its particular demands of unusual working hours, it seems feasible to consider the ageing baby boomers who may be seeking alternative working arrangements. Tourism and hospitality organisations are encouraged to embrace this valuable opportunity to develop and adopt HRM policies and practices which will accommodate the interests and needs of this extending labour force.

Recruitment and selection have long been recognised as being one of the biggest challenges faced by the tourism and hospitality industry (e.g. Baum, 1995; Guerrier, 1999; Iverson & Deery, 1997; Powell & Wood, 1999; Riley, 1996). This challenge will continue to plague the industry unless the industry works toward shifting negative perceptions of the fundamental characteristics and nature of the industry. In 2008, *The International Journal of Contemporary Hospitality Management* published an entire issue on 'Talent Management'. Careful recruitment and selection are an investment in the success of the organisation and ultimately the tourism and hospitality industry. Assiduous recruitment and selection may be more time-consuming and costly than *ad hoc* processes but in the long run benefits will be realised through reduction in absenteeism and labour turnover, and increase in employee satisfaction, customer satisfaction and organisation performance.

The website of 'Cairns Ports' provides an insight into how a tourism organisation approaches management of the employment process. In particular, it provides an overview of part of the recruitment and selection process (see Box 3.1).

BOX 3.1 Managing the process at Cairns Ports

Employment

Far North Queensland Ports Corporation Limited employs approx 65 staff comprising full-time, part-time, temporary and contract positions. These positions cover professional, technical, clerical, administrative and operational roles across our business units.

We consider equal opportunity a basic principle in our overall operations and all our appointments are strictly based on merit.

Applications will only be accepted for advertised vacancies. Job vacancies are advertised in the *Cairns Post* and *Courier Mail* employment sections and our website which is updated weekly.

Please view our Job Vacancies Application Guide which provides a summary of the recruitment procedures at Far North Queensland Ports Corporation Limited.

Job Vacancies Application Guide

Selection Process

The selection process incorporates a variety of selection methods. This may include a written application, structured group or individual exercises, interviews and work samples.

Selection Committee

A selection committee is used to assess applications.

Position Description

This document outlines the purpose, duties, reporting relationships and environment of the job as well as any knowledge and skills required for the position.

Written Application

Written applications provide the basis for assessment regarding job suitability. Once assessed, individuals will then be sorted and interviews offered to appropriate candidates. It is recommended that your written application include the following:

- A cover letter addressing your application for the position
- A resumé or curriculum vitae detailing past work experience. This should include past positions, period of employment and duties and responsibilities performed

Interview

All candidates will be asked a series of questions developed from appropriate selection criteria. As the interview is interactive, supplement questions based on the individual may also be asked.

83

Referee Checks

If a candidate proceeds to the interview stage they will be asked to provide a series of referees. These referees will be contacted to verify any information supplied in the written application and interview.

After the Selection Process

After the selection process both the successful candidate and their unsuccessful counterparts will be notified.

Lodging Your Application

All applications must be received by the date expressed on the corresponding advertisement. Applications are welcomed via email to recruitment@portsfnq.com.au or via hard copy mail.

Source: Accessed on 15.5.09 at: http://www.cairnsports.com.au/content/standard2.asp?name= Employment

Critical note

Best practice in recruitment and selection within the tourism and hospitality sector is not necessarily exemplified by the more traditional, formal, structured and bureaucratic approach recommended by the HRM literature; rather it is worthwhile to consider the interrelationships of internal and external contexts, especially the labour markets; the nature, size, location and ownership of the business; the management structure and style; and the characteristics, knowledge, experience, and tenure of the selector. Hence, consideration should be given to the value of 'social processes' and the associated web of connections to local networks or the 'grapevine'.

Reflection

Consider a tourism or hospitality organisation with which you are familiar. Think of the recruitment and selection approaches they utilise and determine whether they are employing the 'social processes' model. If possible, visit and seek information from the organisation.

INDUCTION

The Department for Education and Employment (cited in Boella and Goss-Turner, 2005: 94) define induction as:

> Arrangements made by or on behalf of the management to familiarize the new employee with the working organization, welfare and safety matters, general condi-

tions of employment and the work of the departments in which he is to be employed. It is a continuous process starting from the first contact with the employer.

This definition suggests that the initial written statement given to the employee should detail the main terms and conditions of employment. This is usually a formal letter offering employment and which is signed by the employee and employer on acceptance and does provide some insights into the job. However, induction is more than this. It involves introducing the new employee to the job, the organisation and their colleagues. Induction is a means of integrating the employing into the organisation and so, consolidating the employment relationship.

A principal component of induction is to ensure that new employees know and understand the requirements and responsibilities of the job. An initial part of induction is to familiarise the employee with the workplace and the people he/she is working with. Boella and Goss-Turner (2005) point out that induction should address the two aspects of a job: the work itself and the peripherals to the job. They note that the elements contiguous to the work include: terms of employment, location and physical layout, colleagues and informal relationships (i.e. the informal organisation), management, supervisors and formal relationships (i.e. the formal organisation), customers, and the company and house rules.

Induction is part of the training and development process and should occur in the initial stages of the employees working life with the organisation. It should expose the new employee to organisational factors such as those outlined in Table 3.2.

Table 3.2 Components of an induction programme

Induction programmes should include:

- the job itself;
- organisational values and culture;
- history of the organisation;
- organisational structure to clarify relationships between staff and departments, lines of communication, and levels of authority and responsibility;
- layout of the organisation;
- health, safety and security practices;
- employee relations: organisational rules and regulations;
- methods of and approaches to work;
- work conditions & entitlements;
- facilities and services; and
- contacts: HR representatives, union representative, social club secretary, key managers, safety officers.

In essence, induction serves to familiarise the individual with the organisation's own particular environment, conditions, rules and methods. It has formal and informal aspects, which managers and supervisors should ensure that the new employee learns.

In the tourism and hospitality industry, all too often, new employees are 'thrust straight into the job without even minimal introduction to the employer's methods and rules, let alone introduction to colleagues and management' (Boella & Goss-Turner, 2005: 94). This approach is of concern and as noted in the case study below is vital if the employee needs training or guidance to meet the requirements of the job effectively and satisfactorily and has been employed with the knowledge that he/she is untrained. A preferable approach would be to allocate an experienced, reputable employee as a 'buddy' or 'mentor' to the new employee so that they can show the newcomer 'the ropes'. Alternatively, organisations may opt for more formal, consistent and systematic training approaches conducted in classroom settings by an appointed individual, generally the HR manager.

BOX 3.2 Case study – Induction oversight!

Sarah was ecstatic. Her ambition was to become the General Manager of an international hotel. She was in the second year of her university degree – Bachelor of Hospitality Management – and finally she had a job in a hotel. It was Saturday and this was her first night. The HR manager had been so nice to her. He seemed to understand Sarah's aspirations and had said that they were easily achievable for her. She had been told that she would begin working in the restaurant and as an opportunity arose she would be provided with training to move to front office and 'learn the ropes' in that department. From there it was a 'hop, skip and jump away' from her realising her dreams.

For the evening service in the restaurant, Sarah was buddied with a waiter called Tim. Sarah soon learnt he had been working in food and beverage for seven years. He told Sarah that he had ample experience with à-la-carte service and had worked in several of the major hotels in town. This had reassured Sarah, as she had never waited on a table before. She started thinking that she should have done a TAFE course to prepare her for this but it was too late now. Besides the restaurant manager knew Sarah had no previous restaurant experience and had said that it was not a problem as she would quickly learn on-the-job.

The evening started off very slowly and it wasn't till around 8:00 that guests started coming into the restaurant. Things were progressing at a steady pace and Tim soon encouraged Sarah to take orders and post them through to the kitchen. She seemed to be doing really well; at least Tim said so.

The settled tempo of service was short-lived. Soon the restaurant began to fill very quickly and it was not long before Sarah found herself delegated to looking after several tables – on her own! Just when she thought she knew the menu, she couldn't remember what some of the terms meant. Ohh! It was like a second language. To make matters worse, as she hurried to process the orders, she was fumbling to note what people wanted and then posting them through to the kitchen was a major drama in itself. Sarah couldn't remember how to enter the details of the orders. She tried to grab Tim's attention but he was too busy with his own tables. The drinks waiter came flitting past but as Sarah asked for help, the lady told her she was there only to serve drinks and knew nothing about the restaurant service. Sarah began to realise she was on her own and she was sinking fast.

Question

1. Discuss the steps which should have been taken to prepare Sarah for service in the restaurant.

Source: Josephine Pryce (2009)

Staff are a key component of organisational success. It is recognised that employees are most productive and satisfied 'when they have confidence in their employer, in their surroundings, and particularly in their own performance of their job' (Boella & Goss-Turner, 2005: 337). Effective inductions play a critical role in introducing and familiarising the new employee with their job and work environment. Hence, taking time to conduct induction programmes has benefits for both the employer and the employee. For the employee it alleviates anxieties and enhances job satisfaction. Induction provides confidence in knowing what the job is about, their responsibilities, duties and competencies. In addition, it establishes the new employee as a member of the team and provides them with a sense of belonging. This in turn, reduces labour turnover.

Ivancevich (2001) notes that making new employees feel part of an organisation impacts positively on labour turnover by reducing associated costs and improves profitability and competitiveness of the organisation. Other benefits to the employer include ensuring meeting of legal obligations and improvement of work standards, staff efficiency, performance and morale. However, in order to achieve these benefits, induction programmes need to be well planned, executed and evaluated and conducted over a period of time. It is easy for a new employee to be weighed down with information. Equally, induction should commence immediately upon the new employee joining the organisation. A study conducted by McGarrell (1983) found that the first 60 to 90 days were crucial in the formation of lasting impressions but in particular, the first day was most important.

> **Critical note**
> Induction is important of an employee's working life in the organisation as it orients the new employee to knowing about the job, the organisation and their colleagues. It is instrumental in promoting positive attitudes and a feeling of belonging, and in minimising problems of poor performance, reduced morale and labour turnover.

> **Reflection**
> As the HR manager of a new tourism attraction, you have been asked to develop an induction programme. What subjects would you cover? Draw up a checklist.

SUMMARY

The job is at the core of the workplace. Job analysis is a key HRM activity as it allows information about the job to be gathered and provides the basis for the development of job descriptions and job specification. These documents supply information about the duties and responsibilities of the job (job description) and the personal characteristics and qualifications (job specifications) employees must possess to satisfactorily perform the job. These job-related criteria provide a platform from which can be made objective decisions about an individual's employment, performance, remuneration and promotion; job design; and how HRM can contribute to the organisation's strategic goals and objectives.

In an attempt to achieve high-performance and healthy workplaces, organisations are encouraged to adopt the various job design strategies: job enlargement, job rotation, and job enrichment. These approaches enhance employees' interest, motivation and quality of work life.

Subsequent to these activities, the HRM process involves recruitment and selection of suitable staff. The job descriptions and specifications inform the recruiter/selector of appropriate methods for attraction and selection of staff. Selection criteria are developed from data about the job and so are valid (job relevant). Efforts should be made to ensure the selection criteria and recruitment and selection processes are equitable and comply with Equal Employment Opportunity legislation.

Invariably, the tourism and hospitality industry presents particular challenges for recruitment and selection. Traditional, formal, structured and bureaucratic models seem to be inadequate in the face of an industry which is dynamic and subject to high staff turnover. Research suggests that a less formal and more unsophisticated approach which engages 'social processes' could be of great value in attracting and selecting the 'right' person.

The managing process continues with the need to orientate new employees. Effective induction serves this purpose and constitutes employees' initial exposure to training. It is critical to promoting a sense of belonging and minimising problems associated with poor performance, reduced morale, and labour turnover.

CHAPTER QUESTIONS

1. Think of a job you are familiar with, preferably one in the tourism and hospitality industry. Comment on how the organisational structure impacts on that job and the role of the person in that position.

2. Use examples to illustrate the meanings of the terms 'job enlargement', 'job enrichment', and 'job rotation'. Explain the differences between these aspects of job design.

3. Choose three methods of recruitment and selection and comment on their suitability for the tourism and hospitality industry.

RECOMMENDED READING

Turco, D.M., Riley, R. and Swart, K. (2002) *Sports Tourism.* Morgantown (WV): Fitness Information Technology Inc.

> The interesting book covers recruitment of staff, including volunteers, in this growing niche area of tourism.

Kusluvan, S. (ed.) (2003) *Managing Employee Attitudes and Behaviours in the Tourism and Hospitality Industry.* Hauppauge (NY): Nova Publishers.

> This treasure of a book recognises the immense value that employees bring to the tourism and hospitality industry. It presents strategies for managing employees' attitudes and behaviours such that there are benefits for employees, customers, and the organisation.

Jones, E. and Haven-Tang, C. (eds) (2005) *Tourism SMEs, Service Quality, and Destination Competitiveness.* Wallingford: CABI Publishing.

> A compelling book which presents the particular challenges of tourism and hospitality's SMEs from all over the world.

Pender, L. and Sharpley, R. (2005) *The Management of Tourism.* London: Sage Publications Ltd.

> This book presents a chapter which focuses on the strategic management of human resources in tourism. It covers a range of issues, including 'aesthetic labour'.

Shone, A. and Parry, B. (2004) *Successful Event Management.* London: Thomson Learning. A pragmatic book with worthy insights for staffing of events.

RECOMMENDED WEBSITES

Canadian Centre for Occupational Health and Safety – http://www.ccohs.ca/oshanswers/hsprograms/

Canada Post Corp Pushing the Envelope – http://www.postalproject.com/documents.asp?d_ID=2457

ETN Global Travel Industry News – http://www.eturbonews.com/

CHAPTER 4

PERFORMING OR IGNORING: MANAGEMENT AND APPRAISAL

LEARNING OBJECTIVES

After working through this chapter you should be able to:

1. Understand the difference between performance management and performance appraisal.

2. Appreciate the strategic perspective of performance management via a systems approach.

3. Identify the steps involved in preparing for and conducting a performance appraisal interview.

4. Explain the major challenges of measuring performance from a human resources management perspective.

5. Identify the key challenges to managing the performance of employees in the tourism and hospitality industry.

6. Identify the key elements of a balanced scorecard approach.

INTRODUCTION

Yourdictionary.com (2005) defines performance as:

Functioning, usually with regard to effectiveness, as of a machine.

Whilst the above is reasonable and allows an understanding of the noun, likening people ('performers') to machines is oversimplifying matters and is certainly at odds with the 'soft' model of human resources management (see Chapter 1). The literature is littered with examples where people are treated as 'programmable' and rational beings often with unfortunate organisational (and societal) outcomes. Indeed, at the turn of the 20th century the 'Classical Management School' held these principles key in understanding and motivating workers and improving organisational performance. Closely related issues have even been taken up by the entertainment industry in such films as *The Matrix*,

Terminator and *Modern Times*! In fairness, the classical approach was appropriate for its time in the context of factory working and managing an intellectually underdeveloped labour force. This is no longer the case particularly in modern service industries where performance is an amalgam of tangible and intangibles and workers are more knowledgeable. Nankervis *et al.*'s (2008: 324) notion that 'Firms are now more complex and ambiguous than at any other time in history' underscores the importance and increasing need for a sophisticated and holistic approach to performance management in the current environment. This is particularly the case in the tourism and hospitality industry as the skills required for effective performance go beyond the purely technical to incorporate essential inter-personal elements (Baum, 2008). 'Performance' is represented as a system in Figure 4.1.

The above components are multidimensional, comprised of technical, emotional and analytical inputs and reflect the role customers play in service delivery. Performance management systems must be able to account for these additional advanced variables and tourism managers must understand:

- the complex nature of the above inputs;
- how they are transformed into outputs;
- what needs to be achieved; and
- what constitutes good performance represented through key performance indicators.

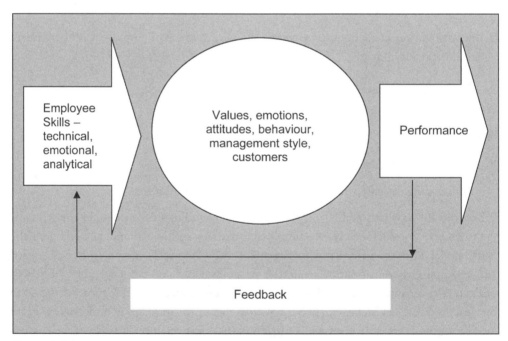

Figure 4.1 A simple systems model of performance

Managers must also ask whether performance can be measured and managed in a meaningful way for all stakeholders?' The answer is of course 'yes' but the journey is fraught with difficulties because ultimately measuring and managing performance involves the judgement of employees by others. Additionally, we all have a tendency to self-appraise and problems may arise where external feedback differs significantly from our own, particularly if it is negative. The challenge then becomes one of reconciling the incumbent's view of performance with those of others. This is arguably the crux of the matter and comprehensive performance management procedures must deal with the issue appropriately through establishing supportive organisational structures so outcomes are not seen as negative, punitive or inequitable.

This chapter begins by introducing performance management using a systems view to emphasise its essential strategic nature. It continues by highlighting some inherent difficulties of establishing performance management systems in the tourism and hospitality industry. Performance appraisals are then discussed together with an outline of key stages of the process. Perennial challenges based on subjectivity, perceptual distortion and context are also overviewed. The chapter concludes by identifying the phenomenon of self-appraisal and how it impacts on the performance appraisal together with a brief review of some common instruments used during performance interviews.

Reflections

Visit three local tourism employers.

1. Ask about their performance management system.
2. Ask whether they hold formal interviews and if so, how often?

PERFORMANCE MANAGEMENT: TOWARDS A DEFINITION

Often, performance management and performance appraisal are taken to be the same thing. Both concepts are linked but appraisals are merely one element of a broader performance management canvass. Essentially, the appraisal is an activity which scrutinises overall ability and potential through assessment of achievements. To be most effective, appraisals must be integrated with the whole performance management system. Interviews usually involve a retrospective comparative view designed to identify gaps between performance and achievements through scrutiny of key performance indicators (KPIs); they should also identify employee training and development needs. Strategically, this is an essential part of human resource planning as it underpins other key decision-making areas including skills audits, job analysis, succession planning, motivational initiatives and so on. Performance management is a much larger framework in which the appraisal plays a key role and is defined in a variety of ways often including terms like:

- meeting goals and targets consistently, effectively and efficiently;
- establishing measurement parameters;
- meeting predetermined goals; and
- linking the goals of employees with those of the firm.

The CIPD (2008) argue that performance management is ultimately about:

- improving the quality of relationships between managers and employees;
- improving the quality of relationships between managers and teams; and
- improving the quality of relationships between individuals within teams.

They also consider that the best performance management systems are continuous and holistic, pervading all aspects of running an organisation. Moreover, these systems must have a strategic focus by considering broader and longer-term issues thus integrating all areas of the firm. In a more pragmatic sense, good performance management procedures eliminate role ambiguity amongst individuals and ensure they have the appropriate skills to carry out their jobs. They also provide contemporary and ongoing feedback to workers and include the opportunity for development. This should result in enhanced employee and organisational effectiveness and ensure that favourable working relationships are maintained amongst employees and managers. A systems model of performance management is shown in Figure 4.2.

Thus, performance management is about more than just appraising work performance. Ideally, it should consider how associated data derived may be used to improve organisational progress. This systemic view of performance management enables the employer to establish specific performance initiatives such as training programmes, career development, and rewards initiatives linked with overall business strategy. Moreover, a strategic perspective is inclusive by definition and permits meaningful measurement at all appropriate organisational levels consistent with generic aims and objectives. This is no different to viewing the process systemically whereby performance management is embedded within a larger super system as shown in Figure 4.2.

Tourism and hospitality

Historically, the tourism and hospitality industry (particularly the unaffiliated hotel sector) appears to have been rather lax in the area of performance management. The process has been ill-defined and its coordination and administration similarly vague with no agreed notion of what performance is. More often than not, managers have relied on 'traditional' financial metrics such as simple ratio analyses and other budgetary information. Peacock (1995) points out that amongst hotel managers, performance is understood to have

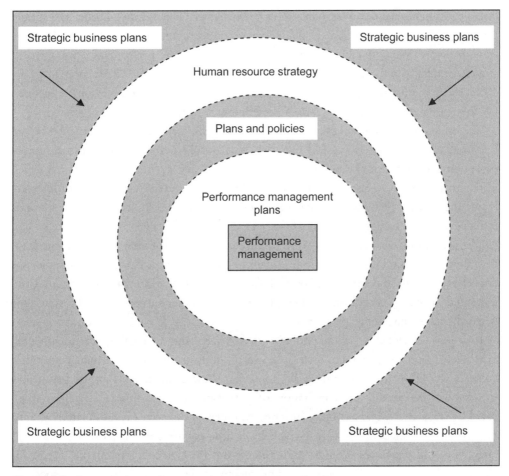

Figure 4.2 A strategic performance management system

a variety of perception-driven meanings. In a telephone interview-based survey, 200 managers were asked to define success through performance. Their responses included:

- financial cost control (36%);
- absence of customer complaints and 'smiling faces' (24%);
- efficiency through an absence of operational problems (16%);
- personal satisfaction with their own job (7%);
- staff retention rates, staff morale and positive feedback from staff (6%);
- advice from superiors such as feedback from performance appraisals (5%); and
- a small proportion whose responses were simply classified as 'other' (6%).

Interestingly, performance appraisal represents the smallest category. Notwithstanding inherent research bias of the research method, this indicates the relatively low value placed on performance appraisals by hotel managers. However, these results also reveal notable differences about what constitutes performance. This is no bad thing and should provide performance management planners with opportunities to consider a broad range of issues which may arguably be features of a sector specific performance management strategy. Similarly in their study of 140 Australian hotels, Davies *et al.* (2001) note that only 40% used some form of performance appraisal or performance management procedure. Of this, only nine used this as part of an employee's career development strategy.

The utility of broad ranging performance criteria depends on whether they are measurable; clearly observation of 'smiling faces' would perhaps not be the easiest or most convincing metric. Nonetheless, it does suggest that customers are satisfied which in no small part is the responsibility of front-line staff. Human resource procedures are increasingly being recognised as having an effect on success in service industries. The intuitive link is through the positive impact increased efficiency and effectiveness of employees has on service quality. Communicated via the customer interface, this leads to improved profitability and overall organizational performance or (for example, see Davies *et al.*, 2001; and Frabotta, 2000). This kind of information could be captured and measured through a combination of employee and customer surveys and fed through the performance management process.

In a sense, Peacock's (1995) findings are not surprising given the well-documented evidence of poor management styles used in the industry but to hold managers totally culpable would be unfair. Baum (2008) notes that some characteristics of the sector may present barriers to the implementation of performance management strategies advocated by researchers. For example, structurally, much of the sector is dominated by small heterogeneous independent firms which have little to offer employees in the way of tangible career structures. Riley (1996) concurs but through a labour market focus. He classifies labour markets for tourism and hospitality as 'weak' characterised by unspecified hiring standards, multiple ports of entry, low skills, absence of on-the-job training. He also notes that there are no fixed criteria for promotion and the influence of unions and other associations on working practices is almost non-existent. Furthermore, jobs (and their tenure) in tourism and hospitality are highly flexible and an excessive use of part-time, casual and outsourced staff (Baum, 2006).

Collectively, these conditions are alleged to conspire against establishing comprehensive performance management programmes. However, we would argue that this situation should not prevent employers from adopting a creative and enlightened way to view these challenges. Indeed, Baum (2008) concludes that tourism and hospitality firms must remain open-minded and inclusive so that all employees have an opportunity to participate in human resource programmes where practicable. Obstacles to the establishment of organisational or even industry-specific initiatives are ever-present. However, this does not mean they should remain unaddressed. Indeed, it could be argued that management abdication in the area of performance management serves to perpetuate high levels of labour turnover, compromised career structures and impoverished working conditions traditionally associated with the tourism and hospitality industry.

Reflections

Visit two local tourism employers.

1. Ask how they measure their firm's performance.
2. Ask whether they believe that appraisal systems are important.

PERFORMANCE APPRAISAL

According to Bratton and Gold (2003), performance appraisal is common but unpopular in organisations. All participants, including managers, seem to merely tolerate it as part and parcel of organisational orthodoxy rather than considering it to be anything of value. Pfläging (2006) considers measurement of individual performance as subjective, assumption-based and difficult to measure. He questions its validity over the establishment of other enablers necessary for good team performance. However intuitively, measurement of performance through appraisals seems a reasonable way to gauge a tourism firm's progress toward achieving targets and objectives. Indeed, Thor (2006) cautions if appraisals are not part of a firm's overall strategic performance management programme a number of key questions remain unanswered. For example, it becomes impossible to know where to allocate or reallocate money and people. Comparisons with other firms are difficult, so too is an understanding of individual performance. Moreover, knowing whether employees value related initiatives such as empowerment, motivation and rewards would be tricky; to say nothing of their personal effectiveness and efficiency.

Critical note

Collectively, weak labour markets and the inability of most tourism firms to provide career structures for employees conspire against establishing comprehensive performance management programmes.

Of course, the above presupposes that organisations are rational, scientific and almost everything is measurable; the reality is far from this ideal. Managers in general like to be in control, if they were not, their careers would be short-lived. Thus, it suits to adopt a lens which perpetuates the idea that people are predictable and not idiosyncratic (see Barlow, 1989 for further discussion). In terms of performance measurement, this view would no doubt support the use of a 'something rather than nothing' approach. While there can be little doubt that appraisals may degrade into little more than a box-ticking exercise they have the potential to fulfil a key strategic role in the organisation as long as they:

- identify elements impacting on individual and organisational performance;
- use a means of meaningful measurement; and
- take account of variables which are overt and relatively easy to measure but also consider those which are infinitely more subtle but still have the capacity to affect organisational outcomes.

Performance appraisals need to be formalised and often this is the case. Typically, large tourism firms will have a yearly or twice-yearly appraisal interview. However, received wisdom suggests that this is a rather contrived format given that people hit targets and reach goals on a much more dynamic and more frequent basis. The performance management system must therefore be able to account for these contingencies and recognise and reward achievement accordingly. Box 4.1 shows a fact-based vignette from a series of management meetings in a public tourism institution.

BOX 4.1 Case study – Performance management planning: the general meeting

General manager: Well colleagues, it's 'performance management planning' time of year again and we have a lot of subordinates to get through. How is the performance team progressing with designing the new appraisal forms?

Manager 1: We have come up with a new simplified one which people should be able to go through fairly easily and quickly; it should be quite painless (laughs).

Manager 2: We had lots of resistance to the earlier version after circulating it for comment; so much in fact that we decided to try and hurry things along by designing a new one.

General manager: So all is ok now with the new one?

Manager 1: We hope so. We contacted human resources for advice on content and layout but they simply said there was no standardised form and that each department tended to go its own way!

General manager: Ok. The appraisal interviews are going to be too much for me alone so I've nominated other people at supervisory level and above to help.

Manager 2: Yes, and we have to inform that a few of them have flatly refused to interview employees on the basis first, that they are not directly responsible for the process and second, they have no skills in either appraisal interviewing techniques nor in the employees area of expertise. They would like clarification how the procedure can be implemented effectively without disadvantaging the staff. Some of us share their views.

General manager: Don't they realise we simply must get the appraisals finished in less than three weeks?

Manager 2: Yes, but we don't really think that is a good reason to push ahead with a flawed procedure.

General manager: You know what some of these people are like, they are well known to me and are always complaining about something or other. This is what will happen, I will conduct as many appraisal interviews as I can and we'll simply email the new form to those who appear to be unhappy. They will be directed to complete, sign and return the forms to me within the week. I'll get my secretary to send out the communication.

Manager 2: Do we have last year's appraisal forms to look through for those of us that have volunteered to help with the interviews?

General manager: I'm not sure, I think we have some but not others. We'll just have to make do with what we can get hold of.

Questions

1. In terms of performance management comment on the likely relationship between the human resources department and the rest of this organisation.
2. What value is perusal of the earlier year's appraisal forms?
3. Identify the major weaknesses and likely outcomes of this performance management planning process.

Source: The authors

The above scenario may be likened to what Härtel, Fujimoto *et al.* (2007) refer to as *the typical appraisal interview* noted as an 'annual fiasco' (p. 334). Although the case is not an interview per se it does recount the lack of planning and attention to detail surrounding such an event. Clearly, the 'something is better than nothing' approach appears to apply in the above case. However, it is evident that both managers and employees are uncomfortable with the rushed arrangements. Additionally, the failure to differentiate between performance appraisal and performance management per se reveals a tacit misunderstanding of their relationship with broad organisational strategy.

Outcomes of this nature are quite common and unfortunately say more about the management regime than anything else. However, one would like to believe that poorly designed procedures are due to incompetence rather than any intent of 'malice'. In any event, simply 'going through the motions' is woefully inadequate when appraising performance. Important issues and inquiries are likely to be missed or misguided resulting a complete failure to understand individual employees or team motivations, attitudes and aspirations. Furthermore, essential 'follow up' interviews (or some other monitoring process) by managers would be unlikely meaning that employee training and development needs could easily be missed or ignored. As discussed earlier in this chapter, appraisals must be part of an ongoing and consistent performance management process where common ground can be established for:

- inclusive negotiated goal-setting;
- institution of KPIs; and
- design of negotiated enabling support structures.

If the above are not achieved, cynicism and negativity will be rife; not a particularly ideal scenario for achieving competitive advantage through the tourism firm's most important asset! Instead of performance appraisals being key in systematically developing and using employee knowledge and skill, they are likely to become short-term and demotivating because they are so poorly executed.

Critical note
Performance management and performance appraisal are linked but appraisals are merely one element of a broader performance management canvas.

Reflections
Visit three local tourism employers.

1. Ask how much planning they undertake prior to conducting appraisal interviews.
2. Ask what key information they use during the interview and how they actually measure the performance of employees.

Steps in the appraisal process

Several steps are involved in appraisal interviews and they may include:

- ascertaining how well workers are performing in their jobs;
- communicating this information to them;
- establishing a mutually agreed plan for improvement;
- implementation of the plan; and
- training and development.

Where formalised, interviews take place between managers and employees once (or more frequently) a year and there are normally two overall foci. The first is a retrospective look at the individual's progress over a specified time period and issues discussed will relate to this area. For example, their behaviour at work may prompt an exchange about promotion opportunities and salary increases. The second is where the developmental requirements of the employee will be reviewed and training opportunities negotiated.

Some organisations may schedule two separate interviews; one judgemental and the other developmental, whilst others may combine the two. According to Bratton and Gold (2003) a key part of a manager's job is to be judgemental; assessment of performance in the appraisal interview is no exception.

Clearly, a critical look at a worker's capabilities, skills and competencies is important. Unfortunately, not many people like criticism in any environment whether work related or not and tend to become demotivated if feedback is something less than expected. For this reason, some believe that only one appraisal interview dealing with both achievements and future employee development is unwise. It is argued that the potential negativity demonstrated by a worker receiving 'bad' news may contaminate the discussion of their future development needs. However, this perspective has little contemporary overwhelming empirical support. Nonetheless, it does highlight how important even an intuitive knowledge of such matters is in conducting an effective appraisal interview. Bratton and Gold (2003) argue that appraisals are difficult because they are based on a confrontational 'management control model' and fail to differentiate between the job and the individual adequately. They cite a summary of Meyer *et al.* (1965) in an attempt to highlight some important issues which may help alleviate challenges during the appraisal process:

- praise has little effect on motivation and performance;
- criticism has a remarkable negative impact on motivation and performance; and must be
  - specific with examples but not directed at the person but their behaviour (the sin, not the sinner);
  - communicated in a simple and direct but supportive manner; and
- goal-setting needs to be participative, specific and achievable if performance is to be realised.

Other steps might include an initial emphasis on positive feedback from managers before the 'honest' discussion to be followed by more positive input so that the interview ends in a constructive and encouraging manner. It might also be useful to enrol managers on developmental programmes designed to improve interviewing skills. This should subsequently improve communication and help clarify misunderstandings between individuals but also help illuminate the links between employee objectives and those of the organisation; often they can be two entirely different things!

Finally, performance-related feedback should not be confined to a once yearly formal interview session. The reality is that individuals in the workplace make judgements about each other and work performance constantly. The more frequent judgements are informal. Indeed, the feedback reporting structure for certain employee tasks may be inappropriately long-term and limited to the formal interview. Feedback is best delivered as quickly as possible (negative or positive) so managers should incorporate this thinking into a more dynamic and continuous approach to appraisals. Ultimately of course this method should become part of the organisational culture as opposed to relying solely on informal input from individual managers.

Härtel *et al.* (2007) suggest that successful appraisal interviews require a three pronged strategy. Prior to the interview, sufficient preparation is an absolute must and thought should be given to who will conduct the session. This could entail the input of one or more people (human resources manager, senior manager, line manager, peers) depending on the specific context. Furthermore, we need to ask 'what is the purpose of the interview?' and 'do we have enough documentation?' For example, does the interviewer have a completed copy of the previous year's (or specified alternative) employee appraisal form and a record of any training undertaken? Additionally, the interviewer must have a clear understanding of the employee's role and performance in the firm though the relevant documents. These authors advocate the SMART (specific, measurable, agreed, realistic, and time-bounded goals) mnemonic to establish performance criteria and to determine the purpose and direction of the appraisal. Assuming the interviewer is competent and insightful, the interview should be used to:

- Obtain input from the worker by allowing sufficient time for self-reflection using an approach which is supportive, passive but probing and constructive.
- Communicate strategically by facilitating an employee-articulated link between individual performance and broad strategic goals. This allows the interviewer to understand the worker's perspective (and any gaps in knowledge) and also assists the latter in making sense of the broader organisational aims in their own terms.
- Provide balanced feedback (see earlier in chapter) and establish clear and systematic protocols for consistently poor performers including:
  - identification of poor performance areas with documented indicators;
  - recording of behavioural episodes with dates, times etc;
  - systematically establishing a benchmark against which poor performance can be checked;
  - consulting with employee outlining their strengths and behaviourally, rather than personally, oriented weaknesses; and
  - mutually establishing ways to improve performance and designing a plan on that basis with targets and deadlines etc.

Adapted from: Hartel *et al.* (2007)

After the appraisal it is essential that all outcomes are acted upon and would typically include: training and development, promotion, salary increases, job enrichment and enlargement, multiskilling, increased autonomy and so on. The key here is for managers actually to follow through with promises based on needs identified between both parties. There is nothing quite as demotivating as failure to deliver in this context. Indeed, employees are more likely to become less alienated from their work had there not been an appraisal interview in the first place! Inaction sends a clear message even if it is an unintended one. For example, a promise of training or conference attendance may have to be broken due to circumstances beyond management's control, such as a series of cancelled tour bookings or accommodation sales. These 'external' mediators must be communicated to employees. Failure to do so either reflects incompetence or a lack of respect; employees will usually understand it as the latter.

Consider the value of the foregoing for this case (Box 4.2) which highlights an increasing use of technology for employee performance management and appraisal.

BOX 4.2 Case study – The Reno-Sparks Convention & Visitors Authority makes employee appraisals exciting and fun

The region of Reno and Lake Tahoe, Nevada is sometimes called 'America's Adventure Place,' offering top-notch skiing, golf, casinos and other attractions for thrill-seekers. But the organisation responsible for luring those thrill-seekers to the area found itself spending too much time and effort on the less than thrilling process of employee performance reviews. The Reno-Sparks Convention & Visitors Authority (RSCVA) was established in 1959 to promote convention and tourism business for the Washoe County area of Nevada and currently employs approximately 400 people at six different facilities and at its Reno headquarters.

When Steve Casper joined the organisation in 2000, only some of the full-time staff were receiving regular employee performance appraisals (part-time staff received no formal feedback). Those appraisals that were being done were paper-based, using standard performance appraisal forms that were laboriously filled out by overworked managers. The process was cumbersome and haphazard. 'We wanted to make the process easier. We wanted to have a system that let the managers focus on the review rather than the forms that needed to be filled out,' Casper said.

So Casper set up a rudimentary performance management system himself, using Microsoft Excel spreadsheets. Some time after he set out to find a better system, with the goal of cutting in half the time that HR staff was spending on managing the annual employee performance appraisal process. It was at the Society of Human Resource Management Convention and Trade Show in 2002 that he first saw a demonstration of Halogen eAppraisal. 'I was immediately attracted to the demo and to the promise of the product.'

'Thanks to Halogen eAppraisal, the time spent by HR staff in managing the annual employee appraisal process has been cut by 75%,' Casper said. 'The process was consuming almost all of our time in HR,' he noted. 'Now, we have time to do a lot of other important things.'

Question

1. Whilst the benefits of such an electronic system are apparent, discuss some of the likely challenges and how they might be managed effectively.

Source: Casper (2009). Copyright 2009 Halogen Software Inc. Used with permission. All rights reserved

Critical note

Performance-related feedback should not be confined to a once yearly formal interview sessions. Individuals in the workplace make judgements about each other and work performance constantly.

Reflections

Visit three local tourism employers.

1. Ask whether they appraise the performance of all employees.
2. Ask them to explain their answer.

APPRAISAL INTERVIEW METHODS

Potential for biased decision-making

Mindful of the careful planning, approaches to and preparation for the appraisal interview, there are a number of methods which can be used. Those chosen depend on the nature and structure of the organisation concerned and the overall business context. Indeed, similar organisations in the same industry will use different approaches. For example in the tourism sector, appraisal methods will depend to a large extent on the size of the firm. Larger corporations are more likely to have a formalised and well-developed procedure whereas smaller firms may take a less formal approach due to resource and skill constraints. Nonetheless, the appraisal interview has the same objective of reviewing performance 'objectively' and developing employees in line with generic organisational strategy.

The notion of objectivity during appraisals remains somewhat problematic and perceptual biases may influence the procedure. Despite the sanctity of the logical rational managerial perspective, most people have perceptual biases; some are significant whilst others are minor and they can have an impact on the appraisal process. Following are some commonly identified distortions:

- selective perception – interpretation based on interviewer's own background, attitudes and experiences;

- contrast/recency – judgements based on most recent critical incidents during the interview;
- projection – interviewer projects own attitudes onto interviewee;
- halo effect – interviewer creates an impression of interviewee based on one characteristic; and
- stereotyping – isolation of one personal characteristic and extrapolating to all members of an ethnic minority, race, gender, age group and so on.

These perceptual distortions may influence both parties during the appraisal interview leading to errors of judgement. They can be particularly acute if techniques incorporated use categories and personality attributes which are difficult to define, for example, dependability, loyalty and decisiveness as judgement criteria (Bratton & Gold, 2003). This creates a situation where subjectivity and thus potential for bias and unfairness may be allowed to flourish.

Internal and external attribution

A need to understand people's behaviour is common to everyone. In the case of the appraisal interview, behaviour proxies as performance. Attribution Theory holds that judgements are made on the basis of 'control', that is, whether behaviour is under control of the person or not (Kelley, 1973). For example, elements attributed to 'internal' forces (under the control of the employee) include, ability, skill, competence, effort, tenacity and so on; those with an external attribution include policies, rules and regulations. The interviewer's judgements about performance will be determined by these attributions but

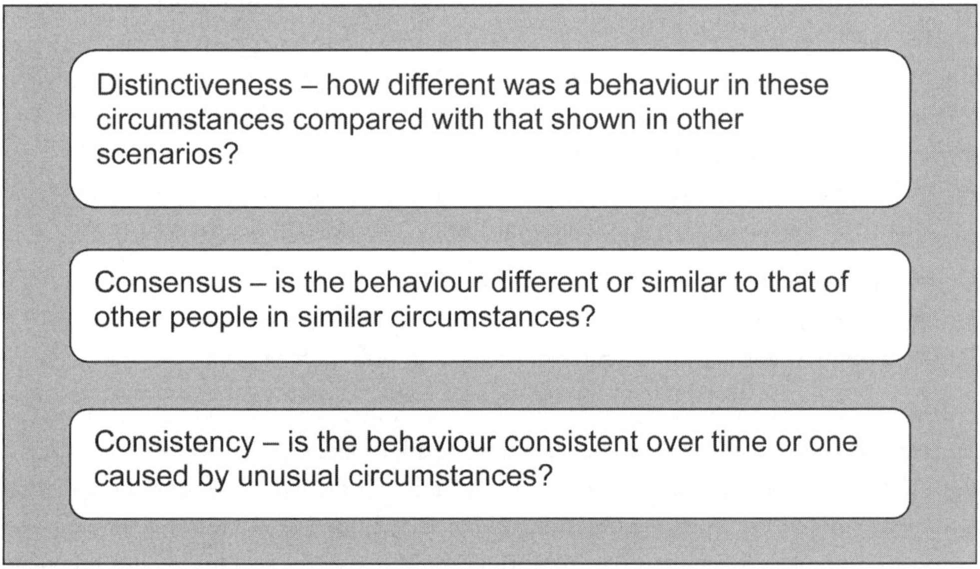

Distinctiveness – how different was a behaviour in these circumstances compared with that shown in other scenarios?

Consensus – is the behaviour different or similar to that of other people in similar circumstances?

Consistency – is the behaviour consistent over time or one caused by unusual circumstances?

Figure 4.3 The three dimensions of Attribution Theory

may also incorporate their prejudices. Three dimensions underpin this theory and they are shown in Figure 4.3.

In the case of a tour bus driver, we may have a situation where a performance target has not been met such as collecting a Japanese tour party from a designated pick-up area. An internal attribution by the interviewer would hold the individual culpable as the behaviour was not distinctive as the driver had also failed to meet other performance targets. Furthermore, they were the only employee to miss the target (consensus) and this behaviour was consistent with a failure to hit a renegotiated performance indicator. However, an interviewer with perceptual distortion may have ignored key factors when making the decision. For example, they may have a learned racist distortion where all members of a certain racial group are viewed as lazy or incompetent in some way. This error would have inevitable consequences if the driver belonged to this particular racial group. On the other hand, there may have been earlier interviews with two other drivers who similarly failed to meet the same or similar targets. On these occasions, one may have been known socially to the interviewer and the other may be particularly personable with a favoured personality characteristic. Objectively, all three should be judged similarly; with perceptual biases, only one driver is deemed to have missed the performance indicator.

Context

Additionally assuming no perceptual bias, other contextual issues may impact unfavourably on the appraised. As already discussed in this chapter, the key for effective appraisal interviews is to obtain results and objective outcomes of work effort, that is, those things that are measurable. However, for tourism and hospitality, outcomes which appear to be measurable objectively can be deceptive. For example, customer satisfaction in a restaurant measured on a numerical Likert-type scale would appear to be results/outcome oriented. A certain benchmark could be negotiated between a front-line employee and manager. For example, a target might be 95% of all customers must be 'extremely satisfied' with service delivered over a given time period. This seems entirely reasonable and objective. However, let us assume that during this period two things happen:

- the restaurant hires an incompetent chef; and
- the *couverts* associated with this particular employee are located in an area of the restaurant adjacent to a drafty doorway and noisy kitchen.

It would be reasonable to expect feedback in this context to be something less than the set target. In this instance, the employee would be adjudged as under-performing. Clearly, the use of additional qualitative information would help the worker during the appraisal interview but the example illustrates the subjective nature of what to all intents and purposes is an objective measure of performance. Moreover, it also invalidates the value of feedback from an 'external' source (the customer).

> **Critical note**
> The notion of objectivity during appraisals remains somewhat problematic and perceptual biases may influence the procedure. Most people have perceptual biases; some are significant whilst others are minor.

> **Reflections**
> In your own work experience
> 1. Do you tend to rate your own performance?
> 2. Are you always satisfied with the way your have performed in your job?
> 3. What are some of the best and worst things about appraisal interviews?
> 4. How have you responded if your ratings of performance differ to those of your employer?

SELF-APPRAISAL

Another obstacle to the appraisal process is that of self-appraisal. Employees have ideas about their performance which do not always tally with those of other appraisers. This can be a significant source of tension especially if it is linked to pay and promotion. On the one hand, some argue that there is no harsher critic than oneself, thus, feedback about performance would be expected to be honest and accurate. On the other, some people have a tendency to exaggerate performance or take liberties with the truth to manufacture a favourable impression of themselves. Whether one person is a harsh critic or another selective with their performance depends on a number of issues not least their personality type. Assuming that individuals choose to be honest there is still an issue of 'self-awareness'. According to Dubrin and Dalglish (2003), this personality trait is linked with task accomplishment and forms the composite whole now known as 'emotional intelligence'. Self-awareness is the ability to understand one's moods, needs and emotions. It is also about seeking and acting on feedback received about behaviour and adapting it accordingly. This trait is present to a lesser or greater degree in most people. However, for those belonging to the former category, their performance on the job may be self-reported as satisfactory when, in fact, it is not. Here, there is no dishonesty but a genuine inability to seek feedback and adapt performance behaviour. This is because the person has little idea of how well their behaviour is being received by others. Therefore, the usefulness of self-impressions for the appraisal depends on whether the information actually reflects performance objectively. Indeed this is the key to all appraisals.

So, how can self-reported feedback be deemed objective? In short, it needs to be corroborated or benchmarked against the reports of others. Typically, this would require performance feedback from more than one person so that comparisons could be made with the self-appraisal. This depends on what organisational framework exists to support such an initiative. One method used increasingly is known as the 360-degree appraisal. Here, performance feedback is received from a number of people usually including supervisors, co-workers, peers, customers, and reporting staff. However, if there are discrepancies between the collective 'external' ratings and the employee, negativity still occurs even with this method. Various authors note that schemes delivering feedback, whether multi source or individual must ensure appropriate training is provided (Bratton & Gold, 2003). Nonetheless, there remain issues over how best to obtain performance data, what individual instruments to use, how to administer the process and how information is shared.

Notwithstanding issues of:

- subjectivity;
- perceptual distortion;
- contextual factors;
- personality type; and
- overly subjective criteria for judgement

the appraisal process remains perennially dogged by the necessary matter of 'judgement'; no one enjoys it even if the outcome is positive. For example, an interviewer may rate a tourism employee's performance favourably even when this is not the case. Counter-intuitively, the employee may become dissatisfied with the manager due to their seeming lack of interest or attention to detail. The interview will be regarded as a farce and of no use in terms of the employee's performance to date and future career development. The key is how to communicate the necessary information to the interviewee in a way that is appropriate. A number of instruments and methods may be used to aid the process. An increasingly popular approach is to use a 'balanced scorecard'.

Balanced scorecard and other techniques

First conceived by Kaplan and Norton (1996), the balanced scorecard is a framework which explains or translates a firm's vision into an inclusive set of measurable current, ongoing and long-term performance indicators divided into categories of:

- finance;
- customer satisfaction;
- internal business processes; and
- learning and growth.

In essence, it was introduced to address the issue of measuring additional and less tangible variables than those used traditionally such as financial indicators. Its benefit largely concerns the holistic perspective on which it is based for example, human resource objectives can be established across all the above areas. The benefit here is that they can be viewed and evaluated within the context of the whole organisation's strategic position. Thus, performance of the employee (and the whole performance management process) becomes strategic by nature of the balanced scorecard approach.

There are a number of websites dedicated to the use of the balanced scorecard and some actually permit free trials with advice on how to design, customise and implement the procedure. Some examples can be found below:

- Balanced Sorecard Designer –
  http://www.strategy2act.com/solutions/hr_metrics_excel.htm
- Cite HR.com –
  http://www.citehr.com/145523-corporate-strategies-hrm-strategies-balanced-scorecard.html
- The Balanced Scorecard Toolkit –
  http://www.w3j.com/6/hr_scorecard.html

A number of specific techniques may be used in conjunction with the balanced scorecard and some are shown below in Table 4.1.

Table 4.1 Some common appraisal techniques

Technique	*Details*
Critical incident	A journal account of effective or ineffective performance – reliance on historical incidents may cause inaccuracies due to memory effects and 'recency' could lead to inappropriate relative weighting
Management by objectives	Outcome oriented through mutual measurable goal-setting – can be seen as 'reward–punishment' if employee has no control over objectives
Semantic differential scale	Trait based on bipolar scales from 'excellent' to 'unsatisfactory' for each. Useful for benchmarking across workforce but careful choice of performance traits is essential for qualitatively different jobs. Also does not provide precise information

Adapted from: Hartel *et al.* (2007) and Bratton and Gold (2003).

Other developments include behavioural-anchored rating scales (BARS) and behavioural observation scales (BOS). Both are competency-based and the former consists of descriptions of 'outstanding' and 'poor' behaviour alongside a numeric scale. For the job of 'tourism planner' a competency descriptor of outstanding (rank 7) might read 'develops thorough verifiable plans, secures authorisation and circulates to all appropriate people'. The counterpart poor (rank 1) might read 'Infrequent finalisation of plans due to disinterest with no effort made to improve'. Other competency descriptions would appear between these two extremes all anchored numerically along the 2, 3, 4, 5, and 6 rankings. The BOS instrument is also based on performance but this time on frequency of observed behaviours on an appropriate scale (for example, 1=never to 7=always). The behaviours may be derived from other techniques such as critical incident or job analysis. The advantage of BOS is its reliance on actual observed behaviour rather than the evaluative orientation of the BARS technique. Bratton and Gold (2003) add further benefits including the specificity of goals developed through BORS when compared with BARS and that several behaviours can be observed simultaneously. This tends to reduce bias and provides more incisive feedback.

Critical note

The balanced scorecard is a framework which explains or translates a firm's vision into an inclusive set of measurable current, ongoing and long-term performance indicators.

Reflections

1. Draft and design two appraisal interview schedules; one for a tourism firm employing only five people and the other with a workforce of 100.
2. Present both schedules to your peers and ask for feedback.
3. What did you learn from this activity?

SUMMARY

Performance management and performance appraisals are terms often understood to have the same meaning. Whilst they are linked the former is an overarching strategic framework in which appraisals are positioned along with other key performance initiatives. This focus is essential if performance appraisals are to be meaningful, measurable and appropriate across all organisational levels linking with generic aims and objectives. Moreover, the strategic perspective is an essential part of human resource planning as it underpins other key decision-making areas including skills audits, job analysis, succession planning, motivational initiatives and so on.

The performance of tourism workers is of key concern if firms are to thrive in an increasingly competitive environment. However, measuring performance accurately has traditionally been fraught with challenges. In a contemporary and dynamic tourism environment where organisations and their structures are in constant flux the importance of performance becomes paramount. Firms with little or no knowledge in this area will find difficulty in comparing their progress against other firms, understanding the performance of individuals and knowing whether employees value other human resource initiatives. However, measuring performance objectively is difficult as employees are now more sophisticated than at any other time and have a wide rage of personal objectives, aims and aspirations. Moreover, the skill sets required at the customer interface go beyond the technical to incorporate less easily identified emotional and aesthetic aspects. Performance management systems must therefore be suitably sophisticated.

Typically, appraisal interviewing is unpopular with both appraised and appraiser. Some argue the process is inherently subjective and despite attempts to minimise this aspect many firms fail to address even the basic elements of both the interview and the planning required. A poorly managed interview can have far-reaching negative consequences upon the motivation and performance of the individual, team and ultimately the whole organisation. Preparation is therefore important and prior to the interview a number of decisions have to be made including who will conduct it, what is its exact purpose and how much prior knowledge does the interviewer need. Interviews may go ahead once these decisions have been made normally in the following stepwise manner:

- ascertaining how well workers are performing in their jobs;
- communicating this information to them;
- establishing a mutually agreed plan for improvement;
- implementation of the plan; and
- training and development.

Some organisations schedule two separate interviews around once a year or at other specified times (not normally more than two). The first is where performance to date is reviewed and the second looks at the training requirements needed and opportunities available. The reasoning behind holding two appraisals is rooted in the major perennial challenge common to all appraisals. By definition, managers make judgements about employees constantly as do they about themselves. However, judgements are only acceptable to the judged if they are deemed to be objective and equitable. If they are in some way thought to be punitive and unfair, negativity is an inevitable outcome for all concerned. It is thought that splitting an interview into two elements helps to diffuse negativity which would otherwise cloud decisions about future employee development. Typically, there is an appropriate time lapse between the two interviews.

Nonetheless, even with approaches like the above, achieving and maintaining perceived objectivity is a problem. A number of factors contribute to this state of affairs including perceptual distortions of stereotyping, projection and specific service work contexts. An increasingly popular method of minimising subjectivity is to use the feedback of more than one person through a 360 degree approach. However, some issues of perceived inequity remain due to the tendency of individuals to self-rate. Clearly, any internal perceptual distortions and associated personality traits may predispose people to rate their performance in a way which may be highly skewed! Additionally, some appraisal techniques and linked rating scales may arguably be overly subjective particularly where criteria are ill-defined and thus difficult to measure.

CHAPTER QUESTIONS

1. Define and discuss the terms performance management and performance appraisal.

2. Outline some key challenges to measuring the performance of tourism employees.

3. Discuss how a balanced scorecard approach helps tourism organisations measure performance.

RECOMMENDED READING

Baum, T. (2006) Reflections on the nature of skills in the experience economy: challenging traditional skills models in hospitality. *Journal of Hospitality and Tourism Management* 13(2), 124–135.
>A discussion of contemporary discourse about skill requirements in the hospitality industry

Bratton, J. and Gold, J. (2003) *Human Resource Management Theory and Practice* (3rd edn). Basingstoke: Palgrave MacMillan.
>A UK-oriented practically focused human resources management text.

Davies, D., Taylor, R. and Savery, L. (2001) The role of appraisal, remuneration and training in improving staff relations in the Western Australian accommodation industry: A comparative study. *Journal of European Industrial Training* 25(7), 366–373.
>A discussion of employee appraisals in the accommodation industry.

Dubrin, A.J. and Dalglish, C. (2003) *Leadership: An Australian Focus*. Australia: John Wiley and Sons.
>A discussion of employee appraisals from a leadership context.

Kaplan, R.S. and Norton, D.P. (1996) Using the balanced scorecard as a strategic management system. *Harvard Business Review,* January–February, 75–85.
>Classic paper discussing and applying the authors' original notion of the balanced scorecard for measurement of organisational output.

RECOMMENDED WEBSITES

An introduction to systems thinking – http://www.systems-thinking.org/intst/int.htm

Performance management systems and tourism enterprises –
http://facta.junis.ni.ac.rs/eao/eao200802/eao200802-04.pdf

'Go2' performance management in tourism –
http://facta.junis.ni.ac.rs/eao/eao200802/eao200802-04.pdf

A guide to performance appraisal –
http://www.doi.gov/hrm/guidance/370dm430hndbk.pdf

Performance appraisals – http://www.businessballs.com/performanceappraisals.htm

CHAPTER 5

TRAINING AND DEVELOPMENT

LEARNING OBJECTIVES

After working through this chapter you should be able to:

1. Explain the need for training and development, particularly for the tourism and hospitality industry.

2. Distinguish between training and development.

3. Understand approaches to training and development.

4. Engage in debates about training, development and education.

5. Consider career development in the tourism and hospitality sector.

INTRODUCTION

Induction and orientation are the initial stages of training and development. These elements, which are recognised as constituents of the human resource development (HRD) process, form part of the organisation's strategic investment in their human resources. Such investment is critical if the organisation is to improve or maintain their success in an internationally competitive environment. In addition, it is now recognised that HRD needs to be a continuous process which is a flexible, adaptable and cooperative endeavour. Organisations are immersed in a dynamic, ever-changing environment. To survive and succeed in such conditions, organisations need to keep their employees up-to-date and reoriented with changing conditions. Further, within the organisation, HRD should be a cooperative effort between HRM, managers and supervisors. Externally, professional bodies, industry collectives and government bodies should ensure that training and development initiatives sustain viable labour markets. They have a responsibility in accepting and contributing to training and development efforts. Equally, individuals are beseeched to engage with lifelong learning to improve their skills, knowledge and attitudes, sustain their employability and enhance career progression. Hence, the talk around HRD entails discussions and debates of training, development, learning and education.

One tourism organisation which has embraced the notion of HRD is the 'Savannah Guides'. This 'is a not for profit member-based organisation comprising a network of professional tour guides and operators with in-depth knowledge of natural and cultural environments across Australia's vast tropical savannahs' (Savannah Guides, 2009). It is an organisation which has taken a holistic approach to HRD, encompassing individual tour guides, operators, the ecotourism industry and national education. The article below in Box 5.1 provides an insight into the organisation.

BOX 5.1 Case study – Savannah Guides

Savannah Guides is a not-for-profit member-based organisation comprising a network of professional tour guides and operators with in-depth knowledge of natural and cultural environments across Australia's vast tropical savannahs.

Savannah Guides Ltd was established in 1988 with its original purpose twofold: to provide access for visitors to unique natural features on private, leased or public property in a manner which protected them; and to provide a benchmark of professionalism and a platform through which members could learn from each other and from specialists. This purpose and philosophy remains today.

Members were initially locals of the Gulf Savannah region but the network has since expanded to encompass tour guides and operators across the tropical savannahs (and abutting regions) of Queensland, Northern Territory and Western Australia. Savannah Guides member enterprises have been developed by privately and publicly owned bodies as either static sites or roving operators conducting tours throughout the region. All Savannah Guides Enterprises must incorporate natural and/or cultural interpretive activities as a prominent part of their business and demonstrate a commitment to conservation values and professional development.

Membership categories/accreditations are separated into businesses (Enterprise Members) and their individual guides. A Savannah Guide is recognised as a person who has the knowledge, professionalism and training required by the organisation, including assessment by his/her peers, and is someone at the pinnacle of the guiding profession. Enterprise and Individual members must meet strict standards of operation and abide by professional Codes of Conduct.

Training, knowledge and professionalism are fundamental to Savannah Guides' operating philosophy. Two training schools are conducted each year, at varying locations across the savannahs, and feature experts in related fields including ecology, land management and tourism. These schools are critical to the training and education process provided to both members and 'friends' of the organisation. In addition, they provide members with an invaluable opportunity to meet, interact with, and learn from each other.

Savannah Guides continues to raise the standards of professional guiding operations throughout Australia and partners with industry and government organisations for continued development and training.

Vision, mission and core values

Savannah Guides Mission Statement was originally drafted in 1992 and has undergone minimal alteration since. It continues to highlight the organisation's purpose.

Vision

Through the promotion of ecologically sustainable tourism principles, Savannah Guides will enhance regional lifestyles and encourage the protection and conservation of the natural and cultural resources of the Tropical Savannahs of Northern Australia.

Mission

To be an economically sound, community based, professional body which maintains high standards of:

- Interpretation and public education
- Training and guiding leadership
- Natural and cultural resource management

Questions

1. Comment on the approach to training and development adopted by Savannah Guides.
2. Discuss why this model is one to be recommended to other organisations in the tourism and hospitality industry.
3. Think of an organisation you are familiar with and reflect on how the Savannah Guides training and development model could be adopted by the organisation.

Source: Savannah Guides (2009). Handout provided by Ms Vicki Jones (Savannah Guides Manager)

The example of Savannah Guides highlights a proactive approach to training and development. Unfortunately, many organisations in the tourism and hospitality industry invest little time, money and effort in training and development. This is exasperated by the labour-intensive and service-oriented nature of the industry, which emphasise the need for such programmes. Further, the industry is renowned for its informal approach towards human resource management, especially with smaller establishments (e.g. Baum, 1995; Jameson, 2000; Lockyer & Scholarios, 2004; Lucas, 1995; Price, 1994).

This chapter will discuss issues associated with training and development. In particular, it will examine approaches to HRD from the tourism and hospitality industry.

> **Critical note**
> HRD is an important consideration for individuals, organisations, professions, industries and governments. It encompasses a holistic approach to training, development, learning and education.

> **Reflection**
> Examine a tourism and hospitality organisation and summarise and assess their approach to HRD.

TRAINING AND DEVELOPMENT

According to Stone (2008: 345) HRD 'includes training and development, career planning and performance appraisals. Its focus is the acquisition of the required attitudes, skills and knowledge to facilitate the achievement of employee career goals and organisational strategic business objectives'. Hence, HRD is an important activity which involves new and existing employees. Training for new employees begins with the induction process as they are oriented to the organisation, the job, the workplace and their colleagues. The basis of training at this stage is to ensure that the new employee has or attains a satisfactory level of knowledge and skills to be able to perform the job effectively (e.g. Boella & Goss-Turner, 2005; Nankervis *et al.*, 2005). Existing employees need continued training as changes occur and they are required to acquire new skills and knowledge. Several reasons could affect training for existing employees, including:

- technological changes, e.g. automation and computerisation;
- enlargement or changing of jobs;
- award restructuring;
- need for multiskilling; and
- jobs being replaced or becoming extinct.

In addition, research highlights the link between investment in HRD and an organisation's profitability (Eldson & Iyer, 1999; Huselid *et al.*, 1997). From a strategic perspective, HRD is regarded as 'a platform for organisational transformation, a mechanism for continuous organisational and individual renewal and a vehicle for global knowledge transfer' (Ready, 1995: 28). Table 5.1 highlights some of the reasons why management training is a valuable tool and some benefits to be gained from training programmes.

Table 5.1 Reasons to develop and implement training programmes

Hussey (1996)	McKenna and Beech (2002)
• implementing a new policy • implementing a strategy • effecting organisational change • changing an organisation's culture • meeting a major change in the external environment • solving particular problems	• helping employees learn jobs more quickly and effectively • improving work performance of existing employees • keeping existing employees up to date in specialist skills • fewer mistakes, less wastage and improved efficiency • reduced turnover and accidents • attracting good workers • receptive attitude to change • operationalisation of management techniques, e.g. quality management

Of particular importance to the tourism and hospitality industry are the links between training and the delivery of service quality. Hall (1975, cited in Lashley, 2002) emphasises that low-skilled and untrained staff have a direct impact on the delivery of service quality in many hospitality organisations. Further, it makes sense that lack of training can result in low staff morale. Low-skilled and untrained staff can be badly prepared for the gruelling demands of service such that this can add stress and dissatisfaction to employees (Hall, 1975, cited in Lashley, 2002).

In addition, research shows that investing in training has positive impacts on wages and job stability (e.g. Booth & Satchell, 1994; Lashley, 2002; Lillard & Tan, 1992; Mincer, 1983). More specifically, some of the research indicates effective on-the-job training can have beneficial outcomes (e.g. Bartel, 1995; Bishop, 1994; Lashley, 2002; Lynch, 1992). Other research has examined training needs in the tourism and hospitality industry (e.g. Amoah & Baum, 1997; Brotherton *et al.*, 1994).

Hence, it is evident that training and development can play a vital role advancing organisation change and promoting corporate culture while empowering and engaging employees and supporting the organisation's business strategies. As Lawrie (1990) noted training and development are concerned with changing or enhancing employee behaviour and improving job performance. In line with this, Stone's (2008) definition of training and development are most apt. He says **training** 'represents activities that teach employees how to better perform their present job [...] [It] typically emphasises immediate improvements in job performance via the procurement of specific skills (for example, computer skills)'; and **development** 'involves those activities that prepare an employee for future responsibilities [...] through the acquisition of new experiences, knowledge, skills and attitudes' (Stone, 2008: 353).

Development involves learning that may be related to future changes in the employee's current job (e.g. new customers or new products) but is not usually associated with the employee's present job. It can entail job experiences and formal education. Often, however, the understanding and use of the terms 'training' and 'development' are blurred. Holden (2004: 313) points out that 'it is difficult to arrive at a consensus definition of terms such as "development" and "training" because of the varied ways in which they are translated into work and life situations'. This is evident in definitions forwarded by other authors. For example, MSC (1981, cited in Armstrong, 1997: 507) define training as 'a planned process to modify attitude, knowledge or skill behaviour through learning experiences to achieve effective performance in an activity or range of activities. Its purpose, in the work situation, is to develop the abilities of the individual and this definition highlights the need for training to develop the organisation's capacity for effectively managing ongoing change, especially change which is driven by external forces'. In this sense, training and development are interconnected and both are important in the development and implementation of HRM policies and practices.

With regards to the tourism and hospitality industry, the literature indicates that generally employees within the industry remain unqualified and that training is limited to large multi-establishment companies (e.g. Lucas, 2004). Further, it seems that casual employees are significantly disadvantaged in relation to employer-endorsed training (VandenHeuvel & Wooden, 1999) as are older workers (Smith, 2003). These issues are compounded by the labour and skills shortage in the tourism and hospitality industry. Ironically, investment in training is critical for building of human capital and as some of the literature has indicated is an instrumental factor in enhancing an organisation's competitive strategies, improving productivity, raising standards of living (especially of low skilled workers) and generating sustainable national economic growth and wealth (e.g. Ramos *et al.*, 2004). Lashley (2002: 105) makes the point that in the tourism and hospitality industry 'managers are themselves inadequately trained and are not naturally convinced of the value of an investment in training activities'. Guerra and Peroni (1991 cited in Mulcahy, 1999: 166) estimate that 'in the UK, approximately 10 per cent of managers have a specific qualification and that 94 per cent of those employed in the tourism industry have no recognised qualification'.

It can further be said that the industry is renowned for its 'short-termism' and the lack of realisation of the benefits and value of training and development. Marhuenda *et al.* (2004: 222) point out that 'the promotion of continuing training, greater recognition of formal vocational education and the development of an entrepreneurial culture are key elements that would enhance opportunities to develop a professional career in tourism'. Despite these training differentials and concerns there are good examples of systematic training and development companies. This is evidenced with Savannah Guides Ltd and their 'Activities' (see Box 5.2).

BOX 5.2 Case study – Activities of Savannah Guides

Savannah Guides provides the following three broad services – Membership and Accreditation; Training and Professional Development; and, Cooperative and Brand Marketing.

Membership and Accreditation – Membership comprises the following categories – Individual, Enterprise, Social (Friends of Savannah Guides), Special and Honorary. Each membership criteria undergoes assessment to maintain standards. To be accredited, individual members must work for an accredited enterprise member, but can maintain their accreditation if they leave its employ. Members are mentored through the membership and accreditation process by senior members and the Board.

Training and Professional Development – The core principle of training is for members to continue to cooperatively share knowledge, experiences and passion in order to develop high levels of competence in interpretation and other skills that are consistent throughout the network.

- *Operator-based Training* – Individual guides are trained by their accredited tour operator/enterprise. Senior Savannah Guides mentor potential members in knowledge, professionalism and the Savannah Guides ethos and passion, before guides undertake a peer assessment.
- *Schools* – Each guide must attend two schools before accreditation. The Schools are professional development conferences that foster the sharing of knowledge between members and from specialists in their fields. The four to five day schools are held at different locations across the tropical savannas twice a year and give participants an opportunity to experience new and existing member locations and develop an intimate knowledge of the local environment and community. Schools are open to all members, all industry guides and operators, tourism students and interested parties.
- *Formal Qualifications* – Members must complete the Certificate III in Tourism (Guiding). The accreditation process is mapped to this and existing members have the opportunity to gain recognition of prior learning for their existing skills. Time pre and post Schools is utilised to provide formal training which is credited towards higher qualifications.

Cooperative and branding marketing – The Savannah Guides brand is marketed to raise awareness of the organisation, and its members, with consumers and in the industry. The brand and professionalism is also marketed as a means of increasing membership.

> The outcome of all of the above services is a network of professional tour guides and tour operators with a collective in depth knowledge of natural and cultural environments who share similar interests, professionalism and passion, and form lasting friendships and business relationships.

Source: Savannah Guides (2009). Handout provided by Ms Vicki Jones (Savannah Guides Manager)

The training and development model realised by Savannah Guides has gained much interest in recent years. For example, Dr Julie Carmody (Postdoctoral Researcher, JCU) is in the process of finalising a paper on the model and how it can be used as a template for other tourism and hospitality organisations to follow. This research follows her earlier work (Carmody & Prideaux, 2008) in which she profiled membership of Savannah Guides. In that report, Carmody and Prideaux (2008: 8) recognised that 'training of Savannah Guides is an important aspect of the organisation. The core objective of training is for members to achieve and maintain a high level of competence in both knowledge and interpretation skills'. Similarly, Hillman (2003: viii) commented that 'the guides have implemented various forms of assessment and training that serve as a measurement of competency and uniformity'.

Training and development also provide opportunities for employees to advance to positions of higher responsibility or to be promoted. This can enhance employee's self-esteem and confidence and promote personal growth. This is evident with Savannah Guides where membership is categorised as 'entry' or 'senior' level and members can work toward achieving the higher level (Savannah Guides, 2009). The Savannah Guides example also introduced the notion that there are different methods of training. In the case of Savannah Guides, this included operator-based training, Schools and formal education. The next section discusses approaches to training.

Critical note

Training and development are processes planned to affect positive changes in employees' attitude, knowledge or skill behaviour so as to improve performance. Training is a response to satisfy current labour needs of the organisation while development involves activities that prepare employees for future or higher job responsibilities.

Reflection

Find a tourism or hospitality organisation and evaluate their training and development programme.

METHOD OF TRAINING

There is a wide variety of methods available to organisations for training and development of staff. All have strengths and weaknesses and so a contingent approach to the development and implementation of training and development programmes should result in the most appropriate method being chosen for the organisation.

There are both traditional more recent methods of training. As our understanding of learning, motivation and other human behaviour increases, newer methods of training and development are advanced. In addition, as technology progresses, more effective and economical methods are developed. Parallel to these factors, management training and development is often approached differently to training of non-managerial staff. Generally, training methods are categorised according to location (on-the-job or off-the-job) and level of formality (formal or informal) as described in Table 5.2.

Table 5.2 Typologies of training methods

Formal on-the-job training	Refers to instruction that takes place at the place of employment with the intention of raising skills levels, e.g. formal induction to a department by the department manager
Informal on-the-job training	Relates to those activities that improve skills and knowledge relating to an employee's tasks, but which involve few organisational inputs, e.g. informal discussion among employees about cashiering procedures
Formal off-the-job training	Refers to instruction that takes place outside the workplace but is designed to enhance skills and knowledge related to employment, e.g. supervisory training courses at the local college or university
Informal off-the-job training	Relates to activities that improves skills and knowledge but do not lead to formal accreditation or are not part of a systematic programme, e.g. sending employees to hear industry speakers

Adapted from: Curran *et al.* (1996, cited in Lashley, 2002: 105)

These approaches are also impacted by several other factors such as whether:

- the person conducting the training is trained to train others;
- the training is structured and systematic;
- the training approach considers training design and delivery; and
- the training monitors and evaluates employee performance and development.

In reality, training will be affected by operational constraints. Principally, optimal training and development will be affected by an organisations capacity to operate while employees are being trained or developed.

ON-THE-JOB TRAINING

On-the-job training is the most commonly used method of training of non-managerial staff, especially in the tourism and hospitality industry. It is sometimes referred to as 'sitting next to Nellie'. It is based on behaviour modelling or observational learning and involves two processes; acquisition and performance. The new employee learns from watching and observing somebody with greater experience perform their work and notes the other's actions and their consequences. Subsequently, the new employee copies the observed behaviour. Such a simple approach is a very popular method for learning new skills, especially for the attainment and development of interpersonal skills (Stone, 2008: 361). It allows employees practise immediately what they have observed and receive simultaneous feedback.

In an industry which is strongly focused on direct customer contact, experience gained from on-the-job training as a basis for learning becomes central to the employees' training and development. Learning through 'real work' situations in a 'real time' environment provides valuable opportunities for new staff to learn to deal with customers. This experiential, approach to learning can be an effective form of training. As well as providing 'hands-on' skills, knowledge and understanding, on-the-job training can work to build positive relationships between people working together. The danger lies in the quality of training being delivered. Disadvantages can include:

- supervisor or 'experienced worker' with poor training skills – leading to piece-meal, inappropriate or inadequate training;
- disregard for or lack of standard job performance criteria;
- inappropriate training environment;
- poor scaffolding of the learning such that the trainee is 'thrown in the deep end'; and
- passing on of bad habits.

Ivancevich (2001) reported that the behaviour modelling approach was most effective for trainers at IBM and General Electric. Supervisors, sales and customer relations skills were learned more quickly and successfully.

Other forms of on-the-job training include job rotation, secondments and mentoring. Job rotation is designed to provide employees with work experience in various parts of the organisation. In so doing, it increases the range of tasks the employee is exposed to and so enables them to acquire additional skills and knowledge. This can lead to multi-skilling or functional flexibility (i.e. deploying employees from one activity or task to another).

Secondments are temporary assignments within the organisation or to another organisation. Again, they provide opportunities for employees to gain skills, knowledge or understanding. Stone (2008: 361) points out that they can assist employees 'to gain specific skills or differing viewpoints'.

Mentoring involves a senior and/or experienced staff taking or being given responsibility for the training and development of an individual. It generally is used to assist an individual with career progression. As noted above with on-the-job training, it allows an employee to shadow the mentor, observe, learn and practice. Tjapukai Aboriginal Cultural Park (Box 5.3) provides an example of a successful approach to on-the-job training. In including this example, acknowledgement is made of the people from the Djabugay and Yirrgandyji people. In addition, recognition is extended to Don and Judy Freeman who were instrumental in the design, production and directing of Tjapukai.

BOX 5.3 Case study – Tjapukai Aboriginal Cultural Park

Tjapukai Aboriginal Cultural Park has been the leading Cultural Tourist Attraction in Australia for 17 years and has grown from a small operation in the basement of a shopping centre to a $10,000,000 25-acre property at Caravonica, just 10 minutes north of Cairns city. Tjapukai has been a national and international tourism and business success from the beginning.

Tjapukai is an incredible success story and the flagship for marketing Australia's Indigenous culture internationally.

From its inception, the Tjapukai Aboriginal Cultural Park has been a co-operative and consultative venture with the local aboriginal people. It is a true partnership owned by the Djabugay and Yirrgandyji people, Indigenous Business Australia, the Chapman Group and Freeman Productions. The Aboriginal people own the land occupied by the park.

As a tourist attraction, Tjapukai enlightens and entertains audiences, crossing cultural barriers and engendering a feeling of warm simpatico and positive regard for a rich and ancient culture and its descendants in a modern world. Its success has eased racial tension, spurred self-determination and has revived an Aboriginal language and a culture that was being lost through the passing of time and generations. The empowerment this attraction provides for the Tjapukai community is wide reaching.

- Tjapukai is one of the largest private employers of Aboriginal people in Australia. It employs nearly 100 staff, of which 85% are Aboriginal. The benefits of self-determination and cultural pride brought about by such valuable deployment of human resources are felt throughout the entire community.
- Under an innovative employment strategy designed specifically for the park, Tjapukai entered into a benchmark agreement with the Federal Department of Employment, Education and Training, which incorporates a series of programme elements including:

- ○ Recruitment to permanent positions in the company in a range of occupations, including management, administration, retail, hospitality, performing arts, grounds and maintenance.
- ○ Development of a variety of skills enhancement and career development programmes, to meet the identified needs of Aboriginal and Torres Strait Islander staff that have been recruited by the company.
- ○ Cross-cultural awareness training seminars for managers, supervisors and co-workers, create a receptive workplace environment, influencing career advancement and promoting harmony and productivity in the workplace.

In recognition of its employment performance and benefits, Tjapukai won the Medium Employer of the Year in the Queensland Training Awards (NQ) in 1999.

The success of Tjapukai has also encouraged the formation of other Aboriginal dance groups in the Tropical North Queensland region, which has created even more new jobs for Aboriginal people in the tourism industry.

Source: http://www.freemanproductions.com.au/tjapukai.html (accessed 22.5.09)

Another aspect of informal learning process is the role played by socialisation. Socially constructed learning is important in the development of skills, knowledge and attitudes. Procedures, practices and technical, conventional and semantical knowledge enable employees to make sense of the work, to contextualise it and to make it relevant to themselves.

Critical note

There are many approaches to training. In the tourism and hospitality industry, on-the-job training is the most popular method.

Reflection

Interview a tourism or hospitality worker and determine what type of training they have received: on-the-job or off-the-job. Ascertain how useful they found the training. What were the advantages and disadvantages for them? How valuable was the approach? How satisfied were they with the training method?

OFF-THE-JOB TRAINING

In comparison to on-the-job training, off-the-job training takes place away from the employee's usual work environment and can be external to the organisation. It can be run by the organisation's training personnel but generally involves training intercessions conducted by external providers or specialist trainers. Formal induction sessions are an example of this type of training. It can also include training to gain proficiency in a particular skill, e.g. new computer system and apprenticeship training.

A variety of methods fall into this category, including: conference or discussion method; classroom training method; programmed instruction method; and, e-learning and adventure training. Box 5.4 highlights some further approaches to off-the-job training. More particularly, highly interactive methods will involve integration of case study analysis, role plays, and simulations. Such approaches are useful for service-oriented organisations, such as those in the tourism and hospitality sector, especially for developing of customer service skills. A further aspect of off-the-job training is to run a series of short (one or two-day) or modular programmes.

Education is a formal off-the-job training, which will be discussed more fully later in this chapter. Suffice to note here that as the tourism and hospitality industry evolves and matures, vocational and higher education courses are critical to the development of the tourism and hospitality professional. They can play a key role in promulgation of competencies, skills and knowledge as well as fostering values akin to a high level of professionalism, a much desired characteristic within the tourism and hospitality industry if it is to be credible and reputable.

BOX 5.4 Types of off-the-job training

The main types of off-the-job training courses are:

(1) Day release (where the employee takes time out from normal working hours to attend a local college or training centre).
(2) Distance learning/evening classes.
(3) Revision courses (e.g. in the accountancy profession, student employees are given blocks of around 5–6 weeks off on pre-exam courses).
(4) Block release courses – which may involve several weeks at a local college.
(5) Sandwich courses – where the employee spends a longer period of time at college (e.g. six months) before returning to work.
(6) Sponsored courses in higher education.
(7) Self-study, computer-based training (an increasingly popular option – given that attendance at external courses can involve heavy cost).

Source: tutor2u: http://tutor2u.net/business/people/training_offthejob.asp (accessed 14.9.09)

The article in Box 5.5 from *HR Monthly* below depicts some off-the-job approaches to training in the current tough economic climate.

BOX 5.5 Case study – On-track in-house

Global financial organisation JP Morgan Chase is meeting 'extraordinary times' with 'extraordinary measures', according to Julia Simpson, the company's Australia/New Zealand Head of HR. 'Developing people is more at the forefront of our thinking right now than ever as we look at creating ways to roll out training and development.' Almost unerringly it's happening in-house – 48% online, 48% in classrooms, with the remaining 4% in virtual programmes, presenting a growing focus.

With a helpful lead coming from the New York head office and a stash of more than 1000 online programmes tailored to Australia where there are some 1320 employees, the company is calling on in-house experts around the world to deliver their know-how in virtual and classroom sessions across a range of topics – business communication, client impact and risk, to name a few. 'We see the leaders as the teachers for how we run our business,' says Simpson, and the process cascades from the top.

When Jane Perry joined the company some 15 months ago as CEO (Australia & New Zealand) of Worldwide Securities, she was dispatched to New York to participate in the inaugural rollout of The Complete Manager, a programme now being delivered through the company by senior executives working with facilitators. 'The programme not only uses in-house expertise but internal case studies and metrics. The learning is embedded inside what we're trying to achieve as a firm. And the cultural pay-off is significant. You don't get the same benefits by driving development through external programmes,' Perry says.

Where specialist technical insights are required, outside experts are brought in. 'We're focused on how to best use the training budget to reflect our vision, our journey and our culture,' says Perry, herself a one-time HR executive. 'For the cost of sending someone to an external course, you can offer five or six people an experience in-house.'

Not surprisingly, the current climate is accelerating training's move from classrooms to the computer. E-learning continues to be regarded with scepticism that's not always founded. When JP Morgan Chase offered newcomers the choice between face-to-face networking opportunities or electronic induction, 96% completed the online option compared with 74% presenting in person.

Adapted from: Tarrant, D. (2009). Trains of thought. *HR Monthly*, May, 28–30

APPRENTICESHIPS

Apprenticeships have been the traditional training approach for learning of skilled trades such as electricians, mechanics, carpenters, plumbers and chefs. Apprenticeships involve on-the-job and classroom training. While on-the-job the 'trainee' is supervised by an experienced worker and he/she gains valuable work experience. The approach to learning is focused on an observation–practice method with generally no structured or systematic instruction from the experienced worker. This is interspersed with periods of time spent in the classroom learning a mixture of occupational specific theory and some generic skills, such as communication, literacy, numeracy and teamwork. This approach enables the trainee to engage in productive work while studying and realising the reward of pay increases as skills are improved.

Within the tourism and hospitality industry there are certainly opportunities and, in Australia, government incentives, for organisations to train apprentices and other trainees to obtain an industry-endorsed qualification. To receive these incentives, employers and registered training organisations (RTOs) must provide evidence of the training. In Australia, apprenticeship programmes rely on a partnership and cooperation between management and the individual, between industry and government and between the company and the TAFE system or other RTOs. Similar apprenticeship programmes are apparent in Europe. DeCieri and Kramar (2005: 399) note that such apprenticeships 'are linked with employment, education and training systems (i.e. systems that provide youths with the schooling needed in order for them to obtain work in the skilled trades)'.

Receptivity on the part of organisations and individuals toward those schemes is documented in the literature for UK organisations. For example, Mason (1997) reports that the Modern Apprenticeships scheme had attracted nearly 7000 young people by 1997 into tourism and hospitality. He highlights the success of De Vere Hotels in recruiting 'trainees' and applauding the opportunity to be able to train people the 'De Vere Way'. Less fortuitously, Mason (2005) presents data which shows that only 4% of UK hospitality employers were offering apprenticeships. More disturbingly, 80% of these did not complete their hospitality apprenticeship. By contrast, Smith (2003) reported that in Australia, one-third of apprentices do not complete their training.

Nonetheless, apprenticeships are a valuable link between individuals, training, education, and employers. For a long time, the Organisation for Economic Cooperation and Development (OECD) has been concerned about the persistent high levels of unemployment and its economic and social ramifications (e.g. OECD, 2002). Apprenticeships are vocational and education training (VET) programmes which can go a long way toward fighting youth education and unemployment and gaining of quality and purpose of life. Together with adult work-based training schemes, apprenticeships provide valuable pathways to work and in career development.

Critical note

Apprenticeships are an effective way of learning because they afford the individual opportunities to learn in the workplace from certified and experienced workers and

---

to learn in a more structured way in the classroom. It enables the individual to gain a qualification while working and earning money.

Reflection

Speak with someone who has undergone or is completing an apprenticeship and ask them what they see as the advantages and disadvantages of this approach to training.

TOURISM AND HOSPITALITY EDUCATION

Growth in tourism and hospitality has given rise to escalating interest in educational aspects of tourism and hospitality and an equally expanding number of education providers in this area. Emerging from this focus are considerations of key aspects of tourism and hospitality education, including curriculum; teaching and learning; assessment; quality; progression; international perspective; resources; qualifications; personal professional development; and, research of education issues. Airey and Tribe (2005) have edited An International Handbook of Tourism Education. This comprehensive volume details the needs and challenges of tourism and related education.

Subsequently, various organisations have emerged to promote tourism and hospitality education and related research. In Australia these include The Council for Australian University Tourism and Hospitality Education (CAUTHE) and The International Centre of Excellence in Tourism and Hospitality Education, THE-ICE. Further abroad, there are associations/affiliations such as The Association for Tourism and Leisure Education (ATLAS) in Ireland; The Tourism Education Futures Initiative (TEFI); The Center for Hospitality Research (CHR) at Cornell University; and Lausanne Hotel School (École hôtelière de Lausanne, EHL).

As the nature of tourism and hospitality has evolved, its scope has extended to include a range of niche areas of interest and study such as adventure tourism, eco-tourism, cultural tourism, heritage tourism, sustainable tourism, and sports and leisure tourism. These developments have opened up potential for rewarding careers in the tourism and hospitality industry. Concurrently, throughout the world tourism and hospitality education has exploded with a variety of courses ranging from diplomas through degrees to masters course and PhD research (e.g. The International Master in Tourism & Leisure, IMTL, from the MIB School of Management – see below). These educational opportunities afford study via various means, e.g. full-time, part-time, and flexible delivery, and can include a component of work experience. There is a plethora of higher education courses, some more specialised than others. Of interest, is that chosen appropriately, these courses are invaluable for anyone serious about a career in this vibrant and diversified industry.

CAREER DEVELOPMENT

Hjalager and Andersen (2000: 115) acknowledge that 'over the past few decades, the professionalisation of the tourist industry has attracted considerable political and research attention'. This section considers the career vocational prospects and pathways for workers within the tourism and hospitality sector. Against a backdrop of changing times, increased needs for flexibility and mobility in the workplace and debates on the meaning of work, contemporary tourism and hospitality workers face a complex framework of career expectations and opportunities, workers' needs, and vocational training and development pathways.

BOX 5.6 Case study – International Master in Tourism & Leisure

SELECTIONS for the IX edition of the Master (2009–10)

MIB School of Management in Trieste, at 11:00 am:

- **14 September**
- **28 September**

The **International Master in Tourism & Leisure, IMTL, is the only master in tourism accredited by ASFOR and UN WTO.** The programme helps participants develop skills for working in tourism and launching into a managerial or entrepreneurial career.

Important international company partners collaborate with the programme through in-class talks, testimonials, interviews for internships and jobs, and company visits and presentations.

The IMTL offers:

- a solid, technical tourism education;
- a solid business-oriented tourism training;
- mastery of management processes;
- specialized working tools for success in the tourism sector;
- reinforcement of personal capabilities;
- opportunities to network with companies offering career opportunities.

Vision and Mission

Tourism is a real business, which deserves passion and talent, and calls for far-sighted and challenge-oriented managers.

The **International Master in Tourism & Leisure (IMTL)** will forge talent, cultivate passion, widen horizons and challenge the real international tourism

---

professionals of the coming years through tourism training and tourism education at international levels.

Accreditations

- ASFOR Associazione Italiana per la Formazione Manageriale – ASFOR certifies top Masters and MBA programmes in Italy through a rigorous system of evaluation.
- UNWTO TedQual Certification – United Nations World Tourism Organization

Question

1. What are the advantages of undertaking a postgraduate course in tourism and hospitality?

Source: MIB School of Management, Trieste, Italy: http://www.mib.edu/cms/data/pages/master_tourism_training_education.aspx (accessed 14.9.09)

Marhuenda *et al.* (2004) analysed factors which influence formation of vocational identities. In their study, they recognised that 'Tourism-related services vary considerably with respect to the kind of ownership of the business, work organisation, training requirements, duration of employment and salary levels' and add that this varies with 'countries and regions' (Marhuenda *et al.*, 2004: 222). They found that larger organisations were characterised by 'professional management structures' and 'formal recruitment mechanisms for finding qualified personnel'. However, with the predominance of SMEs in the tourism and hospitality industry, career paths are generally not well-defined. Castel (1997, cited in Marhuenda *et al.*, 2004) highlights the segmentation of labour markets. Within this context, it is apparent that the nature of the tourism and hospitality industry demands different types of workers. Hence, development or presence of a homogenous occupational group seems impossible. Nonetheless, Marhuenda *et al.* (2004) report that various segments managed to develop and shape their own vocational identities.

Undoubtedly, the issue of meeting the training and development needs of the future in the tourism and hospitality industry remains a contentious and complex imperative. The training, development and education of individuals at all levels within the tourism and hospitality industry are essential for the growth and sustainability of the industry's competitiveness in the international environment. Baum (2006) discusses the positioning of training, development and education as major components of the industry's framework for the future, which encapsulates such issues as macro planning, and social responsibility. He emphasises that through training, development and education 'college students and employees within international tourism, hospitality and leisure have the opportunity for global vocational mobility, either in support of personal aspirations or of company requirements' (Baum, 2006: 203). He argues that while training and education are related, it is often said that 'training is for skills and education is for life' (p. 206) and that development:

> [...] can be seen to have a key role to play at all stages of a person's formal development (while at school, college or university), their vocational development (at vocational school, training centre or in the workplace) and their informal development (in any of the above situations as well as at home and during their social and leisure situations). (Baum, 2006: 213)

The relevance of this to the tourism and hospitality sector is that this industry can provide a vast array of opportunities to meet people's diverse 'career' needs whether it is the career-focused professional, the tradesperson, the individual seeking flexible part-time or casual employment, or young people seeking their first job. In the vocational, occupational or career context, development should be a planned process, i.e. a process which is controllable and monitored and evaluated by the individual or management. It should consider time, place, provider, reason/motivation, costs, methods, and measurement and recognition of outcomes (Baum, 2006: 217). On a positive note, in their study on the growth in professionalisation of the tourism industry in Denmark, Hjalager and Andersen (2000) reported that the period 1980–1995 has witnessed a growing number of employees with informal degrees or diplomas. They found that cooks and waiters constituted the majority of qualified people who have undergone dedicated training. The vignette below in Box 5.7, which is based on a true story, highlights how appropriate training and personal development can help form fledgling careers.

BOX 5.7 Case study – Forward Future: Career in the making

Nervous and eager, Sam arrived at his first day of work. Having chosen to drop out of school at year 11, Sam had decided to try a pathway in hospitality. He had applied to numerous businesses and franchises before being accepted into a fast food outlet a few blocks from where he lived. At the interview the manager had described this job position as a great first job, and a 'foot in the door' for a promising and rewarding future in hospitality. Sam believed this to be a wonderful opportunity and accepted the job. As he learnt more about the industry, Sam realised that there was enormous potential to move up in rank fairly quickly if one worked hard.

It was still early morning, breakfast time, and the customers were steady and few between. Sam was managing well, 'working the till' with another crew member, who had been chosen to train him for this shift. There were points where Sam felt helpless as he entered the wrong order repeatedly, but his trainer was patient and solved his errors quickly, advising him on what to do in the future. Sam's trainer, Amy, had been working in the fast food industry for nearly two years, and was currently studying year 12 at high school. She told Sam that she had just been appointed to crew trainer, but the managing staff were so pleased with how she was handling the increased responsibility and more difficult work that they had asked her to take on the role of manager in a week's time. She spoke of moving on to other areas of hospitality after school. To Sam this was a reassurance. Amy was not much older than him and with persistence and experience, his career too would take off in the near future.

Weeks passed working in the restaurant, and Sam slowly became more accustomed to the procedures, practices, and expectations of the work. It wasn't too long before he was rewarded for his hard work and positive attitude. Within three months Sam was appointed to Crew Trainer. While sitting in the back room on break one afternoon the store manager approached Sam to offer him a position as manager. Sam was greatly enthused at this offer, and accepted willingly. The manager went on to explain the hospitality certificate course he would have to undertake in order to become a manager. The cost of this would be absorbed by the restaurant.

Sam was excited at the opportunity of becoming a manager, and the qualifications he would receive along the way. The hospitality certificate course was sure to open up further doors outside of the fast food industry. He now dared to dream of one day becoming a General Manager for an international hotel chain and knew that one day his dream would come true.

Question

1. Consider the development of a career as a recipe. What ingredients are required for the making of a rewarding and successful career in the tourism and hospitality industry?

Author: Hayley Celeste Pryce, 2009, freelance writer

There are several models of career development within the hospitality industry. For example, Stone (2008: 364) discusses organisations which have proactively partnered with academic institutions to 'gain a competitive edge'. He comments on the partnership formed between InterContinental Hotels and Southern Cross University to create The Hotel School at Intercontinental Sydney. The School's motto is 'A Degree – A Job – A Future'. Read about The Hotel School Sydney below in Box 5.8.

Such establishments are invaluable in providing prospective tourism and hospitality professionals with effective career pathways through the acquisition of certificates, diplomas or degrees. As Van Dyke (quoted in Theibert, 1996: 31) notes, 'It's just common sense that when you have a specialised degree programme, which focuses on improving those skills that people use at work, you're going to end up with higher skilled workers who are well trained to do that particular job much more efficiently and to the best of their ability'. Notably, such programmes and partnerships contribute to the strategic development of the organisation.

Equally, management knowledge, skills and attitudes are not learnt purely from training and development courses. Experience plays a vital role in developing managers for the tourism and hospitality industry. Boella and Goss-Turner (2005: 136) note that 'Most of their [managers'] experience is obtained in the hard practice of managing people in the workplace [...] A management development programme must therefore contain a balance of formal training and planned experience'. As they comment, such development is an ongoing process lasting the term of 'the manager's working life'. A general pattern of progression for potential managers in the hotel industry is outlined in Table 5.3.

Ultimately, however, in the tourism and hospitality industry, management and career development remain the personal responsibility of individuals. With SMEs constituting the greater part of the industry, support for such programmes is constrained principally by financial resources and in some cases, by narrow management perspectives.

BOX 5.8 Case study – A unique partnership

Your success is our success

The Hotel School Sydney is a unique partnership between Southern Cross University and Mulpha Australia's hotel portfolio – Hayman, InterContinental Sydney, Hyatt Regency Sanctuary Cove and Hilton Melbourne Airport – plus Sanctuary Cove and Bimbadgen Estate Wines.

Paid work opportunities are an attractive feature of the programme, as is its proximity to the five-star InterContinental Sydney (adjacent). The school is positioned in the heart of the CBD, with the Harbour, Sydney Opera House and Botanical Gardens on its doorstep.

At inception in 1989, The Hotel School Sydney first operated as an integral part of InterContinental Sydney, but now, due to growth and demand, has close working relationships with many leading tourism organisations in Australia and around the world.

The programme is focused on hotel operational skills, management practice in the tourism and hospitality industry and the skills needed for continued learning in a changing global business environment.

The Hotel School Sydney is renowned for:

- Providing paid work opportunities integrated with university level education.
- Providing high potential graduates for employment.
- Teaching and learning excellence.

- Academic rigour.
- Strong industry links.
- Graduate success.

  We develop dedicated professionals with university qualifications that are recognised and highly regarded internationally. The growth of tourism and our association with major hotel companies are all leading to exciting career opportunities in hotel, tourism and services management. This is demonstrated by the continued success of our graduates.

Source: http://hotelschool.scu.edu.au/index.php/19/ (accessed 15.6.09)

Table 5.3 General progression pattern for potential tourism and hospitality managers

Year	*Position*	*Education*
0–6 months	Frontline worker in one department	Vocational training with a Registered Training Organisation, e.g. TAFE (Certificate); or first year university (e.g. BBus with a major in Hospitality or Tourism
6–12 months	Frontline worker in various departments	Continued training with RTO (Diploma)
2–3 years	Supervisor in a particular department; or trainee in management programme working through various departments	Second & third year university
4 years	Assistant manager of a particular department	MBA
5–6 years	Manager of a department or of a specialised function, e.g. new project or training management	MBA
7–8 years	Assistant to General Manager of hotel	
9–10 years	Managers of medium-sized organisation	

Adapted from: Boella and Goss-Turner (2005: 137, Figure 9.5)

Critical note

Training and development impacts on the tourism and hospitality industry at a number of levels. It also has implications for government policies, especially in relation to vocational training, traineeships, and apprenticeships. In addition, educational institutions, such as universities, can enhance sectoral level training. Collectively, these agencies can and contribute positively to advancing professionalism and professionalisation at various levels and to career development within the tourism and hospitality sector.

Reflection

You have been hired as a consultant to a regional tourism board in Queensland, what recommendations would you make to members on how to enhance career development in tourism and hospitality contexts?

SUMMARY

Training and development are important activities for organisations to pursue, especially in light of the current, dynamic, global environment. They involve the development of skills, knowledge and expertise and so, are powerful contributors to organisational success. In addition, occupations and professions rely on ongoing training and development to maintain a favourable occupational status.

Through training and development, employees are oriented to the job and organisation, adapt more readily to change, realise a sense of belonging, and are happier in the workplace. This enhances staff performance and morale, and reduces absenteeism and labour turnover.

The tourism and hospitality industry is often seen as a refuge for job opportunities. In terms of career choice, however, studies suggest that it is not the first career choice (e.g. Getz, 1994) and is often viewed as a temporary job. Purcell and Quinn (1996) maintained that even those with dedicated training and education in the industry consider it as a stepping stone into other industries and only approximately half of graduate pursue a career in the industry. Hjalager and Andersen (2000: 125) make a point of 'diffuse and possibly unattractive career opportunities [...] [and] the low and decreasing retention rates of personnel with dedicated training'. Nonetheless, as McKercher *et al.* (1995) emphasise there is a need to remain optimistic about the future of training, development and education for the tourism and hospitality industry. Hjalager and Andersen (2000: 125) suggest that there is a 'need to modify our understanding of careers in tourism and to think of training in a wider perspective'. This makes sense and heightens the urgency for the industry to create, develop and promote genuine career trajectories. The article below in Box 5.9 highlights how operators can work collaboratively to promote tourism and hospitality training for the benefit of the region and the industry.

BOX 5.9 Case study – Time to lift customer service

Perceptions of poor customer service among hospitality operators in Cairns have led to calls for workers in the front line to turn frowns upside down.

Visitor Information Centre manager Val Shields said tourists were becoming more selective, making top service and a warm welcome more important than ever. 'At the moment numbers are pretty much on par with last year's and we are expecting them to go up at the end of June, early July,' she said. 'There is still plenty walk-in traffic and they are interested in all the iconic of the region such as the Reef, Skyrail and train, but they are becoming more selective. I think in general the perception of the area is pretty positive – we really only get about three to four complaints a year about tourism operators and most of the talk we hear is from the locals – not the visitors.'

But local restaurateur, Villa Romana Trattoria's Daniel Guerra, disagreed, saying Cairns needed to lift its game in order to attract guests. 'I think there really is a lack of good service in Cairns,' he said. 'People need to be friendlier and businesses, especially restaurants, need to be more flexible. I teach all of my staff to offer the same services they would expect because the more you can offer the more you can sell.'

Cairns Chamber of Commerce president Jeremy Blockey said he did not believe Cairns was viewed any worse than other tourist destinations and said it was up to locals to support and reward good operators. 'Like anything there are positives and negatives but my perception by and large is pretty good,' he said. 'I'm always paying attention to the service I'm offered but I would say the overwhelming majority of times I feel very well looked after but here are a few upmarket establishments that may leave a bit to be desired. When people pay a premium they do expect service that reflects that.'

Black and White Taxi's fleet services manager Chris Simmons said despite cabbies having copped some flack over being discourteous, he believes they are trained to make a visitor's first impression of the city a good one. 'When considering the amount of points of contacts taxi drivers make in a day I would have to say we do pretty well,' he said.

Cairns consultancy and training groups have put their hands up to help the region put their best foot forward. As Tourism Tropical North Queensland (TTNQ) this week pushed Cairns at a travel conference in Melbourne, local businesses were offered free customer service training to dispel any perception of an unwelcoming industry. Web-based training group Etrainu's Steve Corradi said business owners needed to be more pro-active in upskilling their staff. 'The one thing we hear a lot is when it's busy businesses don't have the time to provide extra training and when it is quiet they don't have the money, which is why we thought offering the service for free might help,' he said. 'I don't think this is a Cairns-based issue but we want our reputation to be the best in customer service in Australia and the world.'

TTNQ chairman Stephen Olle backed the idea of free training, saying every little bit helped in the tough economic climate. 'We can always do better – there is never a perfect product so extra training can only be a good thing,' he said. 'At the moment we have about 90 Cairns tourism operators dominating an international conference and trying to push the region to as many new people as we can so the more prepared we are here the better.'

Questions

1. Discuss why training is important for service industries such as the tourism and hospitality industry.
2. Suggest other HRM initiatives which could be implemented to improve delivery of service quality within the tourism and hospitality industry.
3. What role can education providers play in improving the image of tourism and hospitality service?

Source: Pashley, Anita (2009). Time to lift customer service. *The Weekend Post*, June 20. Cairns, p. 14

CHAPTER QUESTIONS

1. Define the terms 'training' and 'development' and discuss how they are different.

2. Much is to be said of the various methods of training: compare and contrast on-the-job and off-the-job training, including the advantages and disadvantages of both approaches.

3. Explain how stakeholders within the tourism and hospitality industry can work collaboratively to attract people (both young and older) to pursue a career in the industry.

RECOMMENDED READINGS

Airey, D. and Tribe, J. (eds) (2005) *An International Handbook of Tourism Education*. Oxford: Elsevier.

A comprehensive volume which covers curriculum, teaching, learning, assessment, and quality in tourism education.

Chandana Jayardena (ed.) (2002) *Tourism and Hospitality Education and Training in the Caribbean.* Kingston, Jamaica: University of the West Indies Press.

A valuable pragmatic insight into the challenges and opportunities of tourism and hospitality education in international regions.

O'Shannessy, V., Minett, D. and Hyde, G. (2008) *The Road to Tourism* (2nd edn). Frenchs Forest (NSW): Pearson Education Australia.

This easy-to-read book provides a worthy outlook into the skills and attitude required to become a tourism and hospitality professional.

Hsu, C. (ed.) (2006) *Global Tourism Higher Education: Past, Present, and Future.* Binghamton (NY): The Haworth Hospitality Press.

A treasured volume focusing on the history and development of tourism but creating awareness of the current and future challenges and opportunities for tourism higher education programmes.

Riley, M., Ladkin, A. and Szivas, E. (2002) *Tourism Employment: Analysis and Planning.* Clevedon: Channel View Publications.

RECOMMENDED WEBSITES

The Association for Tourism and Leisure Education (ATLAS) – http://www.atlas-euro.org/

Council for Australian University Tourism and Hospitality Education (CAUTHE) – http://www.cauthe.com.au/index.html

The International Centre of Excellence in Tourism and Hospitality Education (*THE-ICE*) – http://www.the-ice.org/

Savannah Guides – http://www.savannah-guides.com.au/

The Tourism Education Futures Initiative (TEFI) – http://www.tourismeducation.at/

CHAPTER 6

QUALITY OF WORK LIFE

LEARNING OBJECTIVES

After working through this chapter you should be able to:

1. Examine what is the nature of 'work'.

2. Define 'work–life balance'.

3. Discuss the benefits of work–life balance to employees and the employer.

4. Explain how OHS promotes a safe and healthy workplace.

5. Identify and describe some current health issues affecting workplaces, especially tourism and hospitality organisations.

6. Identify some of the effects of stress and describe ways of minimising these effects.

INTRODUCTION

There is escalating confirmation that individuals are seeking quality of work life. Weaver (2009) examined perceptions of graduates from tourism management programmes on job quality in the tourism industry. Through use of semi-structured interviews he determined that perceptions of job quality included both economic and non-economic factors. Weaver (2009) found that interviewees valued intrinsic rewards, meaningful work, job characteristics and content, significance of tasks, and compatibility with individual's interests and preferences. He acknowledged that job quality is important and has implications for an employee's well-being.

Individuals want organisations to value them and implement policies and promote practices which reflect philosophies that recognise employees as important assets to the company and as 'a total person' (e.g. Dalton *et al.*, 2006; Grant & Shields, 2002; Herrbach & Mignonac, 2004; Reece & Brandt, 2008). The new HR regime endeavours to place people at the core of the organisation and take into account employees' needs and goals while striving to achieve a win-win situation for employee and organisation. Human resource management (HRM) attempts to capture people's attention and 'provide meaning and purpose, a context and frame that encourages individual potential to flourish and grow' (Gratton, 2000: 3). Organisations which pursue sustainable competitive advantage recognise the worth of HRM to the organisation, and value workers' talents, creativity, hopes and aspirations. They recognise that by working toward a win-win situation, they will have higher staff morale, less conflict, and reduced absenteeism and employee turnover. Such organisations recognise that this involves developing and implementing work–life or work–family programmes.

It appears that attaining work–life balance or reducing work–family conflict is a growing issue and fundamental to the quality of work life framework. Attaining a work–life balance can be a precarious journey fraught with the tenuousness of balancing work and life commitments, responsibilities, needs and desires and their associated issues and problems (see Figure 6.1).

In a longitudinal study which examined career progression of Irish tourism and hospitality management graduates, O'Leary and Deegan (2005) found that amongst the major reasons given for drop-out rate from employment in that sector were poor remuneration, unsuitable working hours, poor work conditions and incompatibility with family life. They stressed that these issues have serious implications for tourism and hospitality employers, especially in light of the persistent skills shortage in this sector. Equally, Deery (2008) found that work–family balance played a key role in employee turnover in the tourism and hospitality industry. She recommended that employers develop strategies which focus on work–family balance to minimise the impact on employees leaving the industry. These recommendations include policies which address

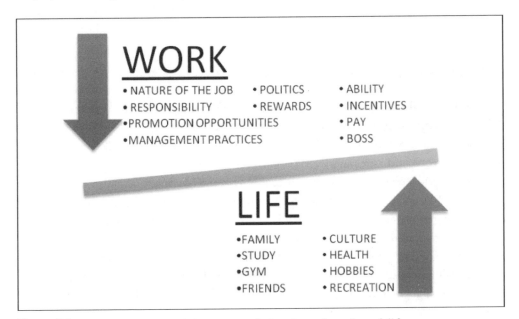

Figure 6.1 Some factors which impact on balancing of work and life

141

work–life balance and strategies such as flexible working hours and arrangements (Deery, 2008).

On another note, research that explored job quality in the tourism and hospitality industry suggests that perceptions of working in the industry are both positive and negative (e.g. Aksu & Köksal, 2005; Choy, 1995; Kusluvan & Kusluvan, 2000; O'Leary & Deegan, 2005). More recently, Weaver's work (2009) supported these findings. He reported that graduates working in the tourism and hospitality industry indicated that working in the industry has positive attributes. Similarly, Boon (2006) found that tourism and hospitality industry affords positive interdependencies between work and leisure. Further and interestingly, research on work–life balance indicates that work–family and family–work positive spillovers can have positive outcomes for organisations and society (e.g. Haar *et al.*, 2008). Some authors argue that having time to attend to or pursue personal or family activities revitalises individuals for their roles in the employment relationship (Greenblatt, 2002; Iwasaki *et al.*, 2005; Trenberth, *et al.*, 1999).

In another vein, Brough *et al.* (2008: 261) point out that 'work–life balance has a direct impact on societal issues, such as delayed parenting, declining fertility rates, ageing populations, and decreasing labour supply'. They confirm that work–life balance policies can have positive impacts on individuals, families, organisations and society but argue that such policies can also 'result in reinforced gender inequities and increased levels of work–life conflict'. Hence, the notion of quality of work life and work–life balance are highly contentious issues which require a comprehensive approach involving workers, managers, company, industry, advocacy and government stakeholders. The following letter (Box 6.1) found on the British 'TourismAlliance' website is testimony to the controversial nature of supporting jobs and working practices in the tourism and hospitality industry.

BOX 6.1 Case study – Letter to MPs: Budget Puts Investment into the Wrong Sectors

A Letter to MPs from Bob Cotton OBE, Chairman, Tourism Alliance
In his Commons speech, the Chancellor of the Exchequer said that his Budget would 'build on the strengths of the British economy and its people, speed the recovery, providing jobs and spreading prosperity'.

One of the strengths of the British economy is the tourism, hospitality and leisure industry. It attracts over £19bn annually in overseas earnings. It is the key economic driver of many regions of the UK. It is one of the country's largest industries, employing over 2m people and valued at more than £110bn. It is currently investing well over £5bn a year in new facilities, providing new jobs throughout the country. Its job-creating potential – at all levels – is significant. They are jobs, both full time and part time, that people want; they are jobs that can fit into any work/life balance pattern.

It is curious, therefore, that despite its size and importance, tourism didn't get a mention in the Chancellor's speech, while other industries – creative, oil, IT, energy – did, with most of them receiving some form of fiscal encouragement from the Chancellor. Tourism was ignored. It was an opportunity missed especially as the weak pound provides the perfect hook to gain more overseas tourists and retain domestic holiday makers this summer.

While Gordon Brown frequently insists that Britain must invest its way out of the economy, the Budget has done little to encourage this in tourism. For example, the hotel industry alone has invested over £25bn in the last five years, and opened over 1000 new hotels. Yet in 2007, the government abolished the Hotel Buildings Allowance and reduced other capital allowances. The investment in tourism facilities – hotels, restaurants, attractions – is essentially long-term. Businesses must invest for the long-term and arrange appropriate long-term finance. The latest Budget has given them little incentive.

At the same time, the tourism industry's short-term needs have also been ignored. The Budget's main focus was to look two, three or more years ahead, but there are more urgent problems. For tourism, the immediate need is to encourage more domestic holidays this year. Frustratingly, the Government is investing heavily in green and hi-tech industries to pull the economy out of the recession (investments that take many years to produce a return) rather than investing in tourism which can produce a near instant return on the Government's investment. For example, a small investment of £20m by the Treasury in 2002 to rebuild tourism after foot-and-mouth outbreak and the attacks of 9/11 resulted in 1m extra visitors to the UK in that year alone. These visitors spent £500m and supported around 12,000 jobs.

If Government wants to rebuild the economy and create new jobs right now, it needs to support real growth sectors of the economy such as tourism by undertaking initiatives such as restoring the Hotel Buildings Allowance, stanching the endless stream of new regulations and providing modest amounts of pump-priming funding for overseas and domestic marketing campaigns by the National Tourism Boards.

Bob Cotton OBE
Chairman

Questions

1. This article highlights the importance of the tourism and hospitality industry to national economies and recognises the need for governments to support jobs in the industry. Comment on how work–life balance can be used as an argument for governments to take investment in the tourism and hospitality industry as a serious matter. Include consideration of the complexity of work–life balance and

its implications for individuals' well-being; the impact of this on social issues and problems and vice versa; and, the potential for tourism and hospitality to assist people in finding the work–life balance through leisure, recreation and holidaying.

2. Assume you are representing the tourism and hospitality industry. Prepare your case for a meeting with government representatives.

3. As a representative of the tourism and hospitality industry, you and your team are now taking your case to the International Labour Organization (ILO, a key partner of UNWTO within the UN family) to advance the Decent Work Agenda. Gather your team and prepare your case.

Source: http://www.tourismalliance.com/showarticle.pl?ft=;id=237;n=10;p=1 (accessed 16.9.09)

The framework of quality of work life issues is complex and involves consideration of factors which affect the welfare, health and safety of employees. It incorporates focusing on issues such as occupational health and safety (OHS), alcohol and drug misuse, smoking, stress and workload. For the tourism and hospitality industry such issues have 'a particular resonance' as the research shows a blurring of work and leisure (e.g. Lee-Ross, 1995), effect of alcohol abuse (e.g. Bignold, 2003) and stress of dealing with demanding customers (e.g. Chappel, 2002). This chapter explores some of these issues with a specific focus on how they influence work, management and development of policies and pro-grammes within the tourism and hospitality industry.

Critical note

As the quality of work life becomes an issue of importance for individuals, organisations and society, businesses turning their attention to the development of policies and programmes to address such issues. Equally, governments are recognising the importance of a safe and healthy work environment and the need to consider the role of work–life balance in the lives of individuals.

Reflection

What do you think is the role of HR in promoting a safe and healthy workplace?

THE MEANING OF WORK

Giddens (1998) highlights that work is a central aspect of people's lives and that it plays an important role within society as a pursuit which affects an individual's identity, self-esteem and standards of living. Weaver (2009: 580) comments that 'For many people, work is a non-discretionary activity, an inescapable dimension of their lives'. This is supported by research which shows that while work can provide some positive and personally rewarding experiences, it can also be burdensome (e.g. Malpas, 2005; Terkel, 1974).

Workers these days have to contend with constantly changing times. Compounded by characteristics of flexible capitalism, issues of instability, fragmentation and uncertainty (Sennett, 2000, cited in Marhuenda *et al.*, 2004) the meaning of work becomes less tenable for contemporary workers. Author and philosopher Charles Handy (2002: 171) states that he maintained: 'Work, I believed, was a fundamental part of life [...] The mistake, my mistake, was to think that there was only one form of work, namely paid work – the job.' He goes on to say that besides paid work, there is home work (labour associated with maintaining family and home), gift work (volunteering for organisations such as charities and clubs), study work or learning (time spent keeping up-to-date in one's area of expertise and upgrading skills).

The emphasis of Handy's approach is for individuals to reflect on and evaluate whether they define themselves by the work they do for money or the work they do for love. Handy's (2002) philosophy is based on the idea the work is defined in terms of how time is spent and not on how one gets paid. In his autobiography *The Elephant and the Flea*, Handy (2002) describes how he sought such definition and illustrates his life in 'fleadom'. As an example, Handy mentions a woman who earns money by packing eggs but defines herself as a writer of TV plays. He says: 'The way she earned her money was not, in her mind, her real work' (Handy, 2002: 177). There are important questions raised by this insight:

- What meaning does work hold for us?
- Will we be like Charles Handy and seek a life in 'fleadom', building our own mixed portfolios based on doing work we love?
- Or will our quest for money rather than leisure prevail?

Handy (2002: 210) comments that it seems that with the current generation 'most preferred more money to more leisure and went on working the 100,000 hours [like their parents] if they could'. The question is what will motivate the next generations. Will it be working long hours with opportunities to perform a myriad of jobs but possibly at the sacrifice of personal, family and leisure time? Or will future generations seek greater harmony between work and life?

Baum offers an interesting insight into the situation. He says that:

Unlike their grandparents, today's school leavers and college graduates are more likely to think of their working lives in terms of finite segments rather than sustained and permanent careers, viewing the future in terms of what has been called, in the Australian context, 'fragmented futures' [...] Working-life segments can contain periods of commitment within different sectors of the economy, periods of study within models of lifelong learning, and periods of travel sabbatical as 'the year-out experience' becomes more and more common to those in their 20s, 30s and beyond. (Baum, 2006: 279)

So it seems that the meaning of work is changing. Barnes (1999, cited in Holland *et al.*, 2007) comments that contemporary employees have needs and expectations different to those of traditional employees and that they behave differently. In addition, Rousseau (1995) noted that these employees are more self-focused than and not as concerned with working conditions and job security as past generations. Of particular interest here are the gold collar workers. The Australian Centre for Industrial Research and Training (1999: 3, cited in Holland *et al.*, 2007: 20) say the following about gold collar workers:

[...] 'gold collar workers' have found high paying jobs which stimulate and challenge them. They often spend extremely long hours at their job, are young, ambitious and very well paid. Their loyalty, however, is owed less to their employer than it is to their career. As a result they are highly mobile, lured by new jobs which offer technical challenges or opportunities for self-development.

This suggests that workers will be more discerning of employers and seek 'employers of choice' who will provide opportunities for developing employees' knowledge, skills and expertise. This 'new paradigm', as Holland *et al.* (2007) refer to it, signifies a 'new psychological contract' which will require 'a new approach' to HRM. Hence, talent and, more specifically, the 'war for talent' are fast becoming a key issue for organisations seeking a competitive advantage and sustainable business performance.

The article below in Box 6.2 from the global recruitment consultancy Robert Walters presents findings on a survey which highlighted that New Zealanders work–life balance as a key factor in employment.

BOX 6.2 Case study – Work–life balance crucial, says survey

29 June 2004

According to the results of a recent survey conducted on their website, global recruitment consultancy Robert Walters has found that on-going personal development and training and a healthy work–life balance are more important factors for consideration in accepting a new job than the basic salary package.

The poll, which surveyed over 8000 people globally, asked respondents 'What's the most important consideration for you in deciding to accept a new job?'

On a global basis, 34% of respondents noted that opportunities for on-going training and personal development were most important, 32% of those polled

---

believed that a work–life balance was paramount, with 26% responding that basic salary was the most important consideration. The vast majority of respondents from New Zealand considered work–life balance and ongoing training the most important considerations.

Norma Aguilar, an International Candidate Manager at Robert Walters London said: 'We have seen an increase in the number of New Zealanders who have been considering returning home recently.'

'Although New Zealand salaries do not compare with those in London, we are being contacted by more and more Kiwis who are seeking to combine a challenging career with the lifestyle choices that New Zealand provides. Often the professionals that contact us have spent between two to five years working in London, they have often managed to save some money and are now ready to go home with a view to settling down, buying a house and starting a family.'

'They are in an excellent position to advance their careers at home as offshore experience, particularly for accounting, sales and marketing, HR and IT roles, is particularly in demand.'

According to Bruce Hall, also an International Career Manager, the employment market in New Zealand is red hot at the moment. 'In Auckland there is a gamete of roles for good quality candidates both on the permanent and temporary side. Currently in finance we are experiencing strong demand for candidates who are chartered accountants with five to eight years of experience.'

Question

1. As a human resource manager for a large hotel in New Zealand, how would you utilise the above information to wage war on the quest for talent and become an employer of choice?

Source: http://www.nznewsuk.co.uk/recruitment/?ID=609&StartRow=51 (accessed 10.9.09)

Critical note

Traditionally work has been an integral part of people's lives. With the progression of the post-industrial age, the meaning of work has been transformed. Post-modernism has heightened the many roles individuals assume in their lives and subsequently witnessed the genesis of multi-faceted meanings of work.

Reflection

Reflect on your 'working life' and think of what work means to you. Discuss the key aspects of why you think work is or is not an important part of your life.

THE CHANGING NATURE OF WORK

In 1889, US workers striked in demand of an eight-hour work day. Their slogan 'eight hours for work, eight hours for rest, eight hours for what you will' was an ongoing driving force for many subsequent industrial disputes and remained at the heart of the fight for appropriate working conditions throughout the Industrial Revolution (Rosenzweig-Fogel & Therstrom, 1985). At the height of the Industrial Revolution, the single 'breadwinner' household prevailed (Creighton, 1999). With the onset of World War II and men being enlisted, women gained a greater prominence in industry. Parallel to these occurrences, employment in tourism and hospitality has its origins in the post-feudal master–servant relationship and the notion of servitude has emphasised hierarchical differences in social relationships. As such, the meaning of work for workers in the tourism and hospitality industry has been framed by Victorian issues of social status and is apparent today in some of the writings about work in this sector. For example, The Work Foundation (2004: 2, cited in Baum, 2006: 113) highlights concerns about the context and security of contemporary domestic work:

> Most domestic relationships are in the informal economy. Whilst this can work well for both sides, we are storing up longer term problems as this sector expands. Those paid cash in hand for household tasks will not be getting National Insurance payments, and are likely to be storing up pension problems – particularly as they are predominantly women, who are already more likely to be in poverty in retirement.

Further evidence of abuse of the relationship is apparent in the current affairs snippets in Boxes 6.3 and 6.4.

BOX 6.3 Perth's hospitality workers short-changed

Hospitality Magazine, **6 April 2009, no author**
A fast-food franchise in Perth has been forced to back-pay many of its teenage workers $50,000 in wages following investigations by the Federal Workplace Ombudsman. After checking employment records, Western Australian Workplace Ombudsman inspectors discovered 33 staff members had been short-changed at the franchise, missing an average of $1500 each. The office is now considering legal action against the franchise, part of a national take-away food chain. The franchise was not the only offender to be discovered by the office in its latest round of investigations.

A bakery in Perth's southern suburbs underpaid 13 junior apprentices and retail sales staff more than $24,000, an average of $1800 each, while a food processing company in Bunbury underpaid 145 of its employees $41,800, an average of $290 each after receiving incorrect advice.

So far this financial year, the office has recovered $1.584 million for 1308 employees, with most claims coming from the retail and hospitality sectors.

Source: http://www.hospitalitymagazine.com.au/articles/Perths-hospitality-workers-short-changed_z475972.htm (accessed 6.4.09)

BOX 6.4 Tavern fined for employing children

3 July 2009. Content provided by AAP
PERTH, 2 July, AAP – The owner of a West Australian tavern has been fined $6000 for illegally employing children. Raydale Holdings Pty Ltd, which trades as the Tambrey Tavern and Function Centre, pleaded guilty on two counts in the Perth Industrial Magistrates Court on Thursday, the WA Department of Commerce said.

'The company had employed two 14-year-old boys to collect cutlery, crockery and empty glasses at the tavern in the Pilbara town of Karratha.'

The courts found one boy had worked had five shifts and another had worked 14, including a Friday night shift finishing at 12.20am.

Under the Children and Community Services Act 2004, it is illegal to employ children under 15 years to work in the hotel and tavern industry.

Labour relations spokesman Joseph Lee said the $6,000 fine should act as a warning to other employers. 'Of particular concern is the environment in which these boys were working,' Mr Lee said. 'There are clear and inherent risks associated with children working in a licensed premise where patrons are consuming alcohol.'

Source: http://www.cch.com.au/au/ContactUs/Print.aspx?ID=32038 (accessed 4.7.09)

The news snippets in illustrate how managers can exploit unsuspecting and vulnerable individuals. Unfortunately, such practices are inherent in the tourism and hospitality industry where there is a labour shortage, turnover is high and there are low skills entry levels.

However, work in the tourism and hospitality sector has other characteristics which afford opportunities for satisfying 'working lives'. Baum (2006: 278) confers that:

> The tourism, hospitality and leisure sector offers many and varied opportunities for rewarding and sustainable working lives across its diverse sub-sectors and at different levels throughout the world. The industry's heterogeneity, geographical spread and stochastic demand provides both opportunity and challenge in terms of mapping the opportunities against the aspirations and expectations of those attracted into the tourism, hospitality and leisure industry, either as new entrants to the labour force or in the context of change opportunities within their working lives.

149

Similarly, Boon (2006) supports the idea that tourism and hospitality can provide a career gateway for individuals seeking a blend of work and leisure. She examined how leisure and work can work as allies for skiers in tourist resort hotels. Boon (2006: 605) found that in the case of ski workers, the employment relationship allowed them to 'ski as much as possible while also being employed', such that the boundaries between work and leisure appeared blurred. She acknowledges that leisure–work relationship may be accentuated by the employment location and that in other tourism/hospitality settings, the relationship may be 'much more subtle and therefore less obvious' (Boon, 2006: 206). Nonetheless, the notion of 'migrant tourist-workers' (Bianchi, 2000; Lee-Ross, 1995) is not a new concept and supports the idea that the tourism and hospitality industry affords opportunities for the *mélange* of work, travel and leisure.

It is acknowledged that in more recent time the three major forces affecting change in the workplace are: demographics, globalisation and technology. In relation to demographics, there has been a marked shift in the number of women joining the workforce, especially mothers. In addition, the traditional 'nuclear family' structure with the stay-at-home mother, working father and 2.5 children has eroded. More commonly, the workforce is characterised by single people, dual-career couples, single-parent families (fathers/mothers), older workers, double-income working parents and the 'sandwich generation'. This latter group are those workers who are caught between works and caring for young children and elderly parents. For each of these groups work can hold varying meanings and maintaining a balance between work and personal life can be a real challenge.

Globalisation has increased competition for businesses, and the increased power of global corporations has placed greater economic pressure on employers to perform. In terms of HR, this has meant the opening of broader labour markets and opportunities to recruit from global rather than national or local labour pools. Equally for employees, globalisation has provided increased mobility and opportunities for finding organisations that value their knowledge and skills. Alongside globalisation, technology has been instrumental in improving recruitment and selection techniques and processes. In addition, technology has enhanced flexibility for both employees and employers in terms of times and places work is performed. For employees therein lies a danger in the possibility of blurring of boundaries between work and home becoming all-consuming.

Concurrently, organisations have been adopting 'just-in-time' workforce solutions such as casual, part-time and contract labour. Along with organisational downsizing and shedding of staff, organisations are flatter, leaner, dynamic and more flexible. Concurrently, work has become less secure and there has been an increase in flexible work arrangements. Despite the negative impacts of such changes, some employees are welcoming the flexibility. For example, in a study conducted in the UK, Meadows (1996) found that greater than 85% of respondents working part-time and on contract were significantly more satisfied working when compared with the respondents working full-time. One of the reasons advanced for this surprising satisfaction with work flexibility is the desire for people to achieve work–life or work–family balance.

> **Critical note**
> Changing demographics in the workplace, globalisation and technology have been major contributors to the changing nature of work.

> **Reflection**
> Consider and discuss the role technology plays in your job.

WORK–LIFE BALANCE

As the separation between work and personal or home life becomes marginalised, there has been a greater emphasis on the need for work–life balance. Further as people's lives become more complex and social changes impact on people's lives, the desirability of achieving work–life balance is becoming even more compelling. However, amongst the rhetoric of work–life balance, it seems that definition of the concept is elusive and that development of policies and implementation of related practices is variable. Bardoel *et al.* (2008) point out that despite the considerable research being conducted in this area, very little has been translated and applied into policy and management practice. In an attempt to define the concept, it is suggested that **work–life balance** refers to the relationship between paid work and people's lives outside of their employment where the sense of balance achieved in this relationship is very much an individual one based on a person's needs, expectations, and aspirations. The term '**work–family balance**' relates to these factors but has a more specific focus on the interface between an individual's work and their family, whether this is children, ageing parents, disabled family member, or partner/ spouse. **Work–family conflict** arises where there are conflicting demands being made on the individual by home and by work and is particularly evidenced in dual-income and single parent families. It should be noted that work–family balance may be less relevant to some workers and that individuals seeking work–family balance may also desire work– life balance. In the quest to achieve work–life balance, individuals may seek activities relating to their hobbies, interests, travel, personal growth, ongoing educating and learning, physical health, religious association, community involvement, social action and aspirations.

In their study on reviewing work–life research, Bardoel *et al.* (2008: 320) drew on various authors to comment that research and interest in work–life has been guided by 'factors such as the increase in the workforce participation of women, changes in household forms, the increase of jobs in the service sector, work intensity (longer working hours), growth in part-time work and alternative work arrangements, and ageing of population'. They identified several themes in work–life research, including organisational approaches to work–life and work–family issues, the job or work itself, occupations or industries, government policies and legislation, health outcomes issues related to work–life, family structure, gender, job or life satisfaction, coping strategies, workaholism and support provided to all stakeholders. Their findings support the need for addressing work–life balance in the workplace. Much of the research indicates that work–life conflict is negative and can be detrimental. Haar and Bardoel (2008: 276) highlight that the negative influence of work–life balance 'intensifies and stigmatises the work–family interface'.

Skinner and Pocock (2008) add to the discussion by exploring whether work time (i.e. flexibility in scheduling or work hours) or work load (quantity of work) contribute to work–life conflict. They found that work load for a person in full-time work is more detrimental to sustaining a healthy work–life relationship than work time is. It promoted emotional strain and exhaustion and combined with long work hours contributed to a poor work–life relationship. Skinner and Pocock (2008: 313) concluded that 'the factors that sustain or impede a healthy work–life relationship are multifaceted, and likely to differ depending on an individual's life circumstances, values and priorities'. They noted that the 'quality' of the work experience or work life (i.e. workload) was more critical than the time spent at work. In addition, they suggested that future research consider specific types of time demands (such as unsocial work times, long hours) and workload demands (such as speed, time pressure, quality requirements). These issues are particularly relevant to work in the tourism and hospitality industry, which is often characterised by working long hours and during times when others are socialising as well as working in a fast-paced, customer-focused environment demanding efficiency, quality and emotional labour.

On a more optimistic note, Haar and Bardoel (2008) present evidence to support work–family positive spillover. They clarify that positive spillover can be from both the workplace into family (work–family) and the family into the workplace (family–work). Haar and Bardoel (2008: 277) point out that spillover can relate to 'values, skills, and behaviours [which] are learned in one role [e.g. home/workplace] might influence other roles [workplace/home]'.

There is universal agreement that there are key issues facing industrialised societies, such as ageing populations, decreasing labour supply, delayed parenting and declining fertility (e.g. Brough et al., 2008). These factors suggest that issues of priority for industrialised countries include rising welfare and healthcare costs, labour shortages and population decline. In an attempt to compensate for some of these factors, governments have sought to increase the workforce by targeting females and older workers into the labour market with family-friendly or work–life balance initiatives. The rationale is that by implementing these strategies economic growth will be enhanced and that costs associated with the ageing population will be met.

There is no doubt that work–life conflict can impact on organisations through decreased productivity and increased absenteeism and turnover. For employees the impact of work–life imbalance can lead to overwork, emotional disorders, physical ill-health and stress. Hence, it makes sense for organisations to adopt genuine work–life balance and family-friendly policies. More so, addressing work–life balance is a societal and government concern and requires input from all stakeholders.

> **Critical note**
> Maintaining a balance between work and life outside of work is critical for an individual's well-being.

> **Reflection**
> You are the HR manager of a high-profile tourist attraction in Tropical North Queensland, which employs 125 staff with diverse needs and interests. Think of work–life and work–family programmes or initiatives that you could develop and implement for your staff.

THE NEW MEANING OF 'CAREER'

As noted earlier, there have been a number of significant economic, social and tech-nological changes in recent times which have influenced the meaning and nature of work. In particular, recent years have seen the emergence of new perspectives on the concept of 'career'. Traditional career development processes have been replaced by such models as Handy's (1995) 'portfolio career' (mentioned above), Arthur and Rousseau's (1996) 'boundaryless career', and Hall's (1996) 'protean career'. The boundaryless career refers to the idea that workers are 'independent agents' responsible for their own careers and free to move between organisations and between careers. Arthur and Rousseau (1996) maintain that within the context of the boundaryless career, workers are self-directed, motivated by skill and personal development, and capitalise on career experiences which have holistic rewards. This was advanced by Marler *et al.* (2002) who noted that the boundaryless career involved lateral as well as vertical moves, radical career changes, and periods of disconnection from the workforce for personal or family reasons. Hence, Boon (2006: 595) comments that work still remains a central life interest of many workers but there are now also many 'who give priority to other life activities'. This is further explained by a statement from Friedman and Greenhaus, (2000, cited in Boon, 2006: 595) 'the traditional concepts, with career progress and success defined so narrowly, do not respond to the fact that there is an increasingly diverse workforce, with different needs, values, and aspirations than in the past.'

Similarly, Hall (1996: 201) acknowledged that individuals were in control of their careers and that 'the protean career is shaped more by the individual than the organization, and may be redirected from time to time to meet the needs of the person'. Boon (2006: 596) notes that:

> [...] rejection of existing career opportunities is not just about families. Learning and community involvement (MacInnes, 2005); personal growth, friendships, political involvement, creative activity and spiritual development (Friedman & Greenhaus, 2000: 193); and travel and adventure (Inkson & Myers, 2003; Richardson & Mallon, 2005) are also important goals affecting working lives.

With new concepts of career being oriented around the individual rather than work or the organisation, it is apparent that contemporary working lives are heterogeneous, flexible and self-directed. The tourism and hospitality industry is particular in that its 24/7 and seasonal variability favour non-standard work arrangements and support the new career concepts and promote quality of work life.

Critical note

Recent economic, social and technological changes have altered that the nature of work and the development of careers. Workers now can no longer rely on organisations for promotions and career progression. Rather, they need to take control of their careers and personal growth. In particular, workers need to be self-directed and flexible.

Reflection

Identify and explain the type of career pattern you would like to pursue.

OCCUPATIONAL HEALTH AND SAFETY (OHS)

Quality of work life extends to maintaining a healthy and safe workplace. In fact, employers have legal, ethical and social obligations to provide a healthy and safe working environment for their employees. Stone (2008: 517) acknowledges that 'Health and safety programmes reflect an organisation's strategic concern for employee productivity and quality of work life'. Such programmes send a message to employees that they are valued and have a positive impact on employment relations, productivity, costs, profits and the organisation's image and reputation. Occupational health and safety (OHS) is the concern of everyone in the organisation: employers, managers, HR manager, safety representatives, and employees. Employers have the ultimate responsibility and duty of care but HR managers can play a key role in promoting OHS in the workplace and making it part of the organisational culture.

Stone (2008: 517) reports that 'There are about 2900 work-related deaths and 650,000 work-related injuries in Australia each year, and annual economic losses of more than $34 billion'. For employees, accidents, injuries and illness resulting from workplace incidences can cause considerable physical and mental suffering. In addition, costs associated with such incidences include increased premiums for workers' compensation insurance and HR-related issues such as loss of experienced workers and decreased morale. Workplace health and safety issues need to be considered jobs are designed and employees are oriented into the organisation and the job and when they are trained.

The following article in Box 6.5 notes an attempt by the hospitality industry in Australia to assist the tourism and hospitality industry with increasing awareness of OHS through the development and dissemination of a 'Hospitality Industry Guide to Safety'.

BOX 6.5 Guide to help hospitality reduce workplace injuries

Hospitality Magazine, **14 May 2009, by Rosemary Ryan**
The latest edition of the valuable 'Hospitality Industry Guide to Safety' has been launched to the industry with a major focus on how hospitality operators can reduce workplace injury and illness.

With injury and poisoning claims accounting for 85 percent of all compensation claims made by the hospitality industry the guide from Pro-Visual Publishing is an important tool. In the last financial year the Australian Safety and Compensation Council reported 5150 injury and poisoning claims made by the Accommodation, Cafes and Restaurants industry.

The safety guide – being delivered free of charge nationally this month – addresses this issue with its focus on subjects like minimising the risk of slips, trips and falls, using chemicals and hazardous substances in the workplace, and how to safely manage biological waste.

The Hotel Motel & Accommodation Association (HMAA) which has been involved in the development of the Guide again this year said the guide was valuable for raising awareness of OHS issues among all personnel within the hospitality industry.

'We encourage all members to display the wall chart in a prominent location so that employees will have a clear, easy to understand, and readily available reference for important issues regarding their every day health and safety,' said HMAA chief executive, Lorraine Duffy.

Other topics featured in this year's guide include workplace bullying, cash handling and managing an armed hold-up. The chart is designed to be displayed at the business to give employees a daily reminder and help employers reduce the costs of workplace accidents, illness and injury.

Source: http://www.hospitalitymagazine.com.au/articles/Guide-to-help-hospitality-reduce-workplace-injuries_z481465.htm (accessed 14.5.09)

CURRENT WORKPLACE HEALTH ISSUES

Providing and maintaining a safe and healthy workplace involves more than just addressing work-related accidents and injuries. As Gomez-Meija *et al.* (2001: 33) note employers need 'to deal with a variety of practical, legal and ethical issues, many of which involve a careful balancing of individual rights (particularly rights of privacy) with the needs of the organisation'. In response, policies need to be developed which address issues such as:

- work–family conflict;
- smoking;
- alcohol/substance abuse;
- sexual harassment;
- AIDs/HIV;
- terrorism;
- violence in the workplace; and
- stress.

Increasingly, organisations are enacting policies that relate to the above issues. For example, smoking has in recent times been a highly contentious issue for the tourism and hospitality industry. Greater awareness of health risks associated with smoking and declining social acceptance of smoking has meant that both employees and customers have demanded smoke-free environments. In Australia, government legislation has directed that organisations provide smoke-free work environments (see articles in Box 6.6). Additionally, some organisations promote 'quit smoking' programmes (e.g. Thompson, 2000).

BOX 6.6 ACT tightens smoking laws in outdoor areas

Hospitality Magazine, **1 June 2009, by Olivia Collings**
Canberra's clubs and pubs are facing further restrictions on where their patrons can light up, with the ACT Government about to introduce new anti-smoking legislation. Under the new legislation being introduced smoking will be banned in outdoor areas

where food and drinks are served, said ACT health minister Katy Gallagher. 'My number one issue is that you can't have food served there, there will be no drinks served there, and that has other impacts in terms of the cleanliness of the venue,' she said. 'We're sort of in the finals stages now and it really is about how big can the area be, the fact that it has to be cordoned off from a whole range of all their other services, and there can be no staff there.'

CEO of Clubs ACT, Bob Samarcq, said the most important thing was for the government to give the establishments time to implement the changes. 'They need to make sure we have enough time between the announcement and the implementation to make sure our patrons are aware of the implications,' he said. As in Queensland, Samarcq would like to see the regulations allow patrons to take their own food and drinks into specially designated outdoor smoking areas, but not receive service there. Samarcq added that the ban would pose a greater threat to hotels and pubs, as clubs generally had larger outdoor areas. 'The most important thing we have asked the government for is a reasonable implementation time, preferably between 18 and 24 months.'

Minister Gallagher said she hoped to get the legislation into parliament in the second half of the year, for implementation in late 2010. ACT is the latest in a string of states and territories to introduce bans in outdoor or alfresco dinning and drinking areas. The West Australian government is in the process of passing the new legislation to ban smoking in alfresco and outdoor areas of restaurant, cafes and hotels.

Source: http://www.hospitalitymagazine.com.au/articles/ACT-tightens-smoking-laws-in-outdoor-areas_z483880.htm (accessed 1.8.09)

Critical note

Developing and maintaining healthy and safe workplaces is in the best interests of employees and employers. In addition, such workplaces serve legal, ethical and social requirements and contribute positively to an organisation's economic performance and employee satisfaction and well-being.

Reflection

Discuss why OHS management is considered to be an integral part of strategic HRM.

STRESS

Stress can be a positive aspect of work and promote energy, motivation and alertness. It is a part of life and is to some extent a driver of day-to-day functioning and survival.

Interestingly, people can be stressed but relaxed. It would seem then that being stressed is neither a good nor bad state of existence. Rather it is the amount of stress and causes of stress which can make stress counter-productive. In this light, Nickson (2007: 266) draws on comments from the Labour Research Department (2006) and says that 'stress is the adverse reaction people have to excessive demands or pressure when trying to cope with tasks and responsibilities in the workplaces'.

In essence, stress can be detrimental to an individual's physical and mental well-being when it is excessive and sustained. Bohle and Quinlan (2000) reported that 75% of all health problems were related to stress. In a similar vein, Nickson highlights findings of the Labour Research Department (2006) and notes that during 2004–2005, there were 12.8 million working days lost in the UK. Likewise, Stone (2008) reports that in 2005, stressed police officers cost the Victorian (Australia) government $6.5 million dollars. Hence, stress is becoming an increasingly major issue of concern in the workplace.

Interestingly, stress levels can increase regardless of whether the circumstances or experience is positive or negative. For example, getting a job (positive) and getting fired (negative) can both equally cause stress and precipitate the same psychological and physiological changes.

In defining stress, authors often elaborate on the causes or stimuli of and the symptoms or responses to stress. For example, Dewe (1989: 494) notes that 'Stress is relational in nature involving some sort of transaction between the individual and the environment'. More specifically, Stone (2008: 537) defines stress as 'a condition of strain that affects one's emotions, thought processes and physical condition'. This aligns with the idea that stress is a physiological phenomenon in which the body reacts either through a 'fight' or 'flight' response to a perceived threat in a stressful situation. Arguably, stress can also affect an individual psychologically. The degree to which stress impacts on an individual's health and working life is very much dependent on their perception of the stressor as a threat or challenge, their ability to deal with the stress and their resilience.

What causes employee stress? Stressors are generally categorised into three groups: those that relate to personal characteristics, those that relate to work, and those that relate to the individual's external environment. Table 6.1 expands on these three categories.

Table 6.1 Categories of employee stressors

Personal factors	*Work factors*	*External factors*
• Needs	• Work load	• Economic conditions
• Type A behaviour	• Shift work	• Government laws &
• Resilience	• Long & irregular hours	regulations
• Health	• Non-flexible work hours	• Community or cultural
• Work–life conflict	• Interpersonal relationships	values

• Education • Emotional competence or intelligence • Locus of control • Diet, rest, relaxation, exercise • Time management	• Treatment by supervisors & managers • Change • Organisational climate • Physical environment • Role ambiguity • Demanding nature of work • Understaffing or staff shortages • Bullying • Discrimination • Customer-related work or activities • Inadequate resources • Undervalued • Pay or salary • Lack of feedback on performance • Lack of management support • Inadequate training	• Travel • Crime • Labour market • Professional or occupational requirements

Source: Adapted from Stone (2008: 538, Figure 13.3)

Factors identified in Table 6.1 apply equally as causes of stress for employees in the tourism and hospitality industry. For example, in their study, O'Leary and Deegan (2005) asked respondents about their views on management jobs within the tourism industry as a career option. They found that 16% of the sample commented that the personally demanding nature of the work was both physical and stressful. Ross (2007) contributed to the research through his study which focused on career stress among hospitality employees and found that strategies for minimising work stress in the industry included role clarity, greater autonomy, increased inter-organisational communication and empathy shown by management toward the needs of workers and their family life. Earlier, Rowley and Purcell (2001) identified that stress and job burnout were contributors to employee turnover in the hospitality industry in Northern Ireland. Their findings emphasised that 'deliberate understaffing, temporary staff shortages and unrealistic task criteria' led to job overload had impacted on staff retention in hotels (Rowley & Purcell, 2001: 169). Additionally, they found that coping strategies included increased consumption of foods high in carbohydrates, sugars and fats and that there was an increased consumption of caffeine drinks, alcohol and drugs.

Mulvaney *et al.* (2006) reported similar findings in that job stress, work–family conflict and characteristics of the job contributed to employees' intention to leave and turnover. Deery (2008: 803) added that stress and its various components (e.g. emotional

159

exhaustion) are of increasing concern in the tourism and hospitality industry and that 'Management need to be aware of the signs of employee stress and have the capacity to provide counselling and stress management activities such as time out and relaxation methods'. Similarly Murray-Gibbons and Gibbons (2007) acknowledged the growing evidence of occupational stress within the tourism and hospitality industry, especially with chefs. They noted that for chefs the greatest sources of stress 'included the norms in the kitchen, hours worked, unsociable hours and the pace of work, together with feeling out of control, being unqualified or working alongside unqualified people' (p. 34).

Stress is often considered a taboo subject, but more and more organisations are realising that it is an issue to be addressed and that there is a need to adopt programmes or initiatives which will minimise stress or assist employees subject to stress. For example, Employee Assistance Programmes (EAPs) are becoming popular. EAPs are services external to the organisation and provided by the employer. The aim of EAPs is to assist employees in identifying and resolving performance-related concerns, including stress. Generally, it consists of a professional, confidential counselling service for employees and their immediate family members, paid for by the employer.

Employers have a duty of care to ensure a healthy and safe workplace for each of their employees. In Australia, breach of this duty of care is a criminal offence and attracts very high penalties. This duty of care includes protection of employees against the risk of physical and mental or psychiatric injury. Hence, it can be argued that an employer has a duty of care to ensure that the employee is not unduly exposed to stress in the workplace.

Critical note

The prevalence of employee stress is a growing concern for organisations, especially those in customer-related industries. In these environments, employees can be subject to conflicting demands from customers and managers.

Reflection

Think about your working life and consider what stressors are present. Are they caused by factors relating to you personally, your work, or externally? What strategies can you adopt to alleviate your stress?

SUMMARY

Maintaining a stable and skilled workforce has been a real challenge for tourism and hospitality organisations. As this chapter has shown, research indicates that perceptions of poor quality of work life has contributed to this ongoing issue and that tourism and hospitality organisations need to pay greater attention to factors affecting quality of work life. In particular, there is a need to develop and implement policies and strategies which address work–life and work–family balance if the image of the industry is to improve.

Quality of work life is influenced by both economic and non-economic factors. Hence, while pay is a significant aspect of work, individuals desire and seek work which is meaningful to them and which is compatible with their needs, interests and preferences. Work–life and work–family balance are key to employee welfare and well-being and can serve as key considerations in the recruitment, selection and retention of valued staff.

This chapter examined the nature of 'work' and sought to understand the importance of achieving a balance between work and life. It discussed some of the benefits to both parties and within the process explored the role of OHS in promoting safe and healthy workplaces. The chapter continued with an analysis of some current health issues affecting workplaces, especially tourism and hospitality organisations. In particular, it focused on stress and discussed how a certain amount of stress is conducive to promoting energy, motivation and alertness. On the other hand, there was an emphasis on the growing concern on the debilitating effects of stress and how this impacts on the workplace. The discussion continued with creating an awareness of the need for managers and organisations to address this issue and put in place policies, activities or programmes which will assist employees in alleviating 'harmful' stress.

In conclusion, it is rationalised that strategic HRM approaches can contribute positively to quality of work life. In this post-industrialist era, it is increasingly evident that individuals are taking charge of their own careers and seek to mingle work and leisure and/or pursue careers which are more leisure than work. Out of this quest, what is emerging for managers and organisations is the necessity to deal with issues relating to work–life balance and work–family conflict.

The tourism and hospitality industry is unique in that it provides a niche for pursuit of careers which balance work and life agendas. The story in Box 6.7 of sommelier Kyriacos Christodoulou illustrates these points. This is not to say that the industry does not need to consider quality of work life. *Au contraire!* As has been mentioned often in this book and the literature, the industry has its own peculiarities and characteristics (e.g. working unsociable hours, management styles and low pay) which present challenges to the industry in attracting and retaining quality workers.

BOX 6.7 Former Maze sommelier heads to Sofitel's No35

Hospitality Magazine, **29 June 2009, by Olivia Collings**
Sofitel Melbourne on Collin's new restaurant No35 now offers the experience and expertise of sommelier Kyriacos Christodoulou.

Christodoulou takes his place alongside No35s restaurant manager, Chris McNally, and chef James Viles at the new restaurant which will offer stunning floor to ceiling views from the 35th level.

Recently returned from London, Christodoulou was previously sommelier at the Michelin star Maze Restaurant and Grill in Grosvenor Square which is renowned for its strong focus on fine food and wine matching.

Prior to this he was wine manager at London's East Room, nominated for two 'Class' bar awards in 2008 including 'Best New Bar' and 'Best Wine Offering' for its outstanding selection – and knowledge of wines.

Christodoulou served a sommelier internship at Jamie Oliver's restaurant Fifteen after working in vineyards across Australia, New Zealand and Europe and completing a Bachelor of Science (Hons) in viticulture and oenology from the University of Brighton's Plumpton College Estate, complete with its own vineyards and modern winery onsite.

Christodoulou's extensive 'hands on' winery experience includes stints at Murdoch James Estate in Marlborough, New Zealand; La Casita Winery in Arribes del Duero, Spain; Ridgeview Winery Estate in Sussex, England; Kyperounda Winery in Cyprus and closer to home, Sticks Yarra Valley Winery in Yarra Glen.

As one of Australia's 'new breed' of young international sommeliers, Christodoulou aspires to create a cellar that explores the diversity and character of Australian regionality combined with celebrated wines from around the world.

'At No35, wine and food are equally important components to the overall dining experience we want to create for our guests,' he says.

Source: http://www.hospitalitymagazine.com.au/articles/former-maze-sommelier-heads-to-sofitel-8217-s-no-35_z488321.htm (accessed 29.6.09)

CHAPTER QUESTIONS

1. Define work–life balance. Provide an example.

2. Discuss how the nature of work is changing. In your response, consider its impact on changing notions of career and quality of work–life.

3. Comment on how you think organisations and employees can address work–life balance issues.

RECOMMENDED READING

O'Connell, F. (2005) *How To Do a Great Job … AND Go Home on Time*. Frenchs Forest (NSW): Pearson Education.

A great book for employees and employers on how to achieve work–life balance.

President and Fellow of Harvard College (2000) *Harvard Business Review on Work and Life Balance*. Boston (MA): Harvard Business School Press.

A good collection of contemporary thought on the balance between employees' work and personal lives.

Kaye, B. and Jordan-Evans, S. (2002) *Love 'em or Lose 'em: Getting Good People to Stay* (2nd edn). San Francisco: Berrett-Koehler Publishers, Inc.

This book suggests innovative ways to assist employees achieve work–life balance.

Rapoport, R., Bailyn, L., Fletcher, J. and Pruitt, B. (2001) *Beyond Work–Family Balance: Advancing Gender Equity and Workplace Performance*. Chichester: Wiley & Sons Inc.

This book presents a novel perspective on work–life balance by talking of work–life integration.

Blyton, P., Blunsdon, B., Reed, K. and Dastmalchian, A. (eds) (2006) *Work–Life Integration: International Perspectives on the Balancing of Multiple Roles*. London: Palgrave Macmillan.

This book extends the idea of work–life integration by examining the challenges of managing multiple roles.

RECOMMENDED WEBSITES

Inside WA tourism and hospitality – http://www.tourism.wa.gov.au/Tourism_Jobs_WA/Pages/Inside_WA_tourism_and_hospitality.aspx

Tourism Australia: No Leave, No Life Program – http://www.media.australia.com/enau/mediareleases/default_1595.aspx

Canadian Centre for Occupational Health and Safety: Work-Life Balance – http://www.ccohs.ca/oshanswers/psychosocial/worklife_balance.html

Graduate Recruitment Bureau (UK) – Travel, Leisure and Tourism – http://www.grb.uk.com/industry_profiles.0.html?industry_id=39

Corporate social responsibility in Asia: Work-Life Balance – http://www.csr-asia.com/index.php?cat=58

CHAPTER 7

INDUSTRIAL RELATIONS AND LEGAL ASPECTS

LEARNING OBJECTIVES

After working through this chapter you should be able to:

1. Understand the nature of industrial relations (IR).

2. Define industrial relations.

3. Explain the main theoretical approaches to industrial relations.

4. Identify stakeholders in industrial relations.

5. Understand the legal framework relating to workplace relations.

INTRODUCTION

Industrial relations (IR) are part of our everyday life. It is an area of competing and compelling ideologies and values that is interwoven into the social fabric of communities, organisations, industries and countries. IR is so entrenched in social systems that it engenders passion and brandishes sensationalism, heated debates, actions, conflict and disputes. This is not surprising as IR is multidimensional and affects everyone. It is an area 'about which almost everyone has an opinion, and often those opinions differ, leading to conflict' (Bray *et al.*, 2009: 5). The legislation and policies which surround IR have outcomes for every member of society because IR is about people and about their welfare and wellbeing.

A step back in time within the tourism and hospitality industry reveals the importance of IR in society. Drawing on the work of Baum (2006), it is evident that there were two streams of entry into the tourism and hospitality workforce. In Britain, there was a noticeable shift of 'domestic servants who worked in the homes of the ruling classes' into the growing hotel and catering industry of the late 19th and early 20th century (Baum, 2006: 42). Concurrently, there was the movement of workers 'from agricultural subsistence of employment to tourism' (Baum, 2006: 43). Synchronously, there was the evolution of industrial societies. This meant that the evolving nature, patterns and scale of work and the associated labour markets forced employers and governments to consider the employment relationship between employer and employee. Often the relationship was wrought with resentment and animosity as wages were low and working conditions were poor. In many cases for workers from industrial townships and cities, this was compounded by their depressed standards of living. It was no surprise, then that as injustices were perceived and conflict arose, workplaces witnessed the rise of unions, employer associations and strike action and so the birth of industrial relations. The objectives of industrial relations systems were (and still are) to protect the employee–employer relationship (Box 7.1).

BOX 7.1 Objectives of IR systems

- Preserve the employment relationship, which allow employers and employees to establish and develop a framework for pay and working conditions.
- Prevent and resolve disagreements that may result in industrial conflict.
- Develop mechanisms for bargaining.
- Preserve the rights and responsibilities of employers and employees for how work is organised.
- Protect employees' pay, working conditions, rights at work, and health and safety by establishing minimum levels that employers must adhere to.

Adapted from: Sappey *et al.* (2009: 5)

The challenge for IR systems is to be able to move with the changing times and accommodate contrasting perspectives and regulatory powers from employees, employers, and the various external stakeholders, such as unions, employer associations, and governments.

Critical note
Industrial relations (IR) is about work and the relationship between employees and employers at work; it affects everyone who receives an income because of work; as such it has implications for the organisation, the employees' working and non-working lives, the national economy, and society at large.

Reflection
Think of an industry with which you are familiar (e.g. tourism and hospitality or retail) and consider the principal IR characteristics of that industry. You may want to consider part of that industry, e.g. frontline work in a hotel or flight attendants job.

DEFINING INDUSTRIAL RELATIONS

In a nutshell, IR is about work, pay and working conditions and the framework within which these factors are developed, determined, exercised and regulated. At the core of IR is the contractual, bipartite relationship between an employer and an employee. Such a relationship is a legal one which details the fundamental conditions of work, such as pay, hours and statutory rights and obligations. Extending from this there is the relationship around the organisation of work, such as tasks to be undertaken, decision-making authority and control.

The employment relationship is described within many contexts, including economic, political, social, cultural, technological and global arenas. Economically, the employment contract legally suggests that an agreed amount of labour performed by an employee is exchanged for an agreed payment by the employer (Keenoy & Kelly, 2000; Balnave et al., 2007). Similarly, Lucas (2004) considers the employment relationship as an economic exchange between the employer (buyer) and the employee (seller). She suggests that this economic exchange is considered the basis of the employment relationship. Equally, Balnave et al. (2007: 3) agree and add that 'the employment relationship is also a power relationship whereby the employee [...] agrees to submit to the authority and direction of the employer'. Gospel and Palmer (1993: 3, cited in Lucas, 2004: 13) note that this labour–reward bargain is 'an economic, social and political relationship, for which employees provide manual and mental labour in return for rewards allotted by employers'. Balnave et al. (2007) refer to this as 'labour power' (the potential to work) and differentiate it from 'labour effort' (actual work effort) in noting that employers hire the former. This is reasonable when one considers that employees 'can modify and restrict' their work effort and that they can unite as a collective to challenge managerial power (Balnave, 2007). So while economic exchange seems quite clear cut, the employment relationship is imbued with social, cultural and political elements such that it can strain the employment relationship and cause conflict.

With variation in interpretation of 'work', 'effort', 'fair' return for labour and the terms and conditions of work (Keenoy & Kelly, 2000) and as the employment relationship has become regulated over time, the employer–employee relationship can be subject to much discussion, contention, heated disagreement, negotiation, and 'acrimonious disputes' (Keenoy & Kelly, 2000: 1). These exchanges have involved actors ranging from employers and employees to state and federal courts of law. They have included governments, politicians, industrial tribunals, professional associations, employer organisations and trade unions. These relationships between stakeholders and institutions have resulted in what is traditionally referred to as 'industrial relations'. In Australia, Labour Day commemorates the granting of the 8-hour working day in the late 1850s (see Box 7.2).

166

BOX 7.2 Labour Day

Labour Day is an Australian public holiday which celebrates the granting of the 8-hour day in the late 1850s. It was originally called 'Eight Hours Day' and represents the achievements of collective efforts to achieve equity for the worker.

Previously, employees worked long and arduous hours each week. The average week consisted of 10 to 12 hour days, six days a week. The move to an eight hour day was immediate but the five day working week did not come into effect until 1948.

The Eight Hours Movement was instigated by Robert Owen, a British socialist, who advocated that workers were entitled to eight hours to work, eight hours for sleep, and eight hours for recreation. His philosophy is said to have been the hallmark of the numbers 888 being inscribed on many union buildings throughout Australia.

The momentous first Labour Day parade was held in Melbourne on 21 April 1956. Today, every Labour Day across Australia is commemorated with parades that remind everyone of the accomplishments made by the unions on behalf of the workers. It is this legacy of the unions' representation by which Australians today enjoy better working conditions.

Each state in Australia achieved the 8-hour day on different dates. Subsequently, Labour Day is celebrated at different times in different states.

Adapted from: http://alldownunder.com/oz-k/date/labour-day.htm

Often, the term 'industrial relations' is used interchangeably with employee relations, employment relations, labour relations and workplace relations. There is much confusion and debate on the meanings and use of these closely related terminologies that are used to describe 'social action at work' (Bray & Waring, 2006: 4).

Industrial relations have traditionally been used to describe the collective relationship between employer and employee (e.g. Boella & Goss-Turner, 2005; Bray *et al.*, 2009). Balnave *et al.* (2007: 2) make a noteworthy point when they say: 'Work is equally important to the functioning of society at large and, as such, becomes a collective concern attracting the attention of the government and other interested groups'. Hence while industrial relations principally includes concern for economic issues it is often extended to encompass political, historical, social and cultural issues which relate not just to the organisation but also to the industry, state and nation.

As noted above, industrial relations have been perceived as the balance of power between employers and employees. As Stone (2008: 471) says, 'traditional industrial relations seems narrow, pessimistic and static [. . .] [it was] centred on conflict inevitability, government intervention and employee representation through trade unions'. For example, until recently, the Australian employee relations landscape has been characterised by a formalised arbitration and conciliation process based on a social justice system which holds 'a fair go for all' as its ethos. In recent times the employer–employee relationship has been reshaped through a number of factors such as changing nature of work, developments in industrial relations, increase in individualised employee agreements and the changing roles and power of trade unions, personnel management and the growing role of HRM (Keenoy & Kelly, 2000; Nankervis, 2005; Sappey *et al.*, 2009).

Critical note

'Industrial relations' as a term refers to the various aspects of the work and includes attention to pay, working conditions and safety. It revolves around the relationship between employers and employees. As work is a critical component of peoples' lives, the implications of this relationship extend beyond the workplace to include various stakeholders such as governments, employer associations, unions, tribunals and other agencies and are influenced by political, economic and social factors.

Reflection

Define the 'employment contract' and explain the work-effort argument.

THE RELATIONSHIP BETWEEN IR AND HRM

There is much debate on the relationship between IR and HRM. Stone (2008) discusses at length the increasing dominance of HRM in the workplace and how its unitarist-oriented ideology positions HRM as the future paradigm of workplace relations. This is a valid stance but IR has a rich history recounting the relationship between employers and employees. Granted this is entrenched in resolving workplace conflicts through various institutions and involving external and internal stakeholders but it should not be ignored.

It can be rationalised that HRM systems such as recruitment, selection, induction, reward, and their related practices all impact on the employment relationship. While this is so, the term 'industrial relations' generally relates to the terms, conditions, rights and management of the employment relationship and because it involves a number of stakeholders it can be suggested that there are both internal and external influences on industrial relations. Further, industrial relations are constantly changing in nature and context. In the broader context, factors such as political, economic, technological, social and historical ones impact on the nature of IR.

As the role of HRM has evolved from personnel management to a more strategic focus, so too there has been a shift away from considering work relations between employer and employee as industrial relations to the broader term of employee relations.

At the turn of the century, Keenoy and Kelly (2000: 2) summed up explicitly the changes in employee relations in Australia:

> In every direction, the contours of the industrial landscape appear to be shifting while all involved adapt to pressures emerging from the global economy. Employers are beginning to reassert their right to manage. Employees and managers are responding to demands to improve productivity. The continued use of industrial Awards is being questioned. Unions are adjusting to the implications of enterprise bargaining and coming to terms with non-union agreements. Meanwhile, amid all this socio-economic and political turbulence, the federal government endeavours to restrain inflation, create employment and stimulate national economic growth and development.

This statement highlights the complexities and interplay of actors in the IR paradigm. As IR has evolved, it is argued that there have been a number of further parallel shifts which have resulted in further debates on the meaning of the various terms. Indeed there have been changes in the employment relationship, the labour force and the work environment and as Sappey *et al.* (2009: 3) note contemporary 'definitions of industrial relations now take account of these changes'. Hence, this text persists with the use of the term industrial relations and provides the following definition:

> Industrial Relations is about work, pay and working conditions and the framework within which these factors are developed, determined, exercised, and regulated. As such it has at its core the relationship between the employee and employer. Principally, this relationship determines how the work is organised and the power balanced between the two central parties. The wider system which informs the relationship may include employee associations (e.g. unions), employer associations, governments, courts, tribunals and other agencies. In essence, the industrial relations system works toward preserving the employment relationship through preventing and resolving industrial conflict, protecting rights and responsibilities of people in the workplace, and setting minimum standards of pay, conditions and safety at work.

This definition highlights the many facets of IR and is enhanced by the understanding that IR is subject of political, economic and social influences and ideologies. An example of the impact of public policy on IR is the introduction of the Work Choices legislation in Australia in 2005. This legislation divided governments and the people and substantiates the notion that IR needs to be efficient in achieving satisfactory overall performance of an organisation but synchronously needs to be equitable in relation to terms and conditions of employment which support quality in employees working lives and welfare (Bray *et al.*, 2009). Bray *et al.* (2005: 4) argue that 'Trade unions and state [and federal] regulations are correspondingly considered essential for maintaining effective labour markets and a fair society'.

Further, the ideological frameworks upon which theory and practice of IR is based reflect social, cultural and political contexts and so there is a need to consider the various perspectives (e.g. unitarist, pluralist or radical/Marxist) and the analytical approaches (e.g. neo-institutionalist). These will be discussed in the next section.

Reflections

Consider the terms IR, ER and HRM. How you would define each of these terms? Why?

PERSPECTIVES ON INDUSTRIAL RELATIONS

With a history of varying predominance of workplace ideologies, there is much debate on the theoretical framework underpinning IR. The 'discipline' of IR is informed by theories and concepts from various traditional social science disciplines. Like other disciplines, IR has evolved its own unique array of knowledge, understanding, skills and practices. Since the genesis of industrial societies, IR has witnessed various theoretical approaches. These have included Dunlop's application of systems theory to IR in the 1950s and application of management theory to IR in the 1980s. The latter has occurred concurrently with the increased involvement of employers in the practice and control of IR and with the emergence of HR. Equally, other phenomena have been applied to IR, such as organisation theory, labour process theory and corporatism; and there is no doubt that, as IR continues to evolve, there will be other theoretical approaches which will influence its development. In the meantime, attention needs to be drawn to three main theoretical approaches which influenced the growth of IR and our understanding of the employment relationship, work and authority relationships in the workplace. These theories form the basis of the unitarist, pluralist and radical/Marxist perspectives and are summarised in Table 7.1.

Table 7.1 The three main theoretical approaches to IR

Ideology	
Unitarist	The unitarists believe that employers and employees share the same goals and so view conflict as a temporary occurrence which strengthens relationships between both parties. Unitarists deem that management has authority and that loyalty is to the organisation only. HRM aligns with this approach and so promotes an organisational culture of commitment, mutual cooperation, teamwork and treatment of the employee as an individual.

Pluralist	The pluralist approach considers conflict as an inherent aspect of employee relations. Pluralists believe that the diversity in needs, interests and goals between employers and employees can be managed and controlled by organisational rules and regulations. Loyalty and sources of authority can vary such that unions are considered to be a legitimate force against management authority and governments and their agencies (tribunals and industrial courts) have a responsibility, in terms of public interest, to intervene through prevention, regulation and enforcement.
Radical/Marxist	The radical perspective regards conflict as a systemic and enduring aspect of the employer–employee relationship. It considers it as a power relationship where there is an imbalance between employers/capital and employees/labour and their representative (i.e. management and unions, respectively). It espouses that such bias is reflective of social inequalities (i.e. status, power, income, and wealth). Radicalists/Marxists argue that 'the rules of the game' (including legislation and management rules) favour capital rather than labour. As such, it is maintained that injustices of IR perpetuate inequity, poverty, and unfairness and can only be realised if society is restructured to minimise or abolish status or class division.

Conflict is an inherent part of any relationship, including the employment relationship. The unitary, pluralist, and radical/Marxist perspectives provide a frame of reference through which can be viewed management of conflict and cooperation in the employment relationship. It is expected that managers in the workplace will respond to conflict based on their ideological perspective: unitarist, pluralist, or radical/Marxist.

Unitarism

Unitarists consider the organisation as a place of order and harmony where everybody shares common values, interests and goals, managerial prerogative is rational and legitimate and employees accept and obey managerial power and authority. The unitarist perspective views conflict as a threat to the status quo and a challenge to managerial legitimacy. As such it is to be quelled or eliminated. This leads to two predominant management styles where on the one hand, management is more aggressive and resorts to use of coercive power and takes an authoritarian, scientific management approach that is considered 'benign and rational' (Nickson, 2007: 219) and 'desirable and justified' (Teicher *et al.*, 2006: 171). On the other hand, managers take a more cooperative, consultative and inclusive approach where 'soft' HRM practices promote human relations. The paternalistic approach, so often apparent in tourism and hospitality organisations is subsumed by unitarist perspectives. Lucas (2004) supports this and suggests that this unitaristic perspective represents a less sophisticated unitarism that is bridled by cost-minimisation, stifles individualism and creates an unpleasant organisational culture and work experience.

A defining characteristic of unitarism is that trade unions are considered to be unimportant, intrusive and disruptive. It is rationalised that since 'the idea that conflict and dissidence are unnecessary, undesirable, irrational and pathologically deviant behaviour', there is no need for unions. Hence, the unitarist approach reflects the 'new realism' in employee relations as described by Legge (1995) and Guest (1995). It supports a more belligerent management style which marginalises collectivism and unionism and promotes commitment to the organisation and individualism.

Pluralism

Pluralists accept that conflict is inevitable because of the plurality and potentially competing values, interests and goals of the various stakeholders in the employment relationship. Subsequently, the resolution of conflict can be approached collectively or individually. Collective approaches allow for union involvement in the bargaining or negotiation process. Fox (1974: 265) describes pluralism as:

> On the basis of a shared confidence that they both subscribe to this philosophy of mutual survival, the parties are able to operate procedures of negotiation and dispute settlement characterised by a consensual code of ethics and conduct.

Hence, pluralism works toward achieving a balance of power between employer and employees, such that marginal groups (e.g. women) are rightfully considered in legislative reforms and government policies. In the workplace, this acknowledgement of pluralism is operationalised through development of appropriate policies and practices, e.g. anti-discrimination and grievance policies, which can potentially stem from the reality of conflict in the workplace. This is further extended in the workplace through inclusive styles of management which enable representation of conflicting interests through a range of channels and mechanisms, including unions.

Radicalism

Radicalists/Marxists view the employment relationship as an extension of the wider social, political and economic structure. Within this broader, radical perspective of 'capitalist society', the focus is on the perceived imbalance of power which is exploitative and favours capital over labour. Hence, conflict in the workplace is considered to be a subset of conflict in society.

Radicalists/Marxists envisage that the only way to overcome this antagonistic struggle for power and achieve equality is for 'annihilation of this suppressive social order' and the working class to gain control utilising unions as the 'vehicles of this social revolution' (Teicher et al., 2006: 172). With such conflict arising from opposing inherent economic interests, the potential to resolve issues between the competing parties becomes difficult.

> **Critical note**
> The theory underpinning industrial relations is based on three predominant ideologies: unitarist, pluralist, and radical/Marxist. Each informs the practice of industrial relations.

> **Reflections**
> Examine the three ideological perspectives (i.e. unitarist, pluralist, radical/Marxist) outlined above and think of your own approach to conflict in the workplace. Which perspective do you align with? Why do you think this is so? Does it parallel the way conflict is generally managed in your workplace.

UNIONS IN INDUSTRIAL RELATIONS

Essentially, the employment relationship is a relationship between the employer and the employee. As explained above this relationship is often complicated by a 'power struggle' where the employer generally has greater power than the individual employee. Hence, when bargaining about terms and conditions of work, employees often seek support and strength from acting collectively and from being represented by a third party such as unions. In their seminal work, Sidney and Beatrice Webb (1894, cited in Nankervis *et al.*, 2005: 75) note that 'A Trade Union [...] is a continuous association of wage-earners for the purpose of maintaining or improving the conditions of their employment'. Nankervis *et al.* (2005: 75) add that 'a union is a work-based organisation, providing a collective voice for employees, and an institution whose purpose is to represent and defend those who work for someone else'.

Solidarity and collective action constitute the foundation of unionism. Unions are principally based on occupations with similar classes of workers being grouped together. Single unions have been known to build alliances with other unions to strengthen their position and become part of a 'union movement'. In Australia, unions have played a focal role in the industrial system. The move away from traditional manufacturing, mining and construction industries toward a service-oriented economy has resulted in the decline in trade union membership. There is uncertainty that as the employment relations landscape changes whether trade unions will regain their ardour. In 2001, The International Labour Organisation estimated that the average union density for the tourism and hospitality industry globally is a low 10%. In 2006, the DTI reported trade union density for the hotel and catering industry as being 4.2% in the UK. In Australia, the ABS (2006) reported that union density in the tourism and hospitality industry as 22.4%. Nickson (2007: 224–225) draws on several authors (including Lucas, 2004) to explain why union membership is low in the tourism and hospitality industry:

- ethos of hotel and catering;
- conservatism, individualism, self-reliance and informality of the workforce encourages employees to represent themselves in negotiating with management;
- predominance of small workplaces;
- industry is principally represented by small to medium-sized enterprises governed by presence of a 'family culture' that endorses the manager's style of management;
- structure of the workforce;
- the workforce is subject to high labour turnovers and is composed of high numbers of people who are not traditionally associated with trade union membership, e.g. young workers, students, part-timers, women, employees of ethnic minorities and migrant workers;
- employer and management attitudes;
- within the unitary framework, employers and managers are anti-trade unionism and will often pursue an active non-union policy;
- role of trade unions; and
- generally acknowledged that trade unions have repeatedly failed to develop effective strategies to organise the tourism and hospitality sector.

Despite these factors, the unions have been strong and successful in some sub-sectors of the tourism and hospitality industry. For example, the UK airline industry has been recognised as having formidable support from trade unions (Baum, 2006); the hotel industry in Australia has engaged union support with enterprise bargaining (Knox & Nickson, 2007); and the unions have negotiated better wages and working conditions for hotel employees in the US (Bernhardt *et al.*, 2003). More recently, the Transport Workers Union (TWU) supported Qantas baggage handlers as they embarked on strike action in protest 'to ensure safety of Qantas customers, its employees and the general public' (see the Case Study at end of this chapter in Box 7.5).

The major stakeholders involved in industrial relations are employees and their trade unions and employers and their associations. The involvement of other parties varies with different countries. In some countries, an important role is played by governments (state and federal) and industrial tribunals. In Australia, governments have always played a significant role in industrial relations, especially through legislation and regulation of industrial awards through industrial tribunals.

INDUSTRIAL RELATIONS PROCESSES

Conflict is a central theme of industrial relations. The theoretical perspectives of IR described above revolve around conflict. Hence, the industrial relations processes relates to the mechanisms for dealing with industrial conflict. Since the birth of the Industrial Revolution in Europe, history is marked with strikes, lockouts, bans and other actions which have heralded conflict of interests between workers and employers. Sappey *et al.* (2009: 397) refer to these manifestations of conflict as 'overt collective forms of industrial conflict'.

Resolution of industrial conflict is often envisaged as a spectrum of approaches and referred to as 'conflict management continuum' as illustrated in Figure 7.1. The techniques indicated range from unilateral approaches which require no third party and are at the personal level (such as negotiations); through to unstructured, informal approaches which are private and require third party intervention (such as mediation and conciliation); to formal, structured third-party intervention in a public forum (such as arbitration and adjudication).

INDUSTRIAL RELATIONS SYSTEM: HIGHLIGHTS FROM AUSTRALIA

Work and work conditions are central to any industrial relations system. What is more, for most workers pay is a key motivational factor for working. Consequently, conflict over pay or wages is one of the major reasons for industrial disputes. In Australia, the past century has witnessed various methods of wage-setting, ranging from centralised wage determination affecting all workers to individual wage agreements between the worker and organisation. Sappey *et al.* (2009: 324) summarise the 'multiple system of wage determination' current in Australia as follows:

- **National wage cases** – these now only apply to minimum wages for workers who cannot conclude an enterprise bargain with their employer.
- **Awards** – a system of award wage determination still exists, largely in the state industrial relations system.
- **Workplace** collective **agreement-making** – agreements between employees and managers, which may involve a trade union and are registered with industrial tribunals (certified agreements) or unregistered collective agreements.
- **Individual agreement-making** – formal agreements (AWAs) that are registered with the Office of Employment Advocate.
- **Informal individual agreements** (common law contracts) – agreements that are largely determined on the basis of accepting a wage offer from management.

Throughout time, the federal industrial tribunal (Australian Industrial Relations Commission – AIRC) in Australia has maintained a key role in the setting of awards. However, in recent times there has been a move toward decentralisation of employee relations from the federal industrial tribunal (AIRC), to the workplace level. The Australian industrial relations system has experienced deregulation of the labour market, i.e. the repeal of laws and regulations that dictated universal standards of employment. This mirrors the rise of neo-liberalism, which saw the adoption of free-market policies, shrinking government regulation, emphasis on managerial prerogative, diminishing role and influence of

Private decision making				Private, third-party decision-making		Legal (public), authoritative third-party decision-making		Extralegal, coerced decision-making	
Consensual (interests)			Alternative Dispute Resolution (ADR) – Tends toward win/win			Adversarial (rights)		Increased likelihood of win/lose outcome	
Conflict avoidance (Fight) Lose/Lose	**Talk** (informal discussion & problem solving)	**Negotiation** (gather & process information so as to work towards win/win)	**Mediation** (a third party alternative where conflicting parties have some control)	**Administrative decision**	**Arbitration**	**Judicial decision**	**Legislative decision**	**Nonviolent direct action**	**Violence** (Win/Lose)

Increased time, resources & coercion →

Figure 7.1 Continuum of conflict management approaches

Adapted from: C.W. Moore. (1996). *The mediation process: Practical strategies for resolving conflict* (2nd Edition). San Francisco: Jossey-Bass (John Wiley & Sons), p. 7, Table 1.1; M.S. Hermann (ed.) (1994) Introduction. In *Resolving conflict: Strategies for local government* (pp. xi–xxi). Washington, D.C.: International City/County Management Association. Accessed on 20.5.09 at: http://www.tonydorcey.ca/595/08Field1.html; and information accessed on 20.5.09 at: http://siteresources.worldbank.org/INTLAWJUSTINST/Resources/adr_chapter1.pdf

industrial tribunals and incorporation of the philosophy into government economic policies.

The enterprise bargaining system was endorsed in 1991 but it was the Industrial Relations Reform Act of 1994 which was instrumental in advancing the enterprise bargaining system because it permitted non-union enterprise agreements. Further to this, the election of the Coalition government in 1996 expedited the process. The Coalition reduced the role of the AIRC. In its place, the Office of Employment Advocate (OEA) was created, which reduced the significance of national wage cases. In addition, trade unions and industrial action were subject to greater regulation. This was particularly, accentuated with the introduction of the WorkChoices legislation in 2005 and the establishment of the Australian Fair Pay Commission (AFPC). All these factors encouraged facilitation of Australian Workplace Agreements.

In 2008, however, the Rudd government commenced its reform of Australia's industrial relations system. It is envisaged that this system will still, in effect, continue to determine wages under a centralised process which is governed by Fair Work Australia. Apart from its responsibility for the annual review of wages and panel membership structure, the role of this new institution is similar to that of the AFPC. Award restructuring within the tourism and hospitality industry has been at the forefront of this reform, as the article in Box 7.3 illustrates.

BOX 7.3 Restaurant industry rallies against award changes

27 April 2009, by Olivia Collings

The restaurant industry is stepping up its fight against proposed award changes with a series of roundtables being held across the country.

Restaurant and Catering Australia held its first roundtable in Sydney this morning, to discuss the current state of the industry and the changes being proposed under the industrial relations reforms by the Federal Government.

Today's roundtable included industry figures such as Matt Moran (Aria restaurant), Brian Trippes (AHL), George Misfud (Compass Group) and Tonic Farak (Wildfire restaurant). More such events will be held in Melbourne, Brisbane and Adelaide in the coming days.

Peter Doyle, president of Restaurant and Catering Australia, said restaurants and cafés were an important part of society and were facing a number of challenges in the current environment.

'We are concerned about the economy, but we are also concerned about the award modifications the government is proposing,' Doyle said. 'We are being grouped under the hotel award, but we want a separate award.'

The award modernisation process that the Federal Government is undertaking is being run by the Australian Industrial Relations Commission and is expected to be implemented by 1 January 2010.

Some of the proposals in the new award the industry are most concerned about are changes to penalty rates on weekends, which would see a 175% penalty rate and an after 7pm penalty Monday to Friday, similar to the Federal Hotel's Award.

The NSW restaurant and catering industry has seen a 17% drop in business, 5% more than other states said Doyle. 'Lunches are down across the city. And it's across the board, not just the top end of town.'

Doyle claims the government is under the impression that restaurants are big profit makers, but most restaurants are only making 2% profit. 'We are not big profit makers, we are big employers,' he said.

2008 saw a big decline in café and restaurant business according to a report by Westpac. Growth fell from a peak in first quarter 2007 of 10.4% to a negative 8.4% in 2008 last quarter.

Doyle said the association hoped to meet with minister for workplace relations Julia Gillard in the next few months to discuss the award.

Source: Collings, O. (2009). Restaurant industry rallies against award changes. *Hospitality Magazine*. Accessed on 28.4.09 at: http://www.hospitalitymagazine.com.au/Article/Restaurant-industry-rallies-against-award-changes/478675.aspx

This case shows that federal regulations do have implications for employment in the tourism and hospitality industry. Despite the new neo-liberal agenda promoting de-regulation and individualisation, the small-medium sized enterprises in the Australian tourism and hospitality industry continue to be governed by awards (van Barneveld, 2006). Some of the bigger companies, such as hotel chains, have moved toward collective union/non-union agreements for frontline staff with individual agreements being reserved for managerial employees. It would seem that neo-liberal policies have 'provided opportunities for employers to strengthen their bargaining power, which in turn has allowed them greater control over the management of production, resulting in increased flexibility and profitability' (De Cieri & Kramar, 2005: 160).

Critical note

Throughout the industrial revolution, trade unions played a critical role in gaining a 'fair days pay for a fair days work' for employees. In recent times several factors have contributed to a marked decline in trade union membership. As the employment relations landscape continues to change, the role of unions within this setting is still evolving.

> **Reflection**
>
> What do you think of the transition from collective regulation and bargaining to individual regulation and bargaining of the employment relationship?

THE LEGAL CONTEXT

One of the earliest pieces of legislation was the Masters and Servants Act, which was passed in Britain in 1823. This Act regulated rights and responsibilities of employers and employees and governed wages and hours of work. Soon to follow was the emergence of the British 'craft unions'. Amongst these was the stonemasons union which in 1856 became the first union in Australia to win the eight-hour day. Equally, strong were the mass unions of shearers, maritime workers, and mining employees. As the employee relationship evolved through the industrial revolution, workers 'became regarded less as servants and more as individuals who sold their labour in exchange for wages by means of a contract' (Teicher *et al.*, 2006: 200). Stone (2008: 113) defines the employment contract as 'an informal (oral) or formal (written) legally binding agreement between an employer and an employee specifying the legal rights and obligations of each party'.

The fundamental premise of the contract of employment is an agreement between the employee and employer over the terms of the contract. It is important to note that terms most explicitly expressed by the parties at the time the contract is created can be implied by either law or fact. These explicit or implied terms constitute the rights and responsibilities that are legally binding. Also, some workers (such as independent contractors) are not employees and their employment relationship is considered to be 'contract for service'. By comparison, that of employees is legally referred to as 'contract of service' and indicates that the rights and responsibilities differ for the employee, non-employee (or contractor) and employer.

Subsequently, disputes between employees and their employers were resolved in courts and led to the emergence and growth of common law, one of the primary sources of employment law. Concurrently, governments created and established laws which regulated the employment relationship. This was the foundation of statute law in the workplace. Such legislation enables governments to execute their policies and principles. It also ensures that employers abide with government policies.

The mechanisms by which the employment relationship is regulated and legislation derived is widely determined by the ILO Conventions. For example, the Minimum Wage Fixing Convention of 1928 is instrumental in the development of legislation and/or collective agreements (Lucas, 2004). The degree to which it impacts on international regulation of employment varies with different national employment systems, institutional roles and cultures. In Australia, the Constitution is the framework from which has emerged laws applicable to HR. De Cieri and Kramar (2005: 87) define the Australian Constitution as 'a set of rules and principles by which a body (e.g. a nation or sports club) may be governed and power relations defined'.

Lucas (2004) presents a detailed comparison of employment law in various countries. She notes that employment law basically differentiates between individual and collective rights. In essence, employment law encourages employers to engage with 'good practice', whether dealing with workers as individuals or collectively. In Australia, laws of significance which affect HR include:

- equal employment opportunity (EEO) laws;
- anti-discrimination laws;
- termination of employment laws;
- occupational health and safety (OHS) laws; and
- workplace bargaining laws.

Each of these areas has their own relevant statute(s) and tribunal(s) where litigation of issues relevant to the Act occurs. In Australia, the legal framework regulating workplace relations is a conglomerate of common and statute law, which is influenced by the legislative powers of the Commonwealth and State governments. Throughout the 20th century common law has been increasingly displaced by statute law in the regulation of the employment relationship. However, the employment contract remains at the legal core of the relationship and employees' and employers' rights and responsibilities are supplemented by legislation. Further to this, the industrial relations system in Australia is framed by a dual system of federal and state compulsory conciliation and arbitration which complicates the balance of power in regulation of employment relations. It has often been suggested that a 'national industrial relations system' be created. As the article in Box 7.4 shows, recent news reports indicate growing support for this proposal.

BOX 7.4 Case study – Go-ahead for national work safety laws

The Age, **19 May 2009, by Ben Schneiders**
Australia will move to a national system of workplace safety laws after state and territory governments agreed yesterday to harmonise their laws in a move designed to reduce business red tape.

But unions criticised the changes, with ACTU secretary Jeff Lawrence saying they would 'significantly undermine protections' for many workers. 'It's unacceptable that health and safety standards would go backwards.' Standards would not improve, Mr Lawrence said, without unions being able to prosecute for breaches of health and safety laws.

'We are also concerned that some of the rights and powers of union representatives and health and safety officials will be reduced under the recommendations.'

Mr Lawrence said the Council of Australian Governments had provided a 'clear commitment' that through national laws, standards would be improved.

Victorian Trades Hall Council secretary Brian Boyd said unions had wanted from a Labor government the 'best possible legislation', and that was not guaranteed.

The changes do not endorse key elements of the pro-employee NSW laws, which have been strongly criticised by business. The Victorian Government said the proposals closely followed its own system.

Last night, relevant ministers released a communique which said the changes would 'address the disparate and inconsistent OHS laws across jurisdictions'.

Finance Minister Tim Holding said the changes backed the Victorian model of occupational health and safety laws.

'This is a resounding endorsement of Victoria's OHS laws, which will provide the building blocks for the new national scheme,' he said.

'The increased certainty of a national scheme based on the Victorian model is a win for businesses and employees, and will ensure that there is no reduction in safety standards for Victorian workers.'

Australian Industry Group chief executive Heather Ridout largely welcomed the changes, in particular that an employer accused in a safety case is innocent until proven guilty – a move criticised by unions. The reverse applies in NSW.

'Safety is too important to have the rules rewritten in every state. It makes compliance a costly and diverting nightmare,' she said.

'While business will continue to have difficulties with some of the recommendations, we need to move forward on this, and the sooner we see the draft legislation to create a national OHS system, the better.'

Ms Ridout said the decision 'finally paves the way' for a genuinely national workplace safety system.

A Victorian Employers Chamber of Commerce and Industry spokesman said the group was 'looking closely at the proposals'. 'We'd be heartened if the proposals were closer to the Victorian model than other state models.'

Safe Work Australia Council will develop the proposed new laws to be introduced in parliaments throughout Australia.

Question

1. Discuss the advantages and disadvantages of a national system of OHS.

Source: This story was accessed on 12.5.09 at: http://www.theage.com.au/national/goahead-for-national-work-safety-laws-20090518-bcr3.html

While the above article focuses on OHS, it highlights the complexities of moving toward a national industrial relations system. This is further complicated by the implementation of laws, standards, policies and procedures in the workplace. For tourism and hospitality organisations the articulation and dissemination of laws has its own particular issues. Tourism and hospitality organisations often seem to lack the formal policies and procedures which sustain legally framed issues. Such issues can range from grievances associated with OHS and EEO matters to disciplinary or dismissal concerns. This is compounded by the predominance of small-medium sized enterprises (SMEs).

Critical note

The legal framework regulating workplace relations is a complex matrix of common and statute laws that are further complicated by the powers of state and federal governments. At the core of this framework is contract law which regulates the individual employment relationship.

Reflection

Think of your own workplace and reflect on the legislation which impacts on your job. How effective is the organisation in communicating to its employees the relevant legislation and the organisational policies and practices which ensure that employees know their rights and responsibilities? How could this communication be improved?

SUMMARY

This chapter explored the nature of industrial relations and how it relates to the tourism and hospitality industry. It investigated understanding of the term 'industrial relations' and how it connects with 'human resource management' and 'employee relations'. From this platform the main theoretical approaches to industrial relations were investigated and the various stakeholders in industrial relations identified and discussed. The chapter concluded with an insight into the legal framework surrounding industrial relations.

Throughout the chapter attention was drawn to the employment relationship and how it is situated at the centre of industrial relations. In addition, it was stressed that industrial relations are instrumental in the establishment and development of working conditions and wages. However, the role of industrial relations within the framework of employment relationships is shifting as changes occur in political, legal and social arenas and these impact on the positioning of authority for decision-making about working conditions, wages and the nature of work itself. This will further affect the handling of and processes associated with industrial disputes.

As long as people have divergent interests and goals, conflict in the workplace will no doubt continue to exist. Of interest, will be the extent to which such conflict develops into industrial disputes in the future. Already in Australia we have witnessed a decline in the number of manifestations of industrial disputes, such as strikes. Further, the role of unions has diminished and there has been a retreat from collective bargaining at the industry and national level toward collective bargaining and individual agreements in the workplace. Government reforms have contributed to suppressing such activities but the question remains as to whether this is indicative of parallel shifts in social ideologies and in the workplace, a move toward a more unitarist perspective.

Changes in industrial relations will have subsequent implications for theoretical frameworks, policies, and practice. The debates focusing on HR, IR and ER are testimony to such changes. Also, the alleviation of market power to an international level and jobs in the service industry has changed occupational and industry structures, such that the future of industrial relations may lie in a broadening of its framework to accommodate individualism as well as diversity within the global economy, i.e. across different forms of work, labour markets, industries and nations.

BOX 7.5 Case study – Qantas baggage handlers walk off job

Article from: Australian Associated Press, 30 March 2009
A Qantas baggage handlers' strike has disrupted terminals in Brisbane, Sydney, Perth and Adelaide.

International delays were also experienced in Sydney and Brisbane.

Qantas baggage handlers, cleaners and caterers went on strike at 9.20am (AEST) and passengers were seen disembarking their flights and leaving without their luggage.

A Qantas spokesman says workers were ordered by the Industrial Relations Commission to resume duties at 2pm (AEDT).

At Sydney airport, up to 300 Qantas workers walked off the job, refusing to unload arriving planes but servicing aircraft due to depart.

The protest initially disrupted traffic at the airport, but the airport roads were clear by 11am (AEDT).

Transport Workers Union (TWU) federal secretary Tony Sheldon said members had a number of concerns, including the outsourcing of more jobs and the failure to security check airport staff.

'The TWU has been seeking assurances from Qantas for a number of years over safety and today we look at what action needs to be taken to create a safer environment for employees and the general public,' he said.

'Four years ago, industrial action was taken to ensure the safety of Qantas customers, its employees and the general public.'

Qantas spokesman David Epstein dismissed union claims the strike had been about security concerns following the fatal bashing of a biker gang member at Sydney airport earlier this month and he said the union was 'exploiting the tragedy'.

Mr Epstein said the TWU leadership's real problem was with Jetstar awarding a contract to another baggage handling company.

This contract had nothing to do with security arrangements, he said.

'The union has never had any problems with the contractor when they have worked for other airlines like Virgin Blue and Tiger so we don't know why they chose to do what they did today,' Mr Epstein told Sky News.

'They make a very unfortunate link to a tragedy [...] it's absolutely extraordinary that they've chosen to do this.'

Mr Epstein apologised to customers, the general public and other staff for the inconvenience.

He said the unauthorised industrial action had caused the airline and passengers considerable financial damage.

'We will be pursuing the union if this sort of financial damage is allowed to continue,' he said.

Qantas flights at the Brisbane domestic airport had been heavily impacted, a spokeswoman for Brisbane Airport Corporation said.

Flights currently impacted at the Brisbane International terminal include Eva Airways BR3 16, Qantas QF 15, Qantas QF 51 and Air New Zealand 136.

'We're advising passengers who were intending to travel today through the airport to check with their airlines with the timing of their scheduled flights – and if they are coming to the airport please be patient,' the spokeswoman said.

Transport Workers Union Queensland spokesman Hughie Williams said the strike was over Qantas's new chief executive officer deciding to outsource work to a cheaper company named Aero-care.

'We have no choice but to do this if we're going to look after our members,' Mr Williams said.

'Whenever there is any security risk the baggage handlers are the first to report anything odd. They're very hard workers.'

Questions

1. Industrial disputes can have broad implications. For example, the 1989 pilots strike had a dramatic adverse impact on businesses and individuals throughout Australia. Its legacy remains etched in the minds of those affected and many other Australians. Explain how workplace conflict can have affect people and organisations outside of the dispute.

2. From a pluralist perspective, what are the issues in this case? Analyse the case from a unitarist perspective; and a radicalist perspective.

3. As the Director of HR for Qantas, what do you see your role as in this dispute?

Source: This story was accessed on 9.4.09 at: http://www.theaustralian.news.com.au/story/ 0,25197,25262298-5006787,00.html

CHAPTER QUESTIONS

1. Comment on the argument that the theory and practice of HR supports a pro-management perspective.

2. Collect new articles which relate to employee relations. Summarise the issues and critically analyse them in terms of contemporary thought on employee relations.

3. Workplace conflict reflects the control-resistance framework. Discuss how organisation of work can affect power and decision-making in the workplace to favour co-operative and productive rather than conflicting and debilitating environments.

RECOMMENDED READING

Tuman, J. (2003) *Reshaping the North American Automobile Industry: Restructuring, Corporatism and Union Democracy in Mexico*. New York: Routledge.
    This book presents an interesting insight into the response of unions and workers to restructuring in an organisation.

Leat, M. (2006) *Exploring Employee Relations: An International Approach* (2nd edn). Oxford: Butterworth-Heinemann.
    This book provides a comprehensive overview of various aspects of employee relations, including the role of the European Union, governments and power in the employment relationship.

Sen, R. (2003) *Industrial Relations in India: Shifting Paradigms*. India: Macmillan Publishers.
    The value of this book is in its presentation of topics related to industrial relations but which are generally absent, e.g. knowledge workers, communication, retirement schemes and quality circles.

Morely, M., Gunnigle, P. and Collings, D. (eds) (2006) *Global Industrial Relations*. South Yarra, Victoria: Palgrave Macmillan.

Kaufman, B. (2004) *The Global Evolution of Industrial Relations: Events, Ideas and the IIRA.* Geneva: International Labour Office.

A treasured volume which follows the development of industrial relations in the global arena.

RECOMMENDED WEBSITES

CSR Europe – http://www.csreurope.org/pages/en/publications.html

Corporate Research Forum (CRF) – http://www.crforum.co.uk/

Industrial Relations Europe –
http://www.watsonwyatt.com/europe/pubs/industrialrelations/

Australian Government: Workplace Authority –
http://www.workplaceauthority.gov.au/pages/default.aspx

Department of Labour (New Zealand) – http://www.ers.dol.govt.nz/

CHAPTER 8

THE SAME DIFFERENCE? DIVERSITY MANAGEMENT

LEARNING OBJECTIVES

After working through this chapter you should be able to:

1. Understand the impact of migration on demographic profiles.

2. Understand the impact of demographic trends on diversity management in the tourism industry.

3. Define modern diversity management.

4. Discuss the major classifications of diversity in the workplace.

5. Identify the benefits of diversity management amongst tourism and hospitality firms.

INTRODUCTION

People choose to migrate for a number of reasons. Often these are linked to increasing individual and family wealth which in turn is associated with overall long-term aspirations. In a macro sense, migration can give rise to benefits including relieving unemployment, providing a source of foreign exchange, acquisition of a skilled workforce and improved wealth by increasing *per capita* income. From the employing tourism and hospitality firm's perspective, immigrant labour allows economies of scale to be realized; prevents wage inflation; and facilitates investment by ensuring that new capacity can be adequately staffed (Choi *et al.*, 2000). However, these potential benefits also present tourism organisations with the challenge of managing a multicultural and diverse workforce.

This chapter begins by contextualising diversity management in the broader category of migration and other demographic changes impacting on tourism firms. A generic understanding of culture is introduced prior to a brief discussion of global firms. Diversity management is defined and benefits accruing to the tourism firm identified. Perspectives of organisational diversity awareness are introduced, followed by some major challenges to the overall notion of diversity management by category.

> **Critical note**
> Immigrants are now arriving from a much broader spread of nations compared to earlier movements usually determined by geographical proximity and historical and cultural ties.

POPULATION MOVEMENTS

In their study of population flows, Salt *et al.* (2004) note that, generically, immigrants are now arriving from a much broader spread of countries compared to earlier movements usually determined by geographical proximity and historical and cultural ties. New migrations are caused by, amongst other things, relaxed visa requirements, skills shortages and asylum seeking. Recent liberalisation of global labour markets, increasing feminisation and an increase in older working individuals have given rise to a pool of human resources with increased cultural diversity.

The movement of population flows to and from various nation states is not a haphazard affair. Migration policies are based on compromises between government and other institutions to achieve particular outcomes through various analyses of external labour demand, unemployment and demographic developments and may include: labour market testing; special schemes to attract the highly and low-skilled workers; quotas and national targets; bilateral agreements; and amnesties. For example, New Zealand's Recognized Seasonal Employer (RSE) scheme was established so that employers could secure a seasonal migrant labour supply if there were local shortages from Vanuatu, Tonga, Samoa, Kiribati and Tuvalu. The scheme both assists New Zealand employers and provides an inflow of funds into these countries for the purpose of economic development (Maclellan, 2008). Similarly, other legislation impacts on population movements and the demographic profiles of nations: for example, in the Republic of Ireland and Northern Ireland less demanding visa requirements for non-EU citizens have resulted in a non-national tourism/hospitality workforce of 27,000 (Fáilte Ireland, 2005; Jarman, 2004).

The above all illustrate how legislation impacts on population flows and how the demographic profile of the workforce can be altered. However, impacts of refugees and asylum seekers etc. are insignificant compared with those resulting from the demographic changes currently being experienced by many Western nations.

The characteristics of a population, whether national or regional, are important when planning a strategy for employment. This not only pertains to the overall supply of labour, but more specifically the supply of differentiated workers. Managers need to know whether there will be enough potential tourism employees with appropriate skills to satisfy the demand across a number of roles and positions. Initially however, it is vital to understand the implications of broad population projections so that likely contingencies may be planned in the event of demographic changes occurring over a specified period of time.

Proportionately, similar to other Western nations, the resident population of Australia will increase from around 21 million in June 2007 to anything between 31 and 43 million by 2056 (ABS, 2008). In the most recent 10 years (until 2007), the population has increased by an average just over 1% per year with approximately half coming from natural increases and the other from net overseas migration (NOM). Since 2005, NOM has marginally overtaken the former contributing 177,600 people to the population. The ageing population in the West is projected to continue due to low levels of fertility and increased life expectancy. Indeed, by 2056, people aged 65+ are set to represent 25% of the population compared to the current 13%. The proportion of those aged 15 and below will decrease from a current 19% to 15% by 2101 (ABS, 2008). The proportion of individuals of working age (between 15 and 65) in 2007 was 68%; by 2101 this is projected to decrease to around 60%. This has implications upon the profile of the oncoming labour force. For example, fewer available people of working age could mean labour shortages. This might translate into higher wages and improved working conditions due to stronger bargaining power. On the other hand, there may be more reliance on older workers, including those over 65 years. Indeed, employers may have no other choice than to tap into hitherto undeveloped caches of human resources.

In short, the workforce is more heterogeneous, diverse and multicultural than at any other time. It is therefore imperative that appropriate diversity management strategies are planned and implemented by those managers charged with such a responsible task. However, some commentators note that comprehensive strategic diversity management activity is regrettably lacking across industry, particularly the private sector. At best it can be described as reactive and designed to merely comply with legislation.

Miller and Rowney's (1999) study of almost 200 firms in Canada reveals that many engage in diversity programs because they are legally obliged to do so despite them being selected in the first instance because of their reputations for engaging in 'progressive human resource management practices' (p. 309). The authors conclude that larger internationalised organisations tend to incorporate diversity management knowledge into their HR procedures and practices (although this was not uniform). Gröschl and Doherty's (1999) study of seven US-based hotels reveals a workforce comprised of African American, Caucasian, Hispanic, Asian, Native American workers (representative of the regional San Fransisco population). Diversity management development in hotels was poor and tended to be reactive. These kinds of practices do not value a diverse workforce and often only include Affirmative Action programmes enforced by law and management training in legal compliance. Gröschl and Doherty (1999) conclude that the hotels in their study have yet to move from 'tolerating' to 'valuing' diversity.

The above is disconcerting because the tourism and hospitality industry has always maintained a diverse and multicultural workforce due to the nature of employment and characteristics of the industry (see Chapter 1). What would formerly be considered a minority group elsewhere, for example: women, individuals with some form of physical or mental impairment, immigrant workers, certain ethnic minority groups and so on, are more likely to be regarded as the norm rather than the exception. We can surmise from the work of Miller and Rowney (1999) and Gröschl and Doherty (1999) this is not necessarily the result of comprehensive strategic diversity management thinking but rather a simple response to demand and supply. One only has to look at the jobs in which ethnic, racial or other minority groups are pigeonholed. These may be described as mostly low skilled with scant opportunity for career development, for example, kitchen portering, housekeeping and the service of food and beverages. This is especially the case in the UK tourism sector where hotels in particular have traditionally employed high proportions of non-national workers. Indeed, such is the nature of the tourism workforce that Devine *et al.* (2007) consider it a key progressive informant of other disciplines and government diversity-oriented legislation! Choi *et al.* (2000) draw similar conclusions after analysing the immigrant workforce in the entire global service industry sector to approximate a tourism/hospitality profile. Using Canada, USA and France they note that an average of around 40% of all service workers are 'foreign' born.

In summary, despite the high proportion of multicultural and other minority group representation in the workforce, evidence suggests that current diversity thinking in tourism and hospitality is somewhat less than acceptable. This unfortunate situation has long been overdue for change and many researchers have forwarded expressions of frustration, exasperation and strategies to improve the lot of the tourism and hospitality workforce. However, these observations and recommendations are now even more important because forces of globalisation have created increased potential for an expanded and thus more diverse pool of labour. According to Holden (2002), in a globalised economy, managing the productivity of service workers will be one of the main tasks of the manager. Moreover, cultures are not determined by nationality but a reflection of other more complex expressions of individuals and groups. In short, a new multicultural and diverse business environment is taking shape.

Critical note
The workforce is more heterogeneous, diverse and multicultural than at any other time in history.

CULTURE, WORKPLACE DIVERSITY AND ITS MANAGEMENT

The anthropological concept of culture has been used as a basis in organisations and has lead to separation by classification of those things which differentiate groups of people. There are many definitions of culture and most draw attention to a number of key factors, namely that members:

- share a set of ideas and values;
- transmit them from generation to generation by symbols;
- 'produce' culture by past actions;
- learn culture; and
- use culture to shape behaviours and their perception of the world.

The key to understanding how culture influences the behaviour of people within firms is to consider the 'invisible' elements rather than that which can be easily observed. The way people understand and interpret their organisational reality by cultural group will have a key impact on those players involved in managing a cross cultural and diverse workforce.

Hofstede's (1980) study of culture has probably been the most influential in the field of management and cross-cultural inquiry where nations were identified along several dimensions. Unfortunately, his work is often criticised for being too general and stereotypical as the model is used to identify only one culture per nation. However, Hofstede (1994) also identifies other overlapping levels of culture which are important when looking through an organisational lens. In addition to culture at a national level, other categories include, regional, ethnic, religious and linguistic affiliation; gender; generational; social class and education and the manner in which employees have been socialised into their organisations (Holden, 2002). So, whilst his often-quoted cultural dimensions of 'power distance'; 'uncertainty avoidance'; 'individualism/collectivism'; 'masculinity and femininity'; 'Confucian dynamism' are insightful, they are merely a guide as intranational cultures can vary significantly (adapted from Holden, 2002: 22).

- 'Power distance' is understood as the extent to which people accept inequality in power;
- 'Uncertainty avoidance' is the degree to which members of a society feel uncomfortable with ambiguity;
- 'Individualism/collectivism' is the degree to which individuality or community prevails;
- 'Masculinity and femininity' is the extent to which (what must be described as stereotypical) male or female values pervade a society; and
- 'Confucian dynamism' is a preference for long or short term societal thinking.

Adapted from: Hofstede (2001)

> **Reflections**
>
> Visit two local tourism employers.
>
> 1. Ask whether they employ immigrants.
> 2. If they answer 'no' ask why this is the case.
> 3. If they answer 'yes' ask from which countries they originate.

GLOBAL FIRMS

An obvious and extreme context for diversity management is the global firm. Indeed some would argue that most firms are either 'global' or at least operate with that potential given the unrelenting internationalisation of commerce and labour. In this particular instance we are referring to the preparation of expatriate managers for overseas assignments. Whilst this chapter does not focus on this area specifically, it is still worthwhile reminding ourselves of the basic issues. This is because it helps identify major challenges which have to be managed in both global and non-global firms. Moreover, it assists us in identifying some associated subtleties which impact significantly on workplace behaviour in the diverse organisation.

If someone is preparing for a global assignment they clearly need to be trained and have a predisposition for diversity and cross-cultural management. However, they must also be trained about the culture, society, politics, and appropriate legislature of the destination country. Commentators note that typically expatriate managers 'fail' for between 40% and 70% of overseas assignments. Reasons vary but often 'trailing spouse syndrome' or the inability of family members to adapt to the host culture are cited. Thus cross-cultural training needs to be extended to all family members (Dessler *et al.*, 2004). Expatriates are likely to remain in demand for the foreseeable future despite the global downturn, therefore pre-assignment training is essential. Dessler *et al.* summarise some key elements of such programmes:

- language skilling;
- cultural awareness;
- multicultural communication skills;
- experiential role playing;
- sensitivity training; and
- country-specific training (politics, business culture and practices).

Holden cites Hannerz (1996) to emphasise the dynamic nature of culture and underscore the challenging nature of cross-cultural management. Thus, culture is no longer understood as a sharing of consistent patterns of behaviour. Rather, it should now be recognised as based on partly shared patterns of meaning and interpretation because cultural 'patterns' are reproduced but continually reinterpreted and changed by those identifying with them during their everyday existence. Affiliations with nation, firm, gender and generation are changing and boundaries between cultural communities are less rigid and more contingent.

Critical note

Culture is most often understood as a shared a set of learned ideas and values transmitted from generation to generation by symbols used to shape behaviours and perceptions of the world.

TOWARDS A DEFINITION

According to the *Cambridge Advanced Learner's Dictionary* (2009), diversity is understood to be:

> when many different types of things or people are included in something.

And workforce as:

> The group of people who work in a company, industry, country.

The Merriam-Webster Online Dictionary (2009) defines diversity as:

> Variety and the inclusion of diverse people (as people of different races or cultures) in a group or organization.

Daft (2005) defines diversity as:

> Differences among people in terms of age, ethnicity, gender, race or other dimensions. (p. 431)

Thomas (1991) considers diversity management to be the efforts by organisations to actively recruit, retain and facilitate working relationships among individuals from a variety of backgrounds. Clearly, managing such a potentially heterogeneous workforce is challenging as individual differences will be numerous and dynamic. Managers must ensure they are inclusive and address all important categories of diversity and some key questions include:

- How many categories exist?
- Can they be prioritised?
- Can they be integrated or generalised and to what extent?
- Do we treat employees as a homogeneous mass or use all of our pre-established categories?

According to Walenta (2008) diversity management discourse now considers six key elements important. Known as the 'big 6', gender, age, ethnicity, religion, disability and sexual orientation are currently enshrined in much diversity-oriented legislation. However, these factors alone fail to capture the nature of diversity, or rather, its management in the workplace. Firms may wish to engage in diversity management so that no individual is discriminated against but it is more than simply an equal employment opportunity (EEO) or affirmative action (AA) matter.

Citing Kandola and Fullerton (1998), Walenta (2008) notes that diversity management may be defined as:

> [a] basic concept [...] [that] accepts that the workforce consists of a diverse population of people. The diversity consists of visible and non-visible differences which will include factors such as sex, age, background, race, disability, personality and workstyle. (p. 383)

Daft (2005) invokes Loden's (1996) 'diversity wheel', which essentially splits dimensions of diversity into primary and secondary dimensions. The former are innate said to shape a person's self-image and world view (age, race, ethnicity, gender, mental and physical abilities and sexual orientation) whilst the latter (work style, communication style, education and so on) are learned and said to be less 'important', although that very much depends on how one understands importance. Clearly, secondary elements can have a crucial impact on the way individuals behave in the workplace. Poststructuralists would probably challenge the above on the basis that it is overly simplistic and fails to address a 'reality' that meanings and identity shift over time. Moreover, key questions would include 'who is the classifier and why?'; 'why have these categories been used?'; 'what is the real purpose of the classification?'; 'does the classification perpetuate existing organisational power structures?'; 'does the classification marginalise the classified?' and so on. While these are important issues, that particular debate is best left for elsewhere. Nonetheless, practical issues such as context, timing and environment are important because they are key enablers of specific diversity management concerns. However and within reason, what specific elements should or should not be included in a diversity management programme is less important than the premise upon which it is founded:

> [...] that harnessing these differences will create a productive environment on which everybody feels valued, where their talents are being fully utilized and in which organizational goals are being met. (Walenta, 2008: 383)

The key here is that modern approaches to diversity management do not seek to integrate a heterogeneous collection of employees into a dominant culture but rather allow the individual to be themselves. Walby (2007) notes that equality is now based on difference rather than uniformity.

> **Reflections**
> 1. Through desk research, identify two major tourism corporations.
> 2. Identify and describe their diversity management programme.
> 3. Approach two local tourism and hospitality employers and identify their diversity management programmes. Compare the corporations and local firms in terms of their initiatives and compare and contrast your findings.

WHY EMBRACE DIVERSITY MANAGEMENT?

As much as organisational artifacts are a mirror of society at large so too is the notion of diversity management. Whilst there is evidence to suggest that some tourism and hospitality firms appear reluctant to embrace diversity in the way this text advocates, ultimately, they will have no choice given the dynamic nature of the workforce. Daft (2005) notes that forces of globalisation and changing demographics are unrelenting and have resulted in a workforce that is older, feminised, ethnic and contains a large proportion of immigrant workers. He cites Judy and D'Amico (1997) who predict the trend of increasing numbers of immigrants in the USA work force of around 50% will continue for the foreseeable future. Moreover, female immigrants represent two-thirds of the immigrant workforce. Additionally, the same authors predict that the USA labour force as a whole will contain approximately an equal proportion of males and females due to the uniform decrease in male employees since the middle of the last century.

The 'new' philosophy of diversity management is to build on cultural and other differences rather than to neutralise them (Schneider & Barsoux, 1997). This is based on the premise that drawing on a collective experience should benefit the firm as the forum for problem-solving becomes more open and positively critical. The naysayers regard workforce diversity as something to be controlled and the more optimistic of us see it as a means of establishing competitive advantage. Wisely cautious commentators such as Dessler *et al.* (2004) consider diversity a 'good thing' (p. 462) but note the quantum leap which has to be made from the idea to the practical outcome. They concede that diversity might give rise to independence within the workplace; an opportunity for firms to be altruistic; a chance to harness loyal and reliable staff; improved economic performance of the firm and society. Daft (2005) agrees and considers common advantages bestowed by a diverse workforce to include:

- higher morale on the basis that people feel valued for their individuality and the exclusive contribution to the firm;
- an ability to attract and retain valuable workers given the sharpened focus on ability above all else (although there are other less obvious issues to consider such as 'cultural fit' discussed in Chapter 2); and

- an ability for greater innovation, creativity and flexibility given the broader and deeper collective wealth of employee experience.

Daft (2005) also considers the more obvious benefits of multicultural input, for example, when planning international marketing campaigns so that cultural sensitivities and literal translations of one language into another does not cause embarrassment or problems. He also notes that employees and customers having the same cultural or ethnic backgrounds are better able to communicate face to face. This is often seen in the tourism industry where foreign-born employees are used in front of house roles or as tour guides.

However, Dessler *et al.* (2004) remain uncertain and regard the success of diversity management to depend upon identifying which groups are present and which deserve attention by HR managers. In a practical sense, effective diversity management becomes about allocation of resources. Gröschl and Doherty (1999) note that many commentators are enthusiastic about diversity management and eager to share the credo that benefits include:

- better staff customer matching;
- improved decision-making;
- reduced turnover and associated costs;
- increased productivity, quality and improvements; and
- a firm which is more creative and innovative.

This array of impressive benefits sounds ideal but interestingly makes no mention of benefits to the workforce as individuals! The authors continue by conceding that the reality is somewhat different as no common view of the objectives and processes of diversity management exist despite the philosophy behind equal opportunity and in particular, affirmative action initiatives.

Equal opportunity is a term which has differing definitions and there is no consensus as to the precise meaning. Equal opportunity practices include measures taken by organisations to ensure fairness in the employment process. A basic definition of equality is the idea of equal treatment and respect (http://en.wikipedia.org/wiki/Equal_opportunity, accessed April 2009).

Affirmative action refers to policies that take gender, race, or ethnicity into consideration in an attempt to promote equal opportunity. The impetus towards affirmative action is to maximise diversity in all levels of society and to redress perceived disadvantages due to overt, institutional, or involuntary discrimination (http://en.wikipedia.org/wiki/Affirmative_action, accessed April 2009).

Dessler *et al.* (2004) also consider diversity management to be flawed due to its relative novelty and that key elements of the process are intangible, difficult to measure and impute causality. Ely and Thomas (2001) and Peppas (2002) are similarly cautious and question the accepted notion that diversity management somehow improves organisational performance.

Whilst there is no doubt that diversity management is morally and ethically the 'right thing to do' in organisations, the outcomes, particularly for individual workers, are not easy to identify. Intuitively, such initiatives make sense but are only likely to be effective if they are given careful consideration during the planning and implementation (and feedback) stages. Despite the predicted benefits of effective diversity management in the tourism industry, there is an equal and opposite portent if the process is bungled. In fact, the outcome is likely to be worse than having done nothing at all! Negative outcomes include a devaluation and demoralisation of workers, stereotyping and an increased likelihood of litigation. Diversity management programmes are intended to address such issues and many do but there are also some unintended outcomes of these approaches when undertaken hastily with an under-prepared team of managers and workers. After reviewing the evidence, Von Bergen *et al.* (2002) identify a number of common mistakes which are shown in Table 8.1.

Table 8.1 Diversity management – some common mistakes

Training
- Trainers' own psychological values used as training templates which may have inappropriate political agendas or support and promote particular special interest groups and may be chosen because they represent or are advocates for a specific minority group.
- Training may be too brief, too late, or only used in response to an existing crisis situation (such as a charge or lawsuit) or as remediation and trainees are considered people with problems, or worse they are considered to be the problem.
- Training does not distinguish among diversity, EEO, affirmative action, and cross-cultural management and may have an overly narrow working definition of diversity, nor is it customised sufficiently for the participants.
- Training that uses hostile confrontational tactics where participants may be forced to reveal private feelings or are subjected to uncomfortable, invasive physical and psychological exercises.
- Resource material contains outdated views and/or information and important issues, such as reverse discrimination, may be ignored.
- Training that negatively targets previously privileged groups (white males in particular) creates an atmosphere of alienation and a bias.

Employees' value
- Equating diversity management with affirmative action (AA) can disadvantage minorities by setting them up to fail as often AA is understood operationally to mean recruitment and promotion according to quotas. Anyone hired or promoted in this way is not taken seriously and tokenised or stereotyped with achievements being treated with suspicion and resentment.

More discrimination
- Affirmative action as a diversity management tool may lead to reverse discrimination as it is often based on the falsehood that workforce imbalances are the result of discrimination against an underrepresented group.
- Creating an environment where nontraditional employees are regarded as 'winners' and, for example, white males as 'losers'. Definitions of diversity should account for the needs and concerns of all employees including previously privileged groups.
- Trainers that encourages antagonism between groups where minorities are encouraged to believe that their value is only worthwhile through discriminating against white males.

Stereotypes
- Training which adopts 'differences' in an attempt to bring understanding and acceptance often elicits anger and divisiveness.
- Inept training informed by contradictory perspectives that, for example, tells participants that it is unacceptable to stereotype on the one hand and on the other to accept individual behavior as an artifact of cultural/racial/sexual differences (which is stereotyping).
- Using ill-informed assumptions of cultural traits including the notion that all women are nurturing, consensus-seeking, and non-detail oriented – even 'positive' stereotypes can be harmful as they obfuscate understanding of individuals.
- The belief that 'fairness' means treating people in the same manner is inappropriate as different groups will have been discriminated against in different ways.

Adapted from: Von Bergen *et al.* (2002)

Unfortunately, many commentators agree that the management of culture and diversity is not done particularly well. Therefore, there must be a shift in thinking about the issue as a problem to the issue as a potential benefit. Firms must be proactive and take a holistic perspective including management of the social and cultural environment rather than simply complying with the appropriate legislation shown in Figure 8.1 below.

Dessler *et al.* (2004) also take a holistic view of diversity management noting that it should be viewed from more than just a business perspective including ethics and morality, benefits to society and legal/regulatory compliance. This systemic view is essential if a proactive climate of openness to change and positive working environment is to be developed and adopted. Gröschl and Doherty (1999) recommend that the following steps be followed by tourism firms considering the transition from legal compliance to becoming culturally predisposed to diversity management:

- organisations must be committed to diversity management in the mission statement;
- organisations must implement supportive policies, procedures and practice to create a climate of respect, training in equitable recruitment and selection and so on;

In Australia, diversity management related legislation is included in the Workplace Relations Act (1996) which was replaced by the Fair Work Act (2009) on 1 July and is available here:

http://www.austlii.edu.au/au/legis/cth/consol_act/wra1996220/. Other Commonwealth laws which are related to diversity management include:

Racial Discrimination Act (1975) – http://www.austlii.edu.au/au/legis/cth/consol_act/rda1975202;
Sex Discrimination Act (1984) – http://www.austlii.edu.au/au/legis/cth/consol_act/sda1984209;
Human Rights and Equal Opportunity Commission Act (1986) – http://www.austlii.edu.au/au/legis/cth/consol_act/hraeoca1986512;
Disability Discrimination Act (1992) – http://www.austlii.edu.au/au/legis/cth/consol_act/dda1992264;
Equal Employment for Women in the Workplace Act (1999) – http://www.eowa.gov.au/About_EOWA/Overview_of_the_Act/Act_At_A_Glance.asp; and
Age Discrimination Act (2004) – http://www.austlii.edu.au/au/legis/cth/consol_act/ada2004174.

State-specific legislation also accounts for these areas, for example in Queensland, the following apply:

Anti-Discrimination Act (1991), details of which can be found at: http://www.austlii.edu.au/au/legis/qld/consol_act/aa1991204/;
Equal Opportunity in Public Employment Act (1992) – http://www.legislation.qld.gov.au/LEGISLTN/ACTS/1992/92AC010.pdf
Workplace Health and Safety Act (1995) – http://www.legislation.qld.gov.au/LEGISLTN/CURRENT/w/workplhsaA95.pdf; and
Industrial Relations Act (1999) – http://www.legislation.qld.gov.au/LEGISLTN/CURRENT/I/IndustRelA99.pdf.

Commonwealth guidelines on diversity management are also available and some sites appear below:

http://www.apsc.gov.au/publications01/diversityguidelines.htm
http://www.dewr.gov.au/dewr/Publications/WorkplaceDiversity/
http://www.ag.gov.au/www/agd/agd.nsf/Page/About_the_DepartmentEmploymentWorkplace_Diversity

Other countries and regions including the UK, European Union and USA have similar provisions governing all aspects of employment and workplace discrimination related to diversity management.

Figure 8.1 Diversity management related legislation

- organisations must acknowledge that such a commitment does not have short-term benefits and should be implemented systemically throughout the whole organisation;
- organisations must have clear plans on how to tackle some of the negative impacts of diversity management including stereotyping;
- organisations must make workers more aware of cultural differences and how to deal with them; and
- where possible organisations must increase use of internal staff exchanges between international locations.

Adapted from: Gröschl and Doherty (1999: 267)

199

Similarly, Daft (2005) considers the following to be important:

- A long-range view that recognises and supports a diverse organisational community through plans to include employees of all groups at every level and a reinforcement of that commitment through practice;
- An openness and positive predisposition toward diversity exhibited by managers illustrated through appropriate behaviour;
- A broad knowledge of diversity and multicultural issues and communication which is respectful of differences; and
- Mentoring and empowering diverse workers to capitalise on their individual skills and talents.

Adapted from: Daft (2005: 455–456)

Moving towards effective diversity management requires first an open and honest acknowledgement that the firm may not be aware of its current position in these terms. Tourism managers or consultants should conduct diagnostics to ascertain the organisation's awareness of diversity management. Dessler *et al.* (2004) recommend that audits should focus on three areas – individual attitudes and beliefs; organisations norms and values; and a critical look at the place where workers and the organisations interact, that is, management practices and policies. Findings could then be matched against a suitable model such as Schwartz's (1992) – based on women's career progression in the USA – which uses five progressive stages of:

- unaware – little appreciation of companies deriving any benefit from developing women;
- regulatory – policies and tracking systems in place to satisfy labour laws;
- morality – where women's needs are beginning to be seen as important;
- multiple initiatives – firms focus on acceptance and a valuing of talent across cultural and other differences with a broader focus than development of women; and
- level playing field.

Adapted from: Miller and Rowney (1999: 310)

Rosener's (1995) model may be used for a similar purpose and is shown in Figure 8.2.

The position of the tourism firm along the above continuum will determine the necessary remedial action required. For example, a firm at Stage 1 of the model is clearly complying with legislation but minorities are viewed as a challenge and only the legal minimum will be employed. Conversely, a tourism firm at Stage 5 will be predisposed, proactive and equally supportive of all individuals regardless of minority group (Daft, 2005).

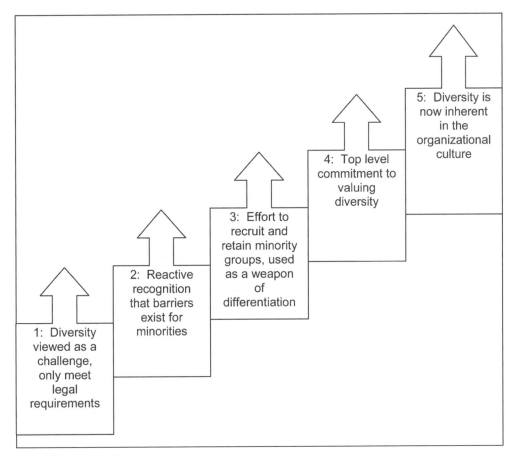

Figure 8.2 A model of progressive organizational diversity awareness

Adapted from: Daft (2005: 452)

The remainder of this chapter introduces some common obstacles to the management of diversity beginning with a discussion of perception. While this is arguably an organisational behaviour topic, it is essential that HR managers are at least aware of its importance in the current context. They need to understand how perception influences the way people make sense of the world and the key role it plays in influencing workplace behaviour.

Critical note

The 'new' philosophy of diversity management is to build on cultural and other differences rather than to neutralise them (Schneider & Barsoux, 1997). This is based on the premise that drawing on a collective experience should benefit the firm as the forum for problem-solving becomes more open and positively critical.

> **Reflections**
> 1. Visit three local tourism employers and ask whether they have provided diversity management training for their staff. If 'yes' why they chose to implement such a programme.
> 2. Ask these employers what are the benefits and challenges of their initiatives.

CHALLENGES TO DIVERSITY MANAGEMENT

A key function of effective diversity management is to eradicate ethnocentricity. This is when an individual or firm believes their own culture to be superior to that of others and attempts to impose it indiscriminately irrespective of global location (imperialism by any other name?). Whilst this is regrettable it is also understandable as we are all predisposed to behave in ways consistent with our core cultural values. However, adherence to a 'one best' prevailing culture is misplaced and will create stereotyping, discrimination, an undermining of employee confidence, alienation and other negative consequences (including an increased potential for litigation).

Perception and Stereotyping

Wood *et al.* (2006) define perception as:

> the process through which people receive, organize and interpret information from their environment. (p. 62)

The way that individuals understand their environment, those in it and themselves depends on many things and is influenced by values, beliefs and subsequent attitudes. Some of the time, different people will perceive their environment similarly. However, there is much potential for perceiving, screening and making sense of even simple messages in a way that is different between people. In the workplace, Wood *et al.* cluster them into three categories of the perceiver, the setting and the perceived. Whilst the first includes attitudes, values, motives and so on, the actual setting can also have an important impact on messages being conveyed. For example, tangible dimensions such as lighting, heating and physical layout will all have an effect. Critical incidents or characteristics of the perceived will also influence the process of perception such as movement, noise, colour and so on.

Given that perception informs attitudes and attitudes inform behaviour, it is vital that HR managers understand the complexities and nuances of the process. In other words, understanding the way people behave due to the way they perceive their world is key if diversity management is to be managed effectively as, even with the best of intentions, there are a number of possible negative outcomes associated with diversity management.

This may be particularly acute wherever perceptual distortion occurs with managers, employees or both. One example is stereotyping where information is organised into different categories depending on the perceiver's dominant perceptual framework or schema. This is important in a diversity management context as managers may erroneously ascribe attitudes and behaviours to organisational groups based on one particular experience. Demographic categories are the most common units for sweeping generalisations. In an organisational context age, gender, ethnicity and so on are often linked with performance stereotypically with predictable results!

Unconscious Discrimination

Discrimination is at its most insidious when it is unconscious. This is because it tends to be inextricably linked with the very cultural foundation of a society or organisation. There are many instances of minority groups (including women) having to outperform their privileged male counterparts for the same rewards or to be taken 'seriously' by CEOs. There are also cases of women having to adopt male behaviours in order to progress their careers. Often, when minorities actually have successful careers, male colleagues objectify or demonise them as a coping mechanism. For example, the former UK Prime Minister Margaret Thatcher acquired the title 'The Iron Lady' from her male counterparts at the time. Arguably Mrs Thatcher had to acquire her particular *modus operandi* in order to succeed in a male dominated profession, that is, she had to adopt the appropriate attitudes and style (which may also be a stereotype, incidentally!). On the other hand, during a particular sitting of Parliament, one member accused her of being a 'giddy girl' in dealings with the then President of the USA Ronald Reagan! The following extract is taken from Hansard (1986):

> Is it not clear from all the statements the Prime Minister has made that her passionate political infatuation with Reagan is leading her to the misjudgements of a giddy girl? Why is she feeding the paranoia of Gaddafi? (p. 734)

Objectifying someone in this manner has the effect of removing them from reality thus allowing the perpetrator liberty to be abusive, condescending and disrespectful; it also devalues their effort, attitudes and behaviours. Additionally, having a family is commonly perceived as a disadvantage for career women whereas for a male high achiever it a positive attribute (Daft, 2005). The rationale being that a woman's commitment to her employer is less than a man's because she will also be committed to her family. One female colleague's tongue-in-cheek comment to the present author sums up the foregoing adequately:

You know the trouble is women have double standards to live up to.

There is also a phenomenon amongst minority groups known as 'biculturalism'. Essentially, this is when the individual is torn between two cultures; that of the workplace which is predominantly male, white and Anglo-Saxon and that of their minority group. Adopting one set of values and attitudes in order to succeed professionally may cause extreme dissonance and other negative outcomes if it extends over long periods. For example, amongst many international indigenous groups individuals adopting a non-indigenous approach often may become estranged from indigenous community because of the significant differences between the two value systems. Indeed, individualism is seen as exploitation and associated personal wealth conflicts with the cultural value of sharing (Lindsay, 2005; Foley, 2003). This ostracism takes a variety of forms, some more extreme than others, and includes the use of derogatory terms by the racial group such as 'Uncle Tom' (African-American) and 'Coconut' (Indigenous Australian).

Critical note

Moving towards effective diversity management requires first an open and honest acknowledgement that the firm may not be aware of its current position in these terms.

Glass Ceiling

Another significant barrier encountered by minority groups is known as the 'glass ceiling' first coined by the *Wall Street Journal* around twenty years ago. Daft (2005) defines it as: 'An invisible barrier that separates women and minorities from top leadership/management positions' (p. 449). The following articles in Box 8.1 provide an insight into this phenomenon.

BOX 8.1 Case study – Glass ceiling clouds over

Despite decades of feminism and apparent attitudinal change, the evidence clearly shows that women are failing to achieve executive management positions. The research from the Equal Opportunity for Women in the Workplace Agency (EOWA) shows women only represent 10.7% of executive managers in Australia's top companies. EOWA describes women's progress as 'glacial'. Moreover, if that's not enough to deter a young, aspiring female manager, then recent trends may do it.

Female representation at executive level in ASX200 companies has actually declined from 12% in 2006. Even more disheartening is that 45.5% of ASX200 companies have no women executive managers, up from 39.5% in 2006. So why have women gone backwards? Jane Caro, co-author of *The F word: How We Learned to Swear By Feminism*, says it's still tough; in fact, very tough. 'It's a pretty hostile environment for women who've risen to a place in senior management. They've had to fight hard

---

to get there' she says. 'We ask women to carry so much responsibility. Men in senior positions represent only themselves.'

Caro sees slow change starting from a very low base. 'There's never going to be a day when men slap themselves on the forehead and say, "Here, girls, have half my power"' she says. 'It always has to be taken. No one is going to give power away.'

Men's attitudes – EOWA research in 2008, *A Gender in the Boardroom*, studied the boardroom experience of women, and men's attitudes towards them.

The research revealed that there are still big obstacles preventing many women from getting to the top, and once they get there, they are still undervalued and underrated. Several chairmen admitted in interviews that there is a tendency for male-dominated boards to continue appointing men, simply because they feel more comfortable in the company of other men.

Claire Braund, Executive Director of a network for boardroom change, *Women on Boards*, says: 'The report certainly highlights that there are some "dangerous dinosaurs" wielding significant influence in who gets a seat in the boardroom of our top companies. Numerous reports outline the strong business case for diversity and its positive effect on company performance, governance and accountability, yet it continues to be ignored.'

However, it's not just old boy networks that may hold women back. Caro suggests that society has high expectations of women and judges them differently, if not more harshly, than men.

'For women there are only two places to be,' she says. 'There's always a dichotomy of expectations; no in-between. Either a good or bad mother, or a ball-breaking bitch or a self-effacing doormat. Unlike men, women are still not allowed to be just flawed individuals.'

Different career paths – So is it different now for younger women? Caro sees many women struggling. She suggests that the concept that there are no barriers – long taught in same-sex schools – does women no favours in the workforce. 'They get an absolute shock in their first management position when they speak in management meetings and realise nobody can hear their voice,' she says.

It appears also today that many women are shifting the context in which they can have a career. Braund says the number of small businesses being started by women in Asia is phenomenal. 'For so many women, the only way they can combine children and a career is to become a successful consultant,' she says.

With no legislated paid parental leave, and a shortage of childcare places, the resulting pace of change for women may be slow. Braund is disappointed that it still has to be like this. 'We are so far behind other countries that it's alarming,' she says, 'When women hit 30 or so, societal norms force them to make a choice, while at the same time pretending to give them access to greater choice. How many women do you know that have a major career and five children?'

Caro suggests that two current strands of thinking around feminism hold women back. 'The first says that you are fully equal. You want career and lifestyle. Make it work.' She says this doesn't take into account that men don't bear the children, and don't do their share of housework.

The second strand is that feminism is a totally flawed experiment. 'Women would have been much better at home. We shouldn't have put such ideas in their heads.' However, Braund says there's a different way of thinking about raising families. 'We still have a perception that you must take time off from your career to have a baby and raise a family, rather than embracing the change that this brings.' Braund suggests that a paradigm shift of thinking is needed along lines seen in Norway, where the government encourages raising children, as part of both men and women's life's work. Norway has heavily subsidised child care and introduced an obligatory six weeks non-transferable parental leave for fathers. These may be two reasons why Norway's labour force participation for women and birth rate are among the highest in Europe.

Given current events, what will a global recession look like for women in management? Braund sees some positives emerging out of the gloom; including the growing recognition that companies who work hard to improve diversity at all management levels will have a better bottom line than more traditional organisations. 'Perhaps the economic crash is a wake-up call that we can no longer continue to fix the problem with the same thinking that created it,' she says.

Questions
1. Discuss the idea that 'enlightened' or progressive diversity management as a policy is essential for all tourism organisations.
2. What impact does government policy have on the existence of the 'glass ceiling'.
3. What organisational factors contribute to the apparent paucity of women in top management jobs in the tourism industry.

Source: Brown (2009)

The second feature in Box 8.2 continues by suggesting some pragmatic tactics for dealing with the challenge in the short term. First, it acknowledges the long held observation that in order for women to be successful in organisations, they must outperform their male counterparts. It also advises women to observe whether the senior management team and board of directors have ethnic minority representation. If not, the pragmatists should opt to quit and find alternative employment. On the other hand where this is not an option, the individual should take advantage of their legal protection under the appropriate national legislation.

BOX 8.2 Case study – The Glass Ceiling for African, Hispanic (Latino) and Asian Americans

The 'glass ceiling' refers to the barriers that often confront Ethnic Americans and women in trying to reach the upper echelons of corporate America. According to a 1995 study commissioned by the Federal Glass Ceiling Commission, 97% of the senior managers of the Fortune 1000 Industrial and Fortune 500 are white, and 95–97% are male. This is occurring while 57% of the workforce is either Ethnic minorities, women, or both. The study also found that African, Hispanic (Latino) and Asian Americans do not earn the same pay for comparable positions, African Americans earning an astounding 21% less than their white counterparts in the same job.

Question

1. What range of option might be open to minority groups who find themselves discriminated against in the workplace?

Source: Tong (2009)

Older Workers

As discussed in the early part of this chapter, demographic changes in the developed world are altering the profile of the general working population. Some refer to this as a gradual 'greying' of the workforce and it is a composite of declining fertility rates, ageing baby boomers and that post retirement-aged people are staying in the workforce is for longer. Reasons cited include the fact that:

- many jobs are no longer in heavy industry, so people have a longer working life;
- repayment of unpaid mortgages; plus
- there is a shortage of younger skilled people to fill employment vacancies.

The situation is little different in the developed world globally. Given the recent economic crisis, employers will have to decide whether they can afford often high earning baby boomers and post retirees embracing the depth of knowledge and reliability they are alleged to possess. The latter is the more likely option given the shortfall of skilled younger people in the workforce. It is also the case that several generations will need to work together. Nelson and Quick (2009) refer to this as the 'job crunch' and predict that the management of such a generationally diverse workgroup will be challenging given their differences in values and attitudes. For example, those born between 1930–1945 (the Silents) will have starkly different attitudes to those born after 1982 (Generation Y-ers). Indeed, the two intermediate categories of Baby Boomers (1946–1964) and Generation X-ers (1965–1976) will also share dissimilar value sets. While the evidence for 'real' differences between the generations is rather patchy (apart from the two extreme categories) HR managers would be foolhardy to treat workers from each generation in the same manner. Shared significant events create markers or 'perspective shapers' through which the world is viewed and decisions are made. For example, baby boomers were influenced by TV, Rock 'n' Roll music, the threat of nuclear war and so on. Influences on generation X include the introduction of the personal computer, AIDs and the downsizing of companies. Similarly for generation Y, significant events such as the advent of the internet, globalisation and the political polarisation of global regions and so on have had a similar effect.

Given the above differences it is almost inevitable that stereotypes and myths abound for each category, especially for older workers. For example, there is a commonly held idea that older workers tend to be 'set in their ways' and resistant to change. Accordingly, they may be less likely to adopt new ways of working. Moreover, they are also accused of being physically and mentally less capable of high performance and creativity in the workplace. However, after reviewing the evidence, Dessler *et al.* (2004) conclude that there is no reason to believe the commonly held belief that older workers are less productive than their younger counterparts when compared along eight criteria shown in Table 8.2. Each one has evidence to support the notion that older workers actually outperform younger ones.

Table 8.2 Eight criteria of effectiveness

1. Adapting to change	**6.** Job turnover
2. Quality of work	**7.** Training and recruitment costs
3. Possessing 'corporate memory'	**8.** Absenteeism
4. Effective matching of employees to customers	**9.** Loyalty to the employer
5. Costs of employment	**10.** Work ethic

Adapted from: Dessler *et al.* (2004: 473–474)

Tourism managers would do well to heed the above by striving to motivate and empower older workers. Ultimately, they will have no choice due to the demographic situation.

Critical note
Discrimination is at its most insidious when it is unconscious. This is because it tends to be inextricably linked with the very cultural foundation of a society or organisation.

> **Reflections**
> 1. Through desk research, identify two major tourism corporations.
> 2. Identify the types and proportions of minority groups represented in their work-force.
> 3. Do similar, by interview, for two local tourism and hospitality employers.
> 4. Compare and contrast your results.

Disability

According to the ICF (2007) disability is a classification of health and health-related domains. These domains are classified from body, individual and societal perspectives by means of two lists: a list of body functions and structure, and a list of domains of activity and participation (http://www.who.int/classifications/icf/en/, accessed April 2009). As a global standard it is a useful and comprehensive benchmark and helps us to understand that disability pertains to categories of aural, visual, mental, allergy, disabling disease, cardiac disease, loss of limbs, psychic and physical. Most common of these are sight and hearing impairment, mobility limitation and emotional and mental disorders. Often, these conditions may limit or erect barriers to achieving job outcomes that would otherwise be the case. However, there is evidence to suggest that these individuals are equally capable as others in particular job types and in hospitality jobs, turnover amongst the group is likely to be lower than people without impairment.

Unfortunately, stereotypical views of this group have evolved and represent a barrier to them obtaining jobs (Mondy, 2008). Once again, HR managers should consider both their own attitudes toward disabled workers and those of potential co-workers as often they are treated with suspicion or patronised. As with all good leadership, managers should lead by example and at least comply with the legislation surrounding disabled workers. There are many stereotypes surrounding disabled individuals but equally there have been several attempts to dispel them. For example, a recent survey by Harris (2008) showed that 90% of firms employing disabled persons are satisfied with their per-formance. Some tourism and hospitality corporations are already actively recruiting dis-abled workers. For example, InterContinental Hotels recently achieved the 2007 RADAR People of the Year Human Rights Award for its success and is currently developing its in house Disability Confidence in Employment scheme so that its employment strategies bestow equal opportunities for all employees (Anon, 2008).

Below is a guide created by the European Leonardo da Vinci programme (Happy Tourist) pitched at tourism employers to encourage them to recruit disabled persons. Its premise is that disabled workers are best placed to anticipate and satisfy the needs of disabled tourists and it shows the benefits that making the first step towards such integration can offer. However, we would argue that this focus is too narrow because disabled employees are more than able to undertake work in particular occupations and are equally effective and efficient in these roles.

BOX 8.3 Excerpt from the Leonardo da Vinci 'Happy Tourist' programme

- 80% of people employing or working with disabled workers think that they are as productive as any other employee;
- Hilton UK & Ireland, which employs more than 15,000 people in 77 hotels in the region, has signed a contract with the Shaw Trust charity to offer thousands of people with disabilities easy access to its job vacancies;
- 82% of the employees working with disabled people, think they are as outstanding as any other colleague;
- In 2007, 37% of the hotels ACCOR employed 6% of disabled people among their staff, and 65% of these disabled workers were working in the group for more than 5 years;
- A management/workforce agreement has been concluded at Disneyland Paris which integrates people with disabilities. Emphasis is placed on the disabled worker's skills and not their disability. Their services are so appreciated that the hotel managers are very willing to take on more;
- 80% of people employing and working with disabled people, say that adjustments made for disabled employees can be beneficial for other people: other employees and disabled customers;
- 77% of the people employing or working with disabled workers don't notice additional workload;
- The hotel 'In Out', in the town of Vallvidriera (Barcelona), is the first establishment in Spain and Europe almost totally managed by disabled workers – 90% of the staff. Many guests from every part of the world come to stay there and are made very welcome;
- 88% of people working with a disabled colleague say that this experience is enriching, likely to modify their opinion of disabled people and to give a new sense of value to their job (60%);
- 91% of people interviewed say they would be ready to help a disabled recently recruited colleague, either in his/her job and daily tasks, or to integrate with the team;
- Aer Rianta, encourages employment of people with disabilities in all its departments. This private Irish airline has 1200 employees, 2.6% have a disability. With the help of social partners, it has developed a special programme, taking action on a number of fronts: employment, customers services and awareness-raising; and

> - 75% of people working with a disabled colleague think that the recruitment of disabled workers in their firm gives a positive image and influences them favourably in the perception of their employer.

Source: http://www.tourismforall.org.uk/10-good-reasons.html (accessed April 2009)

Additionally, many employment agencies and schemes are designed with the aim of encouraging firms to increase their recruitment of disabled people. Some examples include:

- 'Access to work' (UK). The aim of this is to overcome any additional problems associated with employing a disabled person.
- 'Hire Disability Solutions' (USA) employment facilitation service.
- '121' employment advice service for employers and job seekers (Disability Services Australia).
- A dedicated agency to improve and expand inclusive employment opportunities and services for all people with disability (The Association for Supported Employment in New Zealand).

SUMMARY

Diversity management is understood as a process of actively recruiting, retaining and facilitating working relationships among individuals from a variety of backgrounds. The related discourse now considers six key elements important. Known as the 'big 6', gender, age, ethnicity, religion, disability and sexual orientation are currently enshrined in much diversity-oriented legislation. However, these factors alone fail to capture the nature of modern diversity management in the workplace. Human resource managers need to go beyond simple compliance to a situation where diversity is inherent in the organisational culture. This is where the firm is predisposed toward diversity, is proactive and equally supportive of all individuals regardless of minority group. The key here is that modern approaches do not seek to integrate a heterogeneous collection of employees into a dominant culture but rather allow individuals to be themselves.

Many Western nations have an ageing population projected to continue due to low levels of fertility and increased life expectancy. Additionally, evidence suggests that immigrants are now arriving from a much broader spread of destinations compared to earlier movements. The workforce is therefore more heterogeneous, diverse and multicultural than at any other time. It is therefore imperative that appropriate diversity management strategies are planned and implemented by those managers charged with such a responsible task. Managers need to know whether there will be enough potential tourism employees with appropriate skills to satisfy the demand across a number of roles and positions.

Disconcertingly, comprehensive strategic diversity management activity is lacking across industry, particularly the private sector. Tourism is no different and some would describe existing initiatives as reactive and designed to merely comply with legislation. Interestingly, this sector has always maintained a diverse and multicultural workforce due to the nature of employment and characteristics of the industry. Thus, minority group representation is more likely to be thought of as the norm rather than the exception. However, this is not a result of proactive strategic diversity management thinking but rather a response to demand and supply.

So what is the actual value of diversity management to tourism firms? Naysayers regard it as something to be controlled and, through a management lens, the more optimistic see it as a means of establishing competitive advantage. Benefits include higher staff morale, more favourable image as an employer, increased rates of retention and the potential for greater innovation, creativity and flexibility given the broader and deeper collective wealth of employee knowledge.

Whilst there is no doubt that diversity management is morally and ethically the 'right thing to do' in organisations, the outcomes, particularly for individual workers, are not easy to identify because many are intangible and therefore difficult to measure. It is also the case that if diversity management practice is bungled the outcomes are likely to be worse than having done nothing at all (notwithstanding the need for legal compliance).

As with most organisational initiatives, diversity management is fraught with difficulties and an essential element of any is how to deal with unexpected outcomes and negative impacts. Despite the best of intent, one of the most frequent in this area is stereotyping and often manifests itself as ethnocentricity (which gives rise to further discrimination) and will cause employees to be unconfident and alienated. Discrimination will not always be overt but rather, unconscious because it is inextricably linked with the very cultural foundation of a society or organisation. Where climates of this nature exist we would argue that the whole organisation loses but more immediately minority groups based on gender, race, ethnicity, age and disability experience difficulties.

A common gendered form of discrimination is often referred to as the glass ceiling where opportunities for career advancement for women are not forthcoming despite legislation. A racial and ethnic outcome of discrimination is biculturalism where the worker grapples with competing cultures of their employing organisation and traditional background. Another group who commonly experience discrimination in the workplace is the older worker. Individuals are often held to be resistant to change and less capable than their younger counterparts. This is an increasingly important issue given demographic trends as tourism firms will have little option but to employ more aged individuals and even those who are past retirement age. This will have serious implications on existing HR policies and procedure. Employers will need to think creatively about such initiatives. An additional outcome of demography is job crunch whereby more than one generation of individuals works together in the same firm. It will be no easy task to manage such a heterogeneous intergenerational group effectively given their well-documented value and attitudinal differences. Finally, disabled workers arguably remain amongst the most stigmatised group in the organisation. Similar to older workers, many associated myths have emerged about what they can and cannot accomplish in the workplace. Like the former group, most individuals with impairment are perfectly able to perform adequately in their jobs. Indeed some tourism and hospitality firms are beginning to actively encourage and recruit them.

Critical note
Forecasting involves identifying a demand for the tourism product and then deciding how many workers are required to deliver the product.

CHAPTER QUESTIONS

1. Identify the key elements of diversity awareness programmes.

2. Identify some important differences between modern diversity management initiatives compared with earlier more 'traditional' approaches. Discuss how these changes would impact on practice in tourism firms.

3. Several tourism firms employ diversity management initiatives merely to comply with associated legislation. Comment why this is currently the case.

RECOMMENDED READING

Devine, F., Baum, T., Hearns, N. and Devine, A. (2007) Managing cultural diversity: Opportunities and challenges for Northern Ireland Hoteliers. *International Journal of Contemporary Hospitality Management* 19(2), 120–132.
> A discussion of the benefits and challenges of working immigrants in the hotel industry.

Foley, D. (2003) An examination of Indigenous Australian Entrepreneurs. *Journal of Developmental Entrepreneurship* 8, 133–152.
> A discussion of indigenous culture and other characteristics and their impact on entrepreneurship.

Hofstede, G. (2001) *Cultural Consequences: Comparing Values, Behaviors, Institutions and Organizations Across Nations* (2nd edn). London: Sage Publications.
> Classic text discussing the author's national cultural dimensions.

Mapunda, G. (2005) Traditional societies and entrepreneurship: an analysis of Australian and Tanzanian Businesses. *Journal of Asia Entrepreneurship and Sustainability* 1(2), 1–23.
A comparative discussion of indigenous societies and entrepreneurship.

Walenta, C. (2008) Diversity management discourse meets queer theory. *Gender in Management: An International Journal* 23(6), 382–394.
A theoretical review of diversity management from alternative perspectives.

RECOMMENDED WEBSITES

International classification of disability and health –
http://www.who.int/classifications/icf/site/onlinebrowser/icf.cfm

Diversity management –
http://www.diversityworking.com/employerZone/diversityManagement/

International demographic trends – http://gsociology.icaap.org/report/demsum.html

Hospitality workforce and disability –
http://www.disabilityworks.org/default.asp?contentID=88

The 'glass ceiling' – http://feminism.eserver.org/the-glass-ceiling.txt

CHAPTER 9

TO BE OR NOT TO BE? HUMAN RESOURCE MANAGEMENT AND THE ROLE OF ETHICS

LEARNING OBJECTIVES

After working through this chapter you should be able to:

1. Define ethics.

2. Understand the nature of business ethics.

3. Identify key ethical developments in a business context.

4. Discuss important ethical issues in the tourism and hospitality industry.

5. Understand the impact of ethics upon the role of human resources in tourism firms.

INTRODUCTION

Essentially, ethics concerns values and associated derivatives culminating in a decision whether to engage in one course of action (behaviour) or another. Mondy (2008) defines ethics as:

> [...] dealing with what is good and bad, or right and wrong, or with moral duty and obligation. (p. 30)

And those engaged in the process:

> [...] anyone who thinks about what he or she ought to do is, consciously or un-consciously, involved in ethics. (Dessler *et al.*, 2004: 45)

Obligations range from the personal and business to those which are societal and global in nature. We make ethical decisions regularly, relying on personal values which have been learned and shaped by upbringing, culture, religion and the overriding ethical climate. In many cases our behaviour is not difficult to justify because the decision seems obvious amongst an array of competing alternatives, such as a broken promise for a dinner date or other social occasions. Similarly, the decision not to install solar panels or drive a small environmentally-friendly car may not be too difficult. Of course this depends how passionately one believes that carbon emissions are damaging the environment, whether your action makes a significant contribution to environmental well-being, whether you are in a financial position to alter your habits, the pressure exerted by your peer group and so on. On the other hand, decisions having the potential to impact on a grand scale on various groups or individuals may be difficult to make requiring reflection and guidance.

Western leaders believed that invading Iraq in the early part of the 21st century was the appropriate course of action; no doubt many Iraqis felt differently. Since then, former US President Bush, UK and Australian Prime Ministers Tony Blair and John Howard have been accused of duping the public to engender support for the act. Indeed, this begs the question of whether the alliance of the 'willing' would have been so keen if Iraq had not been so mineral rich? Both issues of invading other sovereign states and the use of dubious premises for justification are keenly ethical issues; in principle, all organisations function similarly.

Complex value-laden business (and personal) situations requiring judgement are often referred to as ethical dilemmas because there is always more than one option. In a simple sense, the ethical decision is considered the 'right thing to do'. The complicating matter is for whom is it the right thing to do? This assumes too that it is possible for people to know rationally what this means (Trezise, 1996).

This chapter begins by discussing some generic observed ethical issues and developments in the business community. It continues by adopting a tourism and hospitality focus and highlights some of the main ethical dilemmas therein. Some theoretical approaches to moral development and ethics are then introduced. Human resources (HR) and its ethical role in organisations is outlined together with a focus on codes of ethics/conduct and whistleblowing.

Reflections
1. Consider a topic about which you have a strong ethical opinion.
2. Reflect on why you have this particular view; is it to do with your culture, upbringing or some other influence?
3. Why do you believe your opinion is 'right'?

ORGANISATIONS

Organisations must act in an ethical manner at all times. If they fail, losses in public confidence will result and all stakeholders will suffer. In part, general ethical standards are set by the national culture (which we will return to later in the chapter). A role here is played by people in the public eye, that is, those who are deemed role models for the rest of us. Sports personalities would be an obvious example as their actions influence, to an extent, younger members of society. Unfortunately the behavioural modelling is far from ideal. Perennially, rugby footballers and others come to blows on the field and some are accused of off the field sexual transgressions. This may well perpetuate a culture of violence and disrespect of others (women) in Western society. The unethical behaviour is compounded by newsreaders and commentators minimising incidents. For example in Australia, extreme violence during a match is often referred to as 'a bit of biffo' when in fact these episodes would almost certainly lead to criminal prosecution off the field.

Where unethical behaviour crosses over into illegality, the long-term outcomes are inevitable. One only has to review the popular media to witness disasters or embarrassments experienced by former 'great and good' companies including Enron, HIH, One.Tel, Hewlett-Packard, Australian Wheat Board, and the 'Chinese Milk Product Scandal'; the list goes on and on. Indeed, some commentators are now blaming impoverished ethics for the global economic crisis of 2009 including US President Obama who recently announced sweeping reforms of the US financial regulatory system to prevent similar crises in the future (*Radio National News, Australia*, June, 2009). Unfortunately, if organisations accrue short-term benefits by engaging in unethical behaviour the practice continues and establishes a self-supporting framework. Within such systems, justification of this behaviour becomes relatively easy. This is particularly the case if executives and managers are under pressure to achieve more with less, that is, to improve productivity with ever diminishing resources. Indeed, as early as 1996, Winstanley *et al.* (1996) conclude that business and industry trends give rise for concern from an ethical standpoint. The situation does not appear to have improved since the mid 1990s and some would argue it has become notably worse. Winstanley *et al.* (1996) comment on the main contingencies and they are summarized in Table 9.1.

Table 9.1 Issues of ethical concern

Concern	*Ethical questions*
Increased job insecurity and risk through macroeconomic changes.	Should employees have to accept an increased burden of risk because it suits the employer who is often well-resourced?
Downsizing and increasing use of contingent workers and associated reward systems.	To what extent should employers insist on upholding their own employment standards over those of suppliers and other sub-contractors? Should sound HR practice be upheld for only non-contingent workers?

Increased pressure to reduce lead times when responding to the marketplace.	What 'shortcuts' are possible? How can rules be 'massaged'? How do these impact on employee participation in decisions?

Winstanley *et al.* (1996) also note an increase of management control through use of recruitment and selection techniques like psychometric testing and the practice of inculcating cultural conformity amongst workers. It is argued that the former may be construed as an unwelcome invasion of employee privacy. The latter is criticised due to its manipulative undertones through a seemingly benign process of affecting cultural change through 'empowerment' and other initiatives. The real concern here is the tacit acceptance of diminishing employee autonomy. This is achieved through a series of contingencies which are designed to align the motivations and aspirations of the workforce with that of the employer.

Some argue that these new and 'enlightened' developments are more damaging to employees than an old fashioned autocratic employment relationship. This is because employees are actually taking part in their own downfall. Of course by the time they realise this, their position has become so impoverished there is little that can be done to address the power imbalance. A linked development is the singular focus of companies of increased productivity at all costs. Whilst improvements have undeniable benefits for the employer, workers are commonly expected to toil 'flexibly' over longer hours and over contractual obligation. Overall, Winstanley *et al.* (1996) argue that these developments illustrate a seeming decline in management integrity. That is, employees are constantly urged or manipulated to unify with organisational objectives whilst their employment rights and job security are being systematically undermined.

Critical note
In a simple sense, the ethical decision is considered the 'right thing to do'. The complicating matter is for whom is it the right thing to do?

Reflections
1. Identify three topical business or political ethical issues.
2. Comment on the positions adopted by politicians, business people and others

Tourism

Like other business sectors, tourism and hospitality has its share of dilemmas not least of which concern 'planning' particularly in areas new to the industry. When does it become acceptable to encourage visitation of a pristine area of natural undisturbed beauty? Many planners and tourism operators justify this on economic grounds; many others argue otherwise. Whilst it is true that most developed nations are now moving toward compromise between economic development and sustainability, there remain conundrums and ethical matters which remain controversial.

Undoubtedly, tourism development has positive as well as negative impacts and the planner's job is to make sure that the latter are kept to a minimum or within what is understood to be an acceptable level through consultation and adherence to associated legislation. 'Acceptability' is of course subjective with a host society's perspective likely to be different to a tourism planner, construction company, equipment supplier, transport provider, local government and so on. For example, tourism development can improve a region's infrastructure, provide employment and facilities for hosts as well as tourists. On the other hand, temporary increases in population may cause existing systems to fail due to increased demand for utilities and other products and services. Moreover, business activity is likely to inflate the cost of living and real estate in the region. Locals not yet on the property ladder may have to look elsewhere for their first home particularly if they are working in relatively poorly paid sectors. In the long term there may be a net outward migration leaving an older host society. Less tangible impacts may also occur including open and subtle hostility by locals toward tourists. Indeed, these impacts do not necessarily occur exclusively in developing nations. For example in the 1970s, a number of vacation homes were destroyed in a Welsh village (UK) by extremists as a direct result of the inflationary impacts tourism was having in the region!

Fennell (2006) describes the above considerations as 'associated costs [. . .] [in terms of] socio-cultural, economic and ecological impacts' (p. 1) and there have been various contributors to the discourse each emphasising ethical considerations through benefits and impacts of tourism on destinations, host societies and tourists themselves. More recent concerns are framed in the 'sustainable tourism' paradigm which is rooted in the earlier 'alternative tourism' perspective. Essentially, each has explicit ethical guidelines which may be understood as codes of conduct to discern what is basically 'good' and 'bad' from an ethical standpoint or in the words of Fennell (2006) 'designed to ameliorate the various dysfunctions that characterize the industry' (p. 7). What may be concluded from these approaches is first, that all have challenges and weaknesses; second, they need to account for contextual contingencies necessary to reflect new moralities emerging at a societal level (ethics is a moveable feast!) and third, identification of negative impacts is only part of the ethical dilemma; the other is following through with plans to address them comprehensively satisfying all stakeholders. Fennell (2006) concludes that tourism ethics in a substantive and meaningful sense is a 'much under researched area' (p. 12). Nonetheless, a number of tourism initiatives exist with inherent ethical responsibilities. Many of these are driven by government departments and non-governmental organisations including the UK's Department for Culture, Media and Sport; the European Europarc Federation; and the USA's Office of Travel and Tourism Industries.

Similarly, in Australia Sustainable Tourism Cooperative Research Centres (STCRC) were established with the objective of:

> [...] delivering innovation to destinations, businesses, communities and governments; ultimately enhancing the environmental, economic and social sustainability of tourism in Australia. (http://www.crctourism.com.au/Page/About+Us/Who+we+are.aspx)

It is clear that the suggested ethical considerations above include obligations to individuals, other organisations, government and society in general. A more targeted ethical base is encompassed in the STCRC aim below. In 2003 a strategy for research was agreed and projects commissioned in three general areas of Sustainable Enterprises, Sustainable Destinations and Sustainable Resource Management. The following aim for enterprises is:

> [Sustainable Enterprises] [...] recognises that a sustainable tourism industry is ultimately dependent upon decisions and strategies developed at enterprise level [...] Enterprises that adhere to sustainable best practices, innovate, and harness the latest technologies will be more likely to prosper. In order to enhance enterprise sustainability, benchmarking, risk, evaluation, planning, and management tools will be developed. (*CRC for Sustainable Tourism – Commonwealth Agreement*, 2003: 74)

Globally, the relatively recent adoption of the International Labour Organization's (ILO) 'decent work' initiative by the United Nations World Tourism Organization (UNWTO) is an example of a systemic framework based on the ethically charged notion of social justice (see later in this chapter). A central aim of the initiative is poverty reduction and equitable sustainable development in partnership with key national and international stakeholders. In short, the ILO strives to imbue dignity and self-respect amongst the global workforce through providing worthwhile employment opportunities, job security and ultimately better standards of living. As a multilateral agency, the ILO does this by formulating global labour standards through various conventions and recommendations which establish minimum standards of basic labour rights. Specifically, the decent work initiative promotes rights at work, nurtures opportunities for decent employment and promotes dialogue around the enhancement of social protection and work-related issues. It is hoped that the UNWTO/ILO agenda offers a basis for an equitable, stable and ethically robust framework for the development of global tourism employment.

As an industry, tourism faces a number of challenges. It has already been described as heterogeneous providing a variety of poorly paid jobs and inconsistent career opportunities. Many employers remain relatively undereducated, there are low barriers to entry and a substantial element of employment exists in the black or grey economy. Furthermore, skilled labour supply shortages are common. These conditions may at worst conspire against the ultimate success of the decent work initiative and at best create obstacles which will need to be managed carefully. Arguably the greatest impediment is the current societal perspective of the tourism industry as an employer and its subsequent management of workers. Tourism jobs are still commonly viewed as short-term, 'not career', poorly paid and so on. Furthermore, many employment relationships are alleged to be adversarial and exploitative.

Critical note

Undoubtedly, tourism development has positive as well as negative impacts and the planner's job is to make sure that the latter are kept to a minimum or within what is understood to be an acceptable level through consultation and adherence to associated legislation.

Reflections

1. Consider a topical tourism development plan or project.
2. Comment on the likely positive and negative outcomes.

Business ethics and dilemmas in tourism and hospitality

Business ethics focuses on the role and position of firms at the enterprise level in a societal context. In other words it attempts to address the issue of corporate social responsibility. Understandably this is a complex area. On one hand some believe that ethics and business have irreconcilable differences and the two should be separate and distinct from each other; on the other, organisations have an ethical obligation to engage with, benefit and contribute positively to the community. The latter view is becoming more popular and can be seen in mission statements of many companies. Dessler *et al.* (2004) call this a values driven approach to ethics and advocate its advantages over reactive and *ad hoc* responses. Using visions and mission statements as indicators and fuzzy foci for ethical HR practices is consistent with a strategy of ethics which is important if the firm wishes to create a culture of ethical practice. A review of such indicates areas where firms place ethical emphasis. Anita Roddick's Body Shop corporation arguably has a most society-friendly mission and it is shown below in Figure 9.1.

This perspective is not new and industrial luminaries such as Henry Ford (20th century) and the Cadbury brothers (19th century) were aware of their ethical social obligations demonstrated through various acts of philanthropy and other initiatives. A

> - *Our Reason for Being:*
>   To dedicate our business to the pursuit of social and environmental change.
> - To creatively balance the financial and human needs of our stakeholders: employees, customers, franchisees, suppliers and shareholders.
> - To courageously ensure that our business is ecologically sustainable, meeting the needs of the present without compromising the future.
> - To meaningfully contribute to local, national and international communities in which we trade, by adopting a code of conduct which ensures care, honesty, fairness and respect.
> - To passionately campaign for the protection of the environment and human and civil rights, and against animal testing within the cosmetics and toiletries industry.
> - To tirelessly work to narrow the gap between principle and practice, while making fun, passion and care part of our daily lives.

Figure 9.1 The Body Shop mission statement

Source: http://ergo.human.cornell.edu/Ecotecture/Case%20Studies/Body%20Shop/Body%20 Shop_home.html. Accessed June 2009

selection of mission statements from tourism and hospitality organisations appears below beginning with the Marriott Hotels Corporation:

> Our commitment is that every guest leaves satisfied.
> (http://wiki.answers.com/Q/What_is_the_Marriott_hotel_mission_statement)

Shangri-La Hotels:

> To delight customers each and every time.
> (http://www.wotif.com/hotels/shangri-la-hotel-sydney.html)

Singapore Airlines:

> Singapore Airlines is a global company dedicated to providing air transportation services of the highest quality and to maximising returns for the benefit of its share-holders and employees.
> (http://www.singaporeair.com/saa/en_UK/content/company_info/siastory/ index.jsp)

Interestingly it is only the last mission that specifies employees. In one sense this is understandable because the focus of hospitality services in particular is the customer. Without further investigation it is difficult to ascertain the ethical position of either Marriott or Shangri-La relative to its workers. However, other scientific and anecdotal information rather supports the case for the prosecution!

Whilst it is dangerous to generalise about anything in such a diverse national and cultural sector, Baum (2006: 111) refers to some perennial dilemmas rooted in ethical decision-making:

- A significant characteristic of the tourism industry is the existence of a sizeable black (sometimes referred to as the grey) economy. It is defined in various ways but in essence is the practice of paying an employee a wage which is undeclared by both parties to avoid paying taxes and other issues of 'red tape'. The practice is both illegal and unethical and whilst difficult to be precise, accounts for approximately half of all tourism employment (Lucas, 2004). Convenience is a surmised reason for engagement in the practice but it also affords no legal protection or employment rights to employees.

- Operationally, there is a requirement for the delivery of high quality service through staff trained to provide it. However, training is expensive and the nature of the workforce is transient with the sector as a whole experiencing high levels of labour turnover. Why should employers invest in costly training when the trainee is likely to leave and become employed elsewhere? Thus the employer does not receive the benefits of training, rather, another organisation does. Besides, the more skilled an employee becomes, the more they might be headhunted by others.

- Working conditions are continually documented as poor across the tourism industry (see Chapter 1) with some attempt made at 'gilding the lily' by employers through offering uniforms, accommodation, subsidised meals and so on. Baum (2006) concludes that such conditions will not be tolerated by future employees. As such the current model of human resource management is not sustainable and employee demands may bring about more ethical treatment of workers. However given the characteristics of the industry, we do not share Baum's (2006) optimism. The 'deregulation model' whereby firms improve conditions to attract and retain the best staff and thus remain competitive seems a long way off. Indeed, Baum (2006) laments the fact that tourism firms commonly over use part-time and casual workers where legislation is not strict and also fail to pay overtime rates (p. 127).

Dessler *et al.* (2004) cite Lowry (2001) and her study of casual workers' perceptions of unfairness and injustices in the workplace. The research is particularly appropriate here given the prevalence of employment practices in the tourism and hospitality industry. In short, workers thought that issues of equity, work scheduling and rewards were unfair and discriminated against them. For example, core staff received better pay and opportunities for promotion and training. Casuals were treated as a just-in-time resource and expected to be 'on-call' at any time. Casual workers also complained that they received no or little feedback of any kind, no training and lack of job security.

Another complicating factor is that the tourism industry is dominated by small businesses, many of whom do not have HR specialists; this role is occupied by the owner/manager. In this situation, pressure for organisational performance is paramount and linked strongly to financial markers rather than through a softer approach to HR and its purported consideration of employees' well-being. Much employment is part-time, temporary/casual and this context has a number of ethical challenges. The major one is the power imbalance between employers and workers and how the latter can be dismissed at the discretion of the former. Here, we have a situation where termination is legal but potentially unethical. Furthermore, consistent levels of low pay raise ethical questions (depending on which side of the political 'poverty line' ceiling one ascribes to) not only in terms of the absolute sum but also upon the reliance of customers to subsidise tourism work through tipping. Is it acceptable to expect front-line workers to 'perform' at the customer interface because they receive so little in their pay packet? Baum (2006) notes that this is no more than 'pandering to customers in a way which may be considered demeaning or humiliating' (p. 121). Furthermore, is it reasonable to pressurise customers into tipping 'good' performance? The industry would answer 'yes' because it is a long established tradition. One could also say the same about slavery and children working as Chimney Sweeps prior to the abolition of both!

Other evidence justifies our concern suggesting that ethics is not an issue high on the agenda at either an enterprise or corporate level. For example, Upchurch's (1998) study of 1500 US hotels found that ethical decisions made by managers were mainly based on self-interest. Decisions on this basis are much argued against by the social reformists for being anachronistic. Deregulation of work does not stop exploitation of employees particularly if they have temporary and casual jobs and little union representation Jones et al.'s (2006) more recent study of corporate social responsibility (CSR) amongst the UK's top ten public house operators found wide variation between them. Nonetheless, most did not integrate CSR ethics into the workplace. They advocate the adoption of CSR for tourism firms. They cite the World Bank's (2004) definition and it is appropriate here:

> The commitment of business to contribute to sustainable economic development working with employees, their families, the local community and society at large to improve the quality of life in ways that are good for business and good for development. (p. 330)

A strategy of CSR considers both internal and external ethical responsibilities. These include an external focus on investors, human rights and other stakeholder concerns. Internally this would provide a strategic ethical backdrop for HR managers accounting for areas identified by Upchurch (1998) as:

- sexual harassment;
- empowerment;
- equal opportunities;
- departmental relations; and
- a balance of organisational and personal values.

The benefits of this approach are alleged to range from better financial performance and reduced operating costs to long term sustainability for organisations and their employees. Naysayers argue that CSR is based on a false premise and an unrealistic perspective of issues and events.

Critical note

Using visions and mission statements as foci for ethical HR practices is consistent with a strategy of ethics which is important if the firm wishes to create a culture of ethical practice.

Reflections

1. Identify two local tourism companies and interview their managers of human resource managers.
2. Ask how ethics impacts on their human resource-related decision-making.

MAKING THE RIGHT DECISION

Ethical dilemmas concern the needs of the individual compared with those of the organisation and other stakeholders. Currently, the issue of closed circuit television monitors in public areas is a matter of ethical debate. The reasoning behind increased use of such surveillance is to combat crimes such as theft, violence, public disturbance and so on. Civil libertarians argue that such measures are a violation of a basic human right to privacy. Ethical debates of this nature are often complex as many options and choices are available.

According to Winstanley *et al.* (1996) rights and obligations are not self-evident truths but issues open for debate. Barrett (1999) agrees noting that people differ in their perceptions of 'justice' and what the benefits of a particular course of action might be. According to Härtel *et al.* (2007), ethical behaviour is rooted in culture and religious beliefs which can be categorised as moral development; the overriding ethical climate and national culture. Daft (2005) uses Kohlberg's (1976) three-stage model to explain moral development viewed as an important antecedent of ethical behaviour. The first is known as 'preconventional' where the person follows rules to avoid punishment and is egocentric acting in their own interest. Furthermore, they are likely to be autocratic and use their organisational role to advance their career often to the detriment of others. The second or 'conventional' stage is where living up to the expectations of others such as family and friends is paramount. So too is upholding the law and satisfying duties and obligations of the social system even if it engages in unethical or illegal behaviour. Most people's morals tend to fit into this category. The final stage is known as the 'postconventional' level where behaviour is determined by an independent and internal set of universal principles. Behaviour may at times qualify as illegal. This point is important because at times ethical and legal behaviour coincide but on other occasions they can be disparate. For example, a worker could decide to take strike action to support a colleague or cause which may go against a particular legal act. Conversely, a resort manager may provide live-in accommodation for workers so they can have access to a convenient supply of labour in the event of unforseen demand increases.

Whilst there will be differences in moral development between individuals chief executive officers (CEOs), managers and the human resources department should ideally be positioned toward the highest of the three levels of Kohlberg's (1976) construct. This allows their ethical behaviour to become part of the espoused organisational culture and culture in practice thus creating a positive ethical climate. However, this is only likely to occur if the national culture provides a supporting framework of positive ethical norms and practices both formally through the judicial system and its religious and societal beliefs. In a simple sense employees look toward their managers for guidance, managers seek to establish and/or maintain cultural ethical norms and organisations look to the nation state to provide guidance through the legislative framework. This is not to say that unethical behaviour does not take place amongst individuals and organisations, nor is there any suggestion that workers need guidance from their employers in order to behave ethically. Rather, in contexts (countries) where bribery and other corrupt behaviours ensue, high moral individual development and establishing a positive ethical climate is more difficult due to certain unethical behaviours being accepted as the norm.

Taking personal moral development as a given, how do people make the 'right' choice? There is no simple answer but some guidance may be found amongst competing ethical frameworks. The following descriptions are taken from a number of sources. These include the theoretical approaches of 'teleology' where acts are morally sound if they produce a desired result (realisation of self interest); 'egoism' where actions are acceptable if they maximise total utility (greatest good for greatest number); 'dentology' where individual rights are associated with behaviour rather than on consequences; and 'relativism' where the moral robustness of decisions is based on individual and or group experiences:

- Utilitarian – decisions are made on the basis of who benefits from the outcome. Ultimately the choice is based on the greatest potential benefit accruing to the largest stakeholder group.
- Individualism – here decisions are deemed moral when they are made in the individual's best long-term interests.
- Moral rights – here everyone is assumed to have rights that cannot be removed by another. These are sixfold and in no particular order include, free consent, privacy, freedom of speech, life and safety, freedom of conscience and due process.
- Justice and distributive justice – decisions are made on standards of equity and impartiality. If people are treated differently the process should not be based on arbitrary characteristics.

The two remaining categories of justice are procedural and compensatory. The former holds that rules and regulations should be clear and applied fairly. The latter holds that people should be compensated fairly for any injuries caused by the culpable party. For example, if a hotel employee is injured during the course of their work perhaps by an item of faulty equipment, fixture of fitting, they would, all things being equal be entitled to compensation of some description. It is understandable that the justice approach to ethics underpins that which is legal in the workplace (see Chapter 8) and ethical frameworks applied to HRM have, in the main, taken this form (Barrett, 1999). These rely on the possibility that we know what is good but still provide a basis for organisational codes of conduct.

Critical note

Moral development is an important antecedent of ethical behaviour. The first stage is known as preconventional, the second as conventional and the third as post-conventional.

Reflections
1. Through desk research, identify two well-known tourism entrepreneurs.
2. From the information you have, try and identify their stages of moral development.

ORGANISATIONAL ETHICS AND THE ROLE OF HR

Box 9.1 depicts a hypothetical interview concerning the practice of tourism and hospitality students working in industry as an integral element of their university or college course.

BOX 9.1 The ethics of student placements/work experience

Interviewer: How many students would you typically seek jobs for in a year?
University Placement Coordinator (UPC): Not too many, we only have a small cohort. I'd say about half a dozen or so.
Interviewer: Do you manage to arrange work successfully for them?
UPC: Yes, we have a number of organisations that help us out. Mind you, the working conditions are variable.
Interviewer: What do you mean?

UPC: With the best of intention, we try to ensure that the work experience is comprehensive and sticks to the schedule we set for them. There is an academic imperative here as well you know. However, we accept that sometimes due to circumstances beyond anyone's control, students may end up not always sticking to the 'plan'.

Interviewer: How do students react to that?

UPC: They're usually ok about it. Besides, if we identify issues before hand we can usually take care of the learning objectives in a slightly different way.

Interviewer: What is your relationship like with the organisations used for the period of work placement?

UPC: Pretty good. Some of them are on our external advisory panel for the hospitality programme so at least there is some kind of strategic appreciation of the course and how the placement fits in with the whole thing.

Interviewer: What about those that are not on the board?

UPC: Still ok but sometimes things can get a little fraught. One of the biggest issues for me is to ensure students get paid for working. This issue raises its head when I am seeking new providers. In fact it would be fair to say that most of them, after expressing an initial interest in taking on students, tend to baulk at the idea that a waged placement is what I'm after. For example, one manager seemed really positive about the whole idea of taking on students commenting that it would be 'Good to get new blood into the team' and 'It's always good to have a new breed of youngsters coming through the ranks' and so on. Soon after mentioning the 'W' word, he spent ten minutes talking about how students would detract from his productivity, require hand-holding and generally erode is already inadequate resources.

Interviewer: Not being paid for work experience is fairly common practice though isn't it?

UPC: It depends what sort of experience you are talking about. Typically, work experience is just that, work experience and nothing more, no pay, no nothing. Industrial placements on the other hand tend to be waged. At the end of the day it's all semantics I suppose. I sometimes think it makes employers feel less guilty if they can sign a student up for work experience rather than a placement. It's easier to justify non-payment if that is the accepted norm for one particular label attached to using students in the workplace.

Interviewer: How do you feel about it?

UPC: I think that anyone who uses the services of another should pay for the privilege. I know that may not be a popular view but I'm not talking about a King's ransom here, just a trainee rate. After all these students are trainees are they not? Frankly, we all know that payment and working conditions are poor in the tourism and hospitality industry relative to some other industries and yes, I believe that some will get ripped off once they enter the sector after leaving university. I do not want to begin this process while they are university students. Some might say that I am giving them a false sense of what the industry is about in HR terms but I believe the industry is wrong to perpetuate some of its employment policies. Sure, I am not going to change what has become traditional in the industry but that doesn't change the way I feel about the matter and what I truly believe is wrong. While students are under my remit I will move heaven and earth to see they get paid fairly for what they do.

Questions
1. Who is 'right' and who is 'wrong' in the above; and identify some of the ethical dilemmas faced by employers when establishing remuneration levels.
2. How many ethical perspectives can you identify?
3. Comment on whether you believe rates of pay and associated working conditions in the tourism industry are acceptable?

Source: the present authors

Many researchers and practitioners agree ethics in business is the responsibility of CEOs, managers and employees alike. Upchurch (1998) considers the conduct of managers as a key enabler of the firm's ethical climate. However, HR must be considered the major instigator, contributor and caretaker of organisational values through the establishment of an ethical climate, standard-setting and compliance with legislation. All human resource policy and practice raises unavoidable ethical questions (Winstanley *et al.*, 1996: 8). Mondy (2008) comments:

> Human resource ethics is the application of ethical principles to human resource relationships and activities. (p. 37)

Woodd (1997) believes that without a proactive approach from those who are involved with the people side of the business, employment practice and social responsibilities will seldom be considered. She believes that HR needs to be at the heart of policy design and implementation and refers to HR professionals as the guardians of ethical conduct in the employment of people. This should be the case in both large and small tourism organisations where human resource departments exist or where HR responsibilities belong to only one person. In principle there is no difference between the two scenarios although both present problems specific to their differing organisational structures. Dessler *et al.* (2004) similarly note that HR has many roles but fundamentally their function is two-pronged. The first is an organisational charge which concerns compliance in the form of diversity management and other externally imposed regulations. The other is more problematic as it involves supporting workers often against the actions of managers and employers. The question is, to whom is HR duty-bound? This of course depends on the legality of behaviour by either party but for less clear-cut matters it is a controversial issue. Relative to other departments HR is some way down the organisational pecking order and has only recently achieved quasi-equal status in the boardroom. Realistically, if HR acts as moral guardian for all things employment related, they may find themselves being excluded. Managers may decide to minimise the role of ethics in future decision-making. Of course this would depend on the dominant organisational culture as some firms may encourage their ethical input whereas others may simply want to comply with legislation; these are two quite different things.

Manipulation by management may therefore be likely thus rendering the HR department a highly political instrument. Indeed some would argue that this is the case. For example, if HR were apolitical there would be little need for the existence of unions. Hart (1993) puts the case more strongly considering the concept of HR to be morally bereft noting that both 'hard' and 'soft' models pursue the same unitarist goal. The first achieves this by strong-handed autocratic means and the other by subterfuge. At heart this is a Marxist perspective where objectives of the employer and employee are viewed as fundamentally conflicting. Hart believes that the HR should not be seeking strategic alignment with business goals but instead provoking questions about the current organisational culture and what it should be ethically. In this sense, the researcher is not questioning the ethical aspirations of a modern HR department but rather challenging what, in practice, it has or will become if issues of morality and ethics do not take priority over financial imperatives.

Similarly, Nankervis *et al.* (2008) argue that unless HR practices are linked to broader frames of ethical reference they will be of limited value. After agreeing the underpinning principles, they can be used as guiding frameworks for ethical decisions in areas identified as appropriate. Woodd (1997: 114) cites Townley's (1994) principles designed to inform ethical HR practice:

- visibility – recognising the importance of understated contributions to the organisation;
- voice – employee appraisals and fair treatment of whistleblowers;
- integrity of the individual;
- difference – pay equity for example; and
- rejection of hierarchical privilege.

Inherent in the above are the essentials of legality, loyalty, confidentiality and equity and justice. These values may be expressed and itemised in a variety of ways:

- civil employment rights;
- procedural justice for all employees;
- compliance with legal and social responsibilities;
- generation of social capital through ethical conduct;
- working conditions and occupational safety;

- gender equality, child labour, sexual harassment and diversity management;
- pay differentials; and
- whistleblowing.

Adapted from: Nankervis *et al.* (2008)

Alternatively:

- discrimination;
- recruitment;
- whistleblowing;
- basic rights;
- testing;
- salary and benefits; and
- employee protection.

Adapted from: Dessler *et al.* (2004)

Critical note
The conduct of managers is a key enabler of a firm's ethical climate.

Codes of ethics

Despite the above, instilling and maintaining an ethical climate is challenging. To be achieved, ethical norms must be agreed together with other stakeholders and communicated appropriately (Drumm, 1994). Senior management must support and model appropriate value-based behaviours. The firm should also establish and publish a negotiated code of ethics into which all stakeholders have input. Human resources should take the leading role here.

Mondy (2008) defines a code of ethics as:

A statement of the values adopted by the whole organization about behaviour. (p. 36)

Figure 9.2 shows the necessary steps in the construction of an organisational code of ethics.

An important but often overlooked element of establishing and managing organisational codes is that whilst much remains unchanged contextually, a feedback loop is essential. Not only does this serve to correct any processual or design anomalies but also acts as an environmental barometer to ensure the code reflects broader societal and environmental ethical shifts.

Commonly, firms will have an ethical code of conduct either self generated and implemented or strongly recommended from associated professional bodies and trade associations. Whilst not all elements of these codes are legally enforceable, they nonetheless act as guides consistent with the organisation's espoused culture, vision and

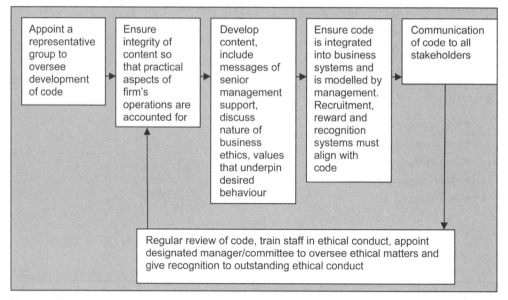

Figure 9.2 Code of ethics management

Adapted from: Lagan (1999) in Dessler (2004)

mission statement. Moreover, for those 'imposed' by professional bodies and other associations, flouting often results in expulsion from the external body. Membership often depends on compliance with the espoused code. For example, Tourism Tropical North Queensland (TTNQ) is the official Regional Tourism Organization for Tropical North Queensland region of Australia. Its key objective is to build destination awareness in Australia and selected international holiday and business tourism markets. Prior to membership, applicants must satisfy the criteria according to the 'TTNQ code of conduct for members'. It is shown in Figure 9.3 below.

Despite codes of conduct, role modelling and associated measures, how should firms respond to unethical behaviour amongst their ranks especially in the public domain? First, related processes and procedures must be checked for inconsistencies, anomalies and errors. If the appointed person finds nothing apparent, Hanson (2003) suggests a five stage process beginning with a condemnation of the action ('not the sinner'). The accused must asked to temporarily take 'leave' until guilt is determined. In this case, the culprit must force a resignation. Thereafter, best ethical practices must be redefined and advocated and the organisation must review them continually to ensure currency.

Critical note

A code of ethics is a statement of values and behaviour adopted by the whole organisation.

Reflections

1. Visit three local tourism operators.
2. Ask whether they have a code of ethics.
3. Ask on what basis were these values derived and who was involved in the process of creating the code.

Tourism Tropical North Queensland's code of conduct outlines professional guidelines to ensure the conduct of TTNQ members will enhance Tropical North Queensland's tourism industry and contribute positively to Tropical North Queensland's community, environment and quality of life.

TTNQ expects Members:

1. To act professionally and with high levels of duty of care, safety and concern towards other TTNQ members, TTNQ staff, customers and the TNQ community.

2. To deliver with integrity, all advertised products and services, meeting all legal responsibilities.

3. To comply with the laws of Australia and to ensure all contracts and terms of business are clear, concise and honoured in full, and ensure all dealings are ethical and fair.

4. To speak and act respectfully and not denigrate or slander anyone or discriminate on the basis of race, gender, religious belief, sexual orientation or political persuasion.

5. To ensure claims in advertising and marketing a product or service are true, and never misleading or exaggerated and are not negative about another member's product or service.

6. To consider the interests of local communities and ensure that the impacts of their businesses on TNQ's community life and environment are positive and beneficial.

7. To manage their businesses effectively and efficiently, enhancing the reputation of tourism in TNQ and to respond and resolve customer complaints in a timely and courteous manner and to change businesses processes and policies when necessary.

8. To operate a humane, safe, healthy and satisfying working environment for staff, customers and the public.

9. To manage their staff/employees fairly and equitably.

10. To operate their businesses guided by environmental best practice guidelines, conserving water, energy and the natural environment. Business operations must balance the rights of future generations with current economic needs, preserving and improving TNQ's quality of life.

11. To be ambassadors for tourism in TNQ and help promote community understanding of the importance of tourism as a vibrant contributor to TNQ's economy and quality of life.

12. To always act with the highest ethical integrity and not misuse authority or office for personal gain when serving on the TTNQ board or associated committees.

13. Refer to company constitution, section 16 and 18 for further information relating to suspension or expulsion of membership.

Figure 9.3 TTNQ code of conduct for members

Source: TTNQ (2009) Reproduced with permission

Whistleblowing

Unethical behaviour is often exposed by a 'whistleblower' which *Wikipedia* defines as:

> A person who alleges misconduct which itself is defined as the violation of a law, rule, regulation and/or a direct threat to public interest, such as fraud, health/safety violations, and corruption. (http://en.wikipedia.org/wiki/Whistleblower, accessed June 2009)

Whistleblowers may be either internal or external. The former report misconduct to a co-worker or other individual within their company. The latter report outside the firm to lawyers, the media, law enforcement or other watchdog agencies. To whom the alleged misconduct is reported depends on the specific subject matter and severity of the incident(s).

Legal protection for whistleblowing is designed to protect whistleblowers from victimisation and dismissal. However, it is not uncommon for whistleblowers to be ostracised by their co-workers, discriminated against by future potential employers or fired from their organisation. After reviewing the evidence, Vinten (1995) points out that retaliation is common in these cases, for example, three surveys of whistleblowers from the US civil service and private sector revealed that virtually all reported subsequent harassment (from peers and managers) with around three quarters of them ultimately losing their jobs.

The following case in Box 9.2 outlines how legislation in the tourism and hospitality industry might impact on employees.

BOX 9.2 Case study – Lawyers predict wave of whistleblowing once smoke ban comes in

Employers who give concessions to 'regulars' will risk being shopped by employees over health and safety. Hospitality employers may face a rise in whistleblowing claims from staff when the blanket smoking ban is implemented across England and Wales next summer, lawyers have warned.

Pub and club staff may feel under pressure to ignore customer breaches of the smoking ban, according to David Appleton, employment partner at law firm Lewis Silkin.

'The pressure is now on for publicans, restaurateurs and hoteliers to compromise customer choice in favour of the rights of their staff,' he said 'Once this law comes into force, I predict a wave of whistleblowing claims as staff get victimised for exposing their bosses for turning a blind eye to their regulars continuing to light up.'

Appleton said the move to implement a total ban will plug a 'major gap' in health and safety legislation. 'The difference in legal terms between exposing staff to

---

asbestos and exposing them to the carcinogenic effects of tobacco smoke has always been illusory,' he said.

Question

1. Discuss some of the likely outcomes for employees who decide to blow the whistle on their employers.

Source: Thomas (2006)

Whistleblowing should be accounted for and forms an important element of a code of conduct in which HR plays a key role (see earlier in this chapter). This is not only important for their protection and ethical treatment but also to identify whether their allegations are valid. Vinten (1996) considers the following questions key in establishing whether allegations are justified:

- How comprehensive is the employee's knowledge of the situation?
- Is the information accurate and substantial?
- What are the unethical practices and why are they so deemed?
- What public values do they harm?
- How substantial and irreversible are the effects of these practices?
- Are there any compensating factors to be considered?

Despite the protective legal framework available to whistleblowers, many end up being persecuted one way or another (there have even been cases of suicide!). Vinten (1996) argues that whistleblowing when institutionalised as part of an open organisational culture is an effective feedback control mechanism. However, if the organisation has no clearly articulated HR policies and procedures in the area, benefits will not accrue and the firm will not learn from its mistakes.

SUMMARY

Those engaged in thinking about what they ought to do is, by definition, being involved in ethics. Obligations range from the personal to societal. Ethical decisions are made based on learned values from one's background and the more general national or global ethical climate. Ethical matters concern the 'right thing to do'; the question is, for whom? How do people make the 'right' choice? There are several competing theoretical frameworks from which guidance can be obtained manifesting as 'utilitarian', 'individualism', 'moral' and 'justice' and 'distributive justice' ethical approaches. The last category underpins much ethical practice in business and HR.

The tourism and hospitality sector has its share of conundrums particularly in the areas of regional planning and development. Tourism has both positive as well as negative impacts. Planners and associated others need to ensure the latter are kept to within an acceptable level. Acceptability is subjective and there is evidence to suggest a person's propensity to act in a particular manner ethically depends on their level of moral development. At an enterprise level, CEOs, managers and HR practitioners need to set high ethical standards. This allows their modelling to become part of the organisational culture thus creating a positive ethical climate.

Business ethics focuses on the role and position of firms at the enterprise level in a societal context addressing matters of corporate social responsibility. Some believe that ethics and business are two different issues and should not be confused. Others consider it paramount for firms to engage with, benefit and contribute positively to the community. The latter view is becoming more popular and is often called a values driven approach to ethics.

At a more focused level, the tourism and hospitality sector has a number of ethically charged characteristics which impact on the employment relationship. These include the existence of a significant black economy, high labour turnover, over-reliance on casual, temporary and part-time working, employee training and domination of small firms.

The HR department has a variety of roles which can be divided into two areas. The first deals with compliance; the other involves supporting workers. This is challenging as it raises the question to whom is HR duty-bound? This is often a matter of controversy in organisations. If HR acts as moral guardian for workers, it will probably become ostracised from management; the key here is appropriate balance.

A key issue for HR is to ensure their practices are linked to broader frames of ethical reference. Some key principles here include legality, loyalty, confidentiality and equity and justice. However, in establishing and maintaining ethical norms it is important to consult stakeholders and communicate standards appropriately. It is essential that senior management supports and models appropriate agreed value-based behaviours. Many firms also publish a HR-led, negotiated code of ethics/conduct which may be used as a guide for all stakeholders.

CHAPTER QUESTIONS

1. Identify the competing ethical frameworks discussed in this chapter and comment on their value towards ethical decision-making in the tourism industry.

2. Discuss the above in terms of their relative contribution to human resources management in tourism organisations.

3. Outline how the human resources department (or those who are responsible for the human resources function in smaller organisations) can ensure its practices are ethically appropriate.

RECOMMENDED READING

Daft, R. (2005) *The Leadership Experience* (3rd edn). Australia: Thomson.
A discussion of ethics from a leadership perspective.

Fennell, D. (2006) *Tourism Ethics*. Clevedon: Channel View Publications.
An incisive generic overview of tourism ethics.

Jones, P., Comfort, D. and Hillier, D. (2006) Reporting and reflecting on corporate social responsibility in the hospitality industry. *International Journal of Contemporary Hospitality Management* 18(4), 329–240.
A review of corporate social responsibility amongst operators in the UK.

Mondy, R.W. (2008) *Human Resource Management*. Upper Saddle River (NJ): Pearson.
A US-oriented HRM text with a practical focus.

Nankervis, A., Compton, R. and Baird, M. (2008) *Human Resource Management Strategies and Processes* (6th edn). Victoria: Thomson.
Useful Australian focused HRM text with a strategic management perspective.

RECOMMENDED WEBSITES

Tourism ethics – http://www.world-tourism.org/code_ethics/eng.html

Tourism and regional development –
http://www.tourism-futures.org/content/view/2048/53/

Business ethics –
http://humanresources.about.com/od/businessethics/Business_Ethics.htm

Chartered Institute of Personnel Development – http://www.cipd.co.uk/default.cipd

Australian Human Resources Institute –
http://www.ahri.com.au/scripts/cgiip.exe/WService=AHRI-LIVE/ccms.r

United Nations World Tourism Organization – http://www.unwto.org/index.php

CHAPTER 10

THE FUTURE OF HUMAN RESOURCES

LEARNING OBJECTIVES

After working through this chapter, you should be able to:

1. Understand and discuss key issues which will affect the future of people and work in the tourism and hospitality sector.

2. Appreciate and debate the key role HRM will play in the future of the industry.

3. Describe the talent shortage and discuss its implications for the industry.

4. Consider the future of the tourism and hospitality professional.

INTRODUCTION

The tourism and hospitality industry is an important generator of jobs and so is a key player in regional, national and global economies. This book has sought to add to contemporary thought, discussion and debate on HR issues in the tourism and hospitality industry. It has aimed to generate critical thinking and engender best practice in HRM rather than provide a prescriptive approach to HRM for the sector. The tourism and hospitality sector is extensive, diverse and complex at various levels. Subsequently, there is a broad range of activities and skills associated with the sector. It is sometimes referred to as the tourism, hospitality, leisure and travel sector. In a similar vein, People 1st (2008) classifies the industry into 14 sub-sectors: hotels; restaurants; pubs, bars and night-clubs; contract food service providers; membership clubs; events; gambling; travel services; tourist services; visitor attractions; youth hostels; holiday parks; self-catering accommodation; and hospitality services. This indicates that jobs within in the industry will vary in relation to skills, attributes, education, qualifications and technical expertise. In addition, the conditions of work within the industry can be diverse because of the range of businesses form small- and medium-sized enterprises to large, global organisations. All of these factors impact on HR approaches, strategies, policies, processes and practices.

Despite this apparent heterogeneity, the industry does present some overarching commonalities, especially in nature of the work and in the experience of working within that industry. Lucas (2004: 4) recognises this in her comment that jobs in tourism and hospitality 'share common attributes and are associated with both hospitality and tourism activities'. The underlying element linking tourism and hospitality workers across the industry is that all jobs are related to the delivery of service to customers. For HR, the implications are that organisational structure, culture and practices should work toward facilitating the delivery of quality service by front-life staff. Some of the issues facing HR in the tourism and hospitality sector have constituted the framework for this book. This final chapter examines the future of HRM in the tourism and hospitality workplace. In particular, it considers the talent shortage and the future of the tourism and hospitality professional.

Critical point

The tourism and hospitality industry is a heterogeneous industry with a variety of stakeholders; however, the characteristics of the industry radiate from its core business, i.e. the delivery of quality service by front-line staff.

Reflection

Consider your work experience in the tourism and hospitality industry (or that of someone you know) and comment on the value that the organisation places on its frontline staff. In particular, reflect on whether the HR practices support frontline staff in their key role of delivery of service.

THE FUTURE WORKPLACE

As mentioned in Chapter 7, three factors have impacted significantly on the nature of work, jobs, employee skills and conditions, conditions in the workplace and workplace structures: demographics, globalisation and technology. In addition, it seems that organisations are driven by competitive strategies which highlight productivity, efficiency, innovation and quality. The quest for achieving these factors is complicated by other influences such as status of labour markets, maintenance of a stable workforce, and building and retention of talented staff. A further implication is demands for labour flexibility, quality of work life, and devolution of HR practices to front-line managers and supervisors.

More recently, the presence of the global economic recession has witnessed the precarious survival or collapse of companies. For many tourism and hospitality businesses, the economic climate resulted in a downturn in business and profits as people have been mindful of how and where they spend their money and travel has been minimised. For example, these turbulent times have forced many businesses to reconsider their current and planned HR practices, and corporate travel for personal growth and development and conference attendance has in many cases been markedly curtailed. The subsequent implication of cutbacks in corporate travel is the loss of business and jobs for the tourism and hospitality industry. On a positive note, however, there are some companies who have still engaged with corporate travel but are being more financially astute about the associated costs. This is illustrated in the article 'Corporates still travelling but looking for a cheaper bed' in Box 10.1.

BOX 10.1 Case Study – Corporates still travelling but looking for a cheaper bed

Hospitality Magazine, **16 July 2009, by Rosemary Ryan**
Business travel in Australia is defying the economic downturn with a new survey revealing most travellers are not cutting back. However, they are looking to save on accommodation costs. More than 70% of regular business travellers say they have not cancelled any business trips due to the global financial downturn, according to the study conducted by serviced apartment company Quest.

The Quest 'Serviced Apartments Business Travel Survey' revealed more than 63% of business travellers except to travel the same amount over the next six months despite the difficult economic climate, with 29% of these respondents saying they planned to stay in less expensive accommodation if they do make a change to their travel habits.

Looking to the future, 73% of respondents said they expected the economic downturn to have no impact on the frequency of their business travel in two years, with 30% of these travellers planning to spend less on accommodation. Meanwhile, an additional ten per cent said they expect to travel more for business in two years. The Quest Serviced Apartments Business Travel Survey polled more than 1000 regular Australian business travellers.

Quest chairman Paul Constantinou said the results reflected a more positive outlook as the new financial year gets underway. 'In most instances, travel is essential to maintaining and growing a business,' Constantinou said. 'While people are still travelling, they are looking at ways to "trim the fat" from their expenses, and are looking more closely at cutting back on unnecessary services,' he said. Constantinou said Quest Apartments – which specialises in corporate accommodation – has maintained high room occupancy during a time when many hotels have been impacted by the downturn. 'We're finding a lot of people are moving toward the serviced apartment option as a way of cutting back on costs, without cutting back on the standard of the accommodation.'

Question

1. In times of economic crisis, organisations should curtail activities related to personal development and training. Discuss.

Source: http://www.hospitalitymagazine.com.au/Article/Corporates-still-travelling-but-looking-for-a-cheaper-bed/490718.aspx (accessed 17 July 2009)

In terms of HRM for the tourism and hospitality industry, the roll-on benefits of corporate travel are apparent in the jobs generated in sub-sectors of the industry. This is critical for an industry with a labour market whose 'lower' end provides work opportunities for those seeking flexible employment (part-timers and casuals), agency temporary staff, and independent contractors.

Aside of the global economic crisis, there are other social influences which affect future workforces. Nankervis *et al.* (2005: 539) points out that:

> Social and demographic changes are likely to result in more educated and more highly skilled employees with increased job expectations vying for a smaller number of jobs and less access to long-term career paths within the same organisation. Schmidt agrees, suggesting that at the 'top' end of the labour market not only will employee be younger and more technologically literate, but they will change their jobs more frequently, and that their loyalty will need to be 'bought' by competing employers on the bases of interesting work projects and competitive employment conditions.

In addition, these educated, mobile employees are increasingly seeking jobs that provide satisfaction, career development and enhanced remuneration and/or benefits. It is from such a base that has emerged the 'War for Talent'. Such activities have presented HR managers with new challenges, such as: recruitment and selection of the 'best candidates'; aligning the employee with rewarding and stimulating work; negotiating of individual contracts that include performance-based pay; and the knowledge that the employee's may be transitory. These issues will require more innovative HRM processes and practices. For the tourism and hospitality sector this provides support for an HR approach which is oriented more toward 'best fit' rather than 'best practice'. Nickson (2007: 294) argues that because of the non-universal nature of the tourism and hospitality industry, 'the "best fit" approach of designing HRM practices which are contingent upon the particular customer definition of 'good service' would seem apposite'. Riley *et al.* (2000) maintain that there is strong 'economic determinism' in the tourism and hospitality industry which governs HR practices. They reason that employees may desire high pay or wages, training, and career progression, the reality is that providing such benefits is generally not cost effective for tourism and hospitality businesses. Having said this, it is here emphasised that this does not diminish the need for good HR practices within the tourism and hospitality sector. The continuing need for the industry to improve its HR practices is supported by a comment from Rowley *et al.* (2000: 13):

> Some of these deficiencies reflect labour market circumstances, commercial constraints and lack of awareness of options, but some reflect poor human resource management, unwillingness to take risks or invest in innovation and short termism; most vividly exemplified by the low pay, crisis management culture of the less impressive establishments.

There is no doubt that environmental factors influence and shape HRM strategies. Further, the diffusion of best practice HR throughout the tourism and hospitality sector is challenging and limited, especially when research presents findings of 'high levels of arbitrary management practice' (Haynes, 1999: 200). Nonetheless, there is wisdom in the words of Worsfold (1999: 346), 'we may need to abandon the search for formal HRM approaches and attempt to establish whether "caring management" can provide the "concern for employee well being" which appears to be linked to service quality'. Nickson (2007: 296) refers to this as the 'economy' version of HRM and suggests that in the case of the tourism and hospitality industry, it may 'offer a more rewarding and meaningful employment experience for the many who work in the sector'. In any case, Schlesinger and Heskett (1991: 72) proffered a view which sustains the 'cycle of quality service':

> Capable workers, who are well trained and fairly compensated, provide better service, require less supervision and [are] more likely to remain on the job. For individual companies, this means enhanced competitiveness.

This comment suggests an integrative approach where the businesses consider employees as vital and valued in achieving their strategic objectives.

Critical point

Several themes and issues are emerging as factors which impact on the nature and experience of work within the tourism and hospitality industry. These have implications for HR strategies within the sector.

Reflection

You are the HR manager of an international tourist attraction, briefly describe the ten key HR processes and practices you would you. Explain why you have focused on these key features.

TALENT SHORTAGE

It is recognised that recruitment and retention are the biggest challenges facing the tourism and hospitality industry (e.g. Baum, 2006). The nature of the industry exacerbates this through factors such as the highly labour intensive nature of the industry (Hughes & Rog, 2008), high turnover rates (Kusluvan, 2003), high mobility to other industries (Baum, 2006), poor perception as industry of choice for employment (Kusluvan, 2003), strong 'economic determinism' (Riley *et al.*, 2000), intensely emotionally labouring (Lashley, 2002), poor promotion and career prospects (Riley, 1996), and poor working conditions (Hughes & Rog, 2008). Irrespective of the causes, the situation for the tourism and hospitality industry is heightened by the current labour shortage, a labour market replete with workers who lack requisite skills and an ageing workforce.

This poses challenges for HR practitioners in hospitality. A report by Towers Perrin (2005) indicates that critical factors for employee recruitment and employee retention may vary. In a study which surveyed 86,000 employees in 16 countries, the report highlights key recruitment and retention drivers (see Table 10.1).

Table 10.1: Critical factors in recruitment and retention

Recruitment drivers	*Retention drivers*
• Competitive base pay • Work/life balance • Career advancement opportunities • Competitive benefits • Challenging work • Salary increases linked to individual performance • Learning and development opportunities • Competitive retirement benefits • Calibre of co-workers • Reputation of the organisation as a good employer	• Base salary • Organisation's success at retaining others with needed skills • Fairly competitive • Manager understands individual employee's motivations • Satisfaction with organisation's people decisions • Fairly compensated compared to others doing similar work in organisation • Opportunities to learn and develop new skills • Retirement benefits • Appropriate amount of decision-making authority to do job well • Reputation of the organisation as a good employer • Senior management acts to ensure organisation's long-term success

Source: Adapted from report by Towers Perrin (2005)

Emerging from this realisation is the impetus to develop and implement effective talent management strategies. Uren (2007) posited that talent management was a means of building sustainable organisational capability and that it consisted of five components: attract, identify, develop, deploy and engage. This suggests that talent management is synonymous with the various processes and practices correlated with 'best practice' HRM. Hughes and Rog (2008: 746) extend this understanding and posit that:

> Talent management is . . . both a philosophy and a practice. It is both an espoused and enacted commitment – shared at the highest levels and throughout the organization by all those in managerial and supervisory positions – to implementing an integrated, strategic and technology enabled approach to HRM, with a particular focus on human resource planning, including employee recruitment, retention, development and succession practices, ideally for all employees but especially for those identified as having high potential or in key positions.

By contrast, Buckingham and Vosburgh (2001: 17) suggest that organisations develop the 'talent inherent in each person'. Similarly, other authors argue that talent management is applicable to all employees (e.g. Evans, 2007; Hyams, 2007). Blyth (2006) and Evans (2007) report on how the Nando's restaurant chain has successfully embraced and 'all-inclusive' approach. This is an important point and highlights that everyone working in the tourism and hospitality industry should be considered as a professional, regardless of whether they are the housekeeper, cleaner, dishwasher, gardener, carpenter, receptionist, restaurant manager, accounts manager or CEO. Baum (2008: 720) adds that 'talent management is an organisational mindset that seeks to assure that the supply of talent is available to align the right people with the right jobs at the right time, based on strategic business objectives'.

Hughes and Rog (2008) emphasise that talent management is achievable through formalised and integrated HR practices which include retention, workforce planning, leadership/high potential development, and professional development. It is interesting to see here the reference to professional development as it supports the idea that there is a responsibility on the tourism and hospitality industry itself to develop and nurture its professionalism, the occupational status of jobs within the industry, and the image of the industry. D'Annunzio-Green, Maxwell, and Watson (2008) build on this by emphasising that all stakeholders in the tourism and hospitality industry (managers, industry and educators) need to embrace the notion of talent management if they are to contend for and build sustainable industry capability.

It is questionable whether talent management is the mainstream driving force of strategic human resource management in the tourism and hospitality industry. This seems unlikely, given that the industry is renowned for its lack of highly developed human resource practices. Nonetheless, there are encouraging indications that some companies are striving to adopt talent management strategies. For example, Maxwell and MacLean (2008: 823) report on findings from CIPD (2006) research which showed that '75 percent of large organisations are active in some form of TM [talent management]'.

As noted earlier, the literature indicates that HR practices will act to direct implementation of the quest for talent. It highlights that it begins with attracting the right people and persists with a focus on employee development. In Tropical North Queensland, an example of such initiatives is evident in the 'Employment' webpage of 'Skyrail', a top tourist attraction in the region. Of particular interest here is the 'Skyrail Employment Philosophy' and 'Skyrail Career Opportunities', which suggest that within this organisation, employees are valued and that there is strong support for personal development and career progression (Box 10.2).

BOX 10.2 Employment at Skyrail

Skyrail Employment Philosophy

Skyrail was founded on a basis of innovation, hard work, persistence and a pursuit of excellence.

Today, the Skyrail team continues to endorse these principles and ensure the Skyrail experience continues to deliver exceptional service and exceed customer expectations.

The Skyrail workplace is a progressive and challenging environment and provides staff members with rewarding and exciting career opportunities.

Skyrail's core employment principles and philosophies are:

- Attract the right people for the right job
- Provide permanent, stable employment – 95%+ of Skyrail's 100 staff members are permanent employees
- Recognise and reward superior work performance
- Provide the opportunity for career development
- Provide on-going training and continual skills development
- Encourage individuals to perform to a superior standard and promote a strong team working environment

Skyrail Career Opportunities

The Skyrail business has many different facets and team members are employed in a variety of job positions.

Skyrail employs over 100 team members all with unique personalities but a range of different backgrounds and job skills. Below we have listed some of the key individual performance criteria demonstrated by team members.

Questions

What type of people suit the Skyrail team?

- People who like a busy and demanding work environment

- People who are guest (customer) focused
- People who are looking for career progression within the tourism industry
- People who possess a positive outlook, willing to take on challenges and strive for improvement
- People who are innovative and communicate well
- People who thrive in a team environment
- People who have a 'yes I can', 'nothing is too much trouble' approach to work
- People who want be part of an multi-award winning team

Source: http://www.skyrail.com.au/employment.html (accessed 16 June 2009)

Further to the example above, research indicates that there are tourism and hospitality organisations that are exemplars of a talent management approach. For example, Storey (2007: 110) reports on the 'action-oriented talent management' approach of the international Royal Bank of Scotland which has contributed to the organisation's business success. Equally, Yeung (2006: 267) identifies the tourism management strategy adopted by the Portman Ritz-Carlton Hotel in China as the driver of companies' 'excellent customer service and ... profitable growth'. All of these initiatives are valuable and are to be commended; however, there is an acute need for the tourism and hospitality industry to be seriously concerned about talent management and to address the issue collectively. Maxwell and MacLean (2008) present important actions for the industry to consider. These include:

- There is recognition that the Scottish tourism and hospitality sector can benefit from using a TM strategy as a proactive and attractive way of presenting careers in the industry than others.
- Individual hospitality and tourism organisations must recognise the value of TM to the industry as a whole rather than solely for the recruitment, development and retention of talent in their own businesses.
- Industry bodies and leaders present exemplary practice in TM.

Liaising with industry, educators develop toolkits for the implementation and evaluation of TM initiatives.

While Maxwell and MacLean's (2008: 828–829) focus is on the tourism and hospitality industry in Scotland, the points they make are relevant to all participants in the industry in all parts of the world. As such, the industry would benefit from embracing the suggestions proposed by Maxwell and MacLean (2008: 828) if it is to improve its image and 'perceptions of the industry as an employer and a service provider'. The next section continues with this theme and examines the future of the tourism and hospitality professional.

> **Critical point**
>
> Traditionally, HR practices within the tourism and hospitality industry have been short-term, ad hoc and economically determined. Changing labour markets and the 'quest for talent' are dictating that the industry reconsider its approach if it is to sustain its competitiveness in the delivery of quality service.

> **Reflection**
>
> Consider the characteristics of current labour markets in the tourism and hospitality industry and the paradox this presents for organisations which seek to attract and retain staff, provide a quality service to customers, and achieve profitability. How do you think this paradox can be dealt with?

THE FUTURE OF THE TOURISM AND HOSPITALITY PROFESSIONAL

It is well documented that recruitment and retention are the major challenges facing the tourism and hospitality industry (e.g. Powell & Wood, 1999; Hughes & Rog, 2008). Fuelling these challenges are characteristics of the industry, such as its labour intensive nature, high turnover rates, emotionally demanding nature of customer service work, working long and unsociable hours, poor pay and work conditions, lack of opportunity for promotion and career progression, and low-status nature of hospitality work. All of these factors contribute to the perception that the industry is not a favourable place to work. In addition, the industry's employment challenges are likely to continue and possibly intensify if the industry does not address these issues and work toward improving its 'industry brand' as an industry of choice for workers. As noted in Chapter 5, it is not just the 'employer brand' that needs to improve, it is the 'tourism and hospitality brand' itself which needs to be enhanced so that individuals view the industry as an industry worthy to be employed in. Further, 'the tourism and hospitality professional' needs to be developed and branded. In so doing the industry can be viewed as one in which it is possible to pursue a profession of worth, value and status. Professionalization of the industry is a must if the industry is to advance and attract talent.

It is imperative that the industry gives prominence to how the vocational/professional identities of the tourism and hospitality workers are shaped and perceived. Development and shaping of identity has been related to the role and influence of others and education; and, the sharing of common interests, experiences, practices and knowledge. Meriot (2002, cited in Marhuenda *et al.*, 2004) considers identity as linked to factors which are socially constructed. Equally, professional identity provides a sense of belonging to a collective. In his *Theory of Human Motivation* Maslow highlighted the importance to humans of having their social needs fulfilled. He stressed that humans need to feel a sense of belonging and acceptance and that this could be from small or large social groups. It follows that if the industry were to embrace the notion of professional identity, it is these factors of social belonging and professional identity which may very well prove to be the industry's saving grace.

Equally, HR policies, processes and practices play a critical role in how the future of the tourism and hospitality professional will unfold. Despite the research and literature which support the benefits of best HR practice, it remains questionable to what extent the hospitality industry engages with these practices. It is acknowledged that there are internal and external factors which can act as driving or restraining forces which impact on HR policies and practices. Internal factors include alignment with strategic business goals, leadership, CEO active participation, organisational culture, organisational structure, and knowledge, skills and experience of the HR practitioner. External factors include the state of the economy, mergers and acquisitions, global expansion strategies and global events (e.g. swine flu of 2009). The economy can have a dramatic impact on the supply and demand for human resources and implications for how companies handle their valued staff during good and turbulent times. For example, the current economic climate of 2009 has impacted on many companies and industries. In an article written for *HR Monthly*, Ross (2009: 3) notes that 'times of crisis brings out the best and worst in people. The trick is to mine the best in people'. An excerpt from the article appears in Box 10.3.

BOX 10.3 Team building in turbulent times

HR Monthly, June 2009, by Emily Ross
Rila Moore is one of the countless Australian human resources directors having an extremely tough year. As executive general manager of HR for the $5.3 billion listed property group Stockland, Moore has had to oversee 150 voluntary and involuntary redundancies across Australia and the United Kingdom. 'We have lost 10 percent of our staff in the past 12 months,' she says. Stockland's head count is down to 1400.

The federal employment minister Julia Gillard sums up the mood: these are 'dreadful days'.

Moore has made one brilliant discovery through this challenging time. Without a budget for annual team-building conferences, weekend retreats, golf or paintballing, Stockland has found a far more effective way to boost staff morale, cement relationships and improve communication. Stockland staff are instead having powerful team-building experiences through the company's established volunteering programmes. Rather than messing around with their colleagues at a retreat, groups of staff are actually making a difference to their local communities.

Stockland staff are entitled to two paid personal volunteering leave days each year, which equates to 3500 Stockland staff hours worth an estimated $1.7 million. The company has partnerships with non-profit organisations United Way and the Australian Business and Community Network across Australia; projects include renovating accommodation for parents of seriously ill children; a grant scheme, as well as mentoring and literacy work with underprivileged students around the country. The enthusiasm and commitment to the volunteer projects sees high levels of discretionary effort. The tasks strengthen teams, making people want to work together and get the job done. That attitude then flows into Stockland workplaces. 'The feedback from staff is incredible,' says Rilla Moor. 'We know it works, our people want to do it and it helps people get things into perspective. We get so much out of it.'

Adapting in hard times

With global financial turmoil and the worst drought and bushfires of modern times, large numbers of Australians have been fighting for survival. Times of crisis bring out the worst in people – the firebugs, embezzlers, sub-prime mortgage lenders and beggars who ride in private jets. These times also bring out the extraordinary, the true leaders, many of whom are working well away from for-profit organisations.

In paid emergency and unpaid volunteer roles there are clear shared goals, a sense of purpose to make a real difference – to put out fires, to feed and shelter, to offer resources, support, protect and unite. These groups face a visible enemy – for example fire, illness or poverty. Fighting against such clear adversaries is a powerful motivator for staff, in most cases a more compelling motivator than doing a job to make profits for a company.

The passion, commitment and engagement of emergency and volunteer workers are hard to cultivate in the corporate world where the bottom line is always the bottom line. However there are traits of effective non-profit and emergency organisations that apply to build resilient corporate organisations. These qualities include perseverance, thrift and a commitment to open, two-way communication. Regardless of the organisation, whether charitable or listed business, chief executive of the Australian Red Cross Robert Tickner believes that 'people need to know how they fit in and contribute to the success of the organisation'.

Through this year's bushfire crisis, Tickner led a team of more than 1000 volunteers in 20 locations around the affected regions.

Source: Adapted from AHRI's *HR Monthly* magazine (June 2009: 14–16)

At the external industry level, an online article from CCH Australia on 15 June 2009 reported on the need for the tourism industry to implement 'fundamental reforms' if it is to be a destination of choice, continue contributing to the nation's GDP, and provide ongoing tourism-related jobs. In relation to HR, the article highlights recommendations from the report which acknowledge that consideration needs to be given by the industry to the development of a sustainable skills base and labour pool. The article appears in Box 10.4.

BOX 10.4 Massive job losses if Australia doesn't lift tourism – report

15 June 2009. Content provided to you by AAP

CANBERRA, June 15, AAP: Australia's tourism industry is at risk of losing thousands of jobs and billions of dollars in income unless it undergoes fundamental reforms, a new report says. The government-sponsored Jackson Report produced by the Long Term Tourism Strategy Steering Committee makes 10 recommendations to enhance research, online capability, skills and investment.

Tourism Minister Martin Ferguson welcomed the report chaired by former Qantas chairwoman Margaret Jackson, saying the government and the industry need to focus on improving productive capacity and international competitiveness. 'The tourism industry's contribution to the Australian economy is immense, with the sector generating more than $40 billion in gross domestic product and directly employing around half a million people,' Mr Ferguson said.

The sector also generates more than $23 billion in exports. Still, Australia's share of global tourism dropped 14 per cent between 1995 and 2008, and as a proportion of GDP has been in decline since peaking in 2001.

'Even more worrying, despite a long economic boom, Australia's domestic tourism performance has flatlined over the past ten years, while outbound travel has soared,' Ms Jackson said. 'A generation of young Australians is growing up without a tradition of an annual local holiday.' However, she said Australia still had a strong international brand and was regarded as an aspirational destination.

'In our consultations we heard a universal view that Australia needs to focus more clearly on developing our tourism industry products based on our competitive advantages – our indigenous culture, landscapes, sophisticated cities and regions, and diverse and friendly people.' She said a vital step is to boost tourism industry research to enable quality decisions across policy, planning and investment.

The Steering Committee also believes a concentrated effort is required to accelerate online capacity of the tourism industry for marketing and booking. Global key performance indicators and targets need to be set up for the industry, and develop plans based on Australia's competitive advantages and priority destinations.

'More effort is required to develop the long-term skill base and labour pool the industry needs,' Ms Jackson said. 'Governments at all levels and the tourism industry will need to collaborate more closely to ensure tourism considerations are factored into the wide range of planning, investment and development processes.' She said that the tourism industry's importance to Australia was widely under-estimated as it brought enormous benefits in terms of job creation and support for small businesses. 'If Australia does not make the necessary changes between now and 2030, we risk forgoing 3.6 million international visitors, $22 billion of tourism's contribution to GDP, and as many as 100,000 tourism jobs,' she said.

'This cannot be allowed to happen.'

Minister Ferguson said the Jackson report was a valuable contribution to the ongoing development of the National Long-Term Tourism Strategy, which will be finalised later this year.

Source: Online article from http://www.cch.com.au/au/ContactUs/Print.aspx?ID=31589

Equally, it seems worthy to acknowledge Morton's (2004) recommendations that efficient and effective processes are engaged by organisations in all HRM areas and that these include a comprehensive review of HR practices (e.g. in recruitment, selection, retention, compensation, performance management and succession planning) and the adjustment of the organisation's approach if need be to reflect an informed, formalised and integrated perspective rather than *ad hoc* or reactive tactics. As Dell and Hickey (2002: 10) note reactionary approaches such as 'raises or other sweetening of the compensation package are common responses when a valued employee shows signs of leaving'. However, such tactics undermine the benefits of effectively developed and implemented HR processes, which include improved employee recruitment, increased employee retention, enhanced employee engagement and subsequent elevated organisational performance.

Further it needs to be stressed that an effective management of HR processes involves all members of the organisation, from the CEO through senior management, middle management, and supervisors to employees. An employee-oriented mindset that values HR processes must permeate the organisation, with the CEO as an active and visible participant, supporting, committed and providing leadership to the process. Hughes and Rog (2008) point out that line managers can play an integral role in implementing comprehensive and integrated HRM policies and practices because they are in a good position to understand what motivates individuals, ensure access to learning opportunities, and treat people with respect.

Also, part of the problem is that HR practitioners lack the skills associated with some of the requirements of their job (Morton, 2005). This is understandable as the HR profession is itself an evolving profession (see AHRI, HR monthly magazine) and then to work in a neonatal industry such as tourism brings further challenges for the HR practitioner. How this is to be addressed remains an issue for further investigation.

Earlier in the book, the point was made about the urgency for the industry to create, develop and promote genuine career trajectories. Hjalager and Andersen (2001) suggest that the industry is 'its own worst enemy' because of the poor employment conditions and HR practices. In line with this, Ross (1997) argues that the industry is ill-equipped to cater for the needs of new generations, especially in relation to provision of job autonomy and learning potentials. This is heightened by Purcell's (1996) comments that the paternalistic management styles inherent in the industry hinder career opportunities and possibly discourage women. Compounded by low pay and nature of employment (part-time, fixed term or temporary contracts, agency work), the prospects for careers for employees seem grim. Hjalager and Andersen (2001: 116) talk about the current presence of 'a persistently "contingent" workforce, employed under very flexible conditions, on non-standard terms and on a part-time of seasonal basis ... [and] the lack of substantial and straightforward career opportunities'.

Against such a pessimistic outlook, it seems that there is hope. Hjalager and Andersen (2001: 127–128) argue that:

> The nature of the employment tends to fit well with an emerging youth culture in which rapid shifts are seen as a positive advantage (Ritzer, 1993). The younger generation looks down on rigid careers, and is critical about the compulsory elements in well-established career tracks. Alternative concepts are emerging under various labels: protean careers (Hall & Moss, 1998), contingent working (Pfeffer, 1994), virtual organisations (Hedberg et al., 1997), and boundaryless careers (Arthur and Rousseau, 1996). According to the new career concepts, less attention should be paid to the 'oldfashioned' understanding of the perfect career, defined by traditions and institutions. Rather, careers should be personally specified paths that transcend organisational, occupational and geographical restrictions and boundaries. The emergence of boundaryless careers also legitimises the blurring of work and leisure activities, as for example utilised in the 'casting' for staff for the Disney theme parks. Lifestyle entrepreneurship can hardly be found anywhere than in the arts and tourism (Weiermaier, 1999). Due to its structure, rapid shifts and the social character of its jobs, tourism seems to be an industry that, more than any other industry in the economy, attracts the ultramobile, the virtual, and the boundaryless.

In line with this it seems that it is now timely for the tourism and hospitality industry to engage with the 'war for talent', or perhaps a more apt term would be the 'quest for talent'. The labour market landscape is changing and complicates challenges facing the industry. Implications are emerging from factors such as the shortage of talent, the expectations of career development and work-life balance, an ageing working population, and Generation Y with particular ideas of work. Responding to these demands requires a strong commitment and effort from all industry participants and stakeholders, including

HR managers, frontline supervisors and managers, CEOs, organisations and corporations, industry leaders and educators. D'Annunzio-Green *et al.* (2008) have provided a worthy blueprint for the industry's to progress on the practical implementation of strategies in their 'quest for talent'. The framework has four key areas:

- Talent Management stakeholders with employees, managers, and strategists at the core of the blueprint.
- Talent management pipeline with HR activities such as attraction, selection, engagement, development, retention, work-life balance, and career management.
- Organisational influences including culture and values, talent management strategy, leadership, and mindset.
- Industry influences highlighting industry image, career opportunities, labour market characteristics, educational outputs, and individual expectations.

Together with the recommendations made by Maxwell and MacLean (2008), Hughes and Rog (2008), Deery (2008), Barron (2008), Baum (2008) and other researchers in the industry, the industry is now well positioned to make a fervent commitment to becoming an 'industry of choice' for employment.

There is no doubt that the nature of the journey is complex and the road to professionalism is fraught with difficulties and challenges. However, with a collective approach, the creation of the future tourism and hospitality professional is promising and presents a brilliant opportunity for showcasing best practice in human resource management.

Critical point

If the tourism and hospitality industry is to move forward in the creation of the future tourism and hospitality professional, it requires a strong commitment and effort from all industry participants and stakeholders, including HR managers, frontline supervisors and managers, CEOs, organisations and corporations, industry leaders and educators. In addition, it needs to view everyone working in the industry as a valued professional, regardless of whether they are the housekeeper, cleaner, dishwasher, gardener, carpenter, receptionist, restaurant manager, accounts manager or CEO.

Reflective practice

You are the HR Director of a five-star resort with strong links to various other tourism and hospitality stakeholders in the region. What would you do to promote the industry as one of choice for employment?

SUMMARY

This chapter considered the key issues which will affect the future of people and work in the tourism and hospitality sector. It debated the key role which HRM will play in the future of the industry and the role of the industry in promoting itself as one of choice for employment. In so doing, the chapter touches on the talent shortage and discusses some of the implications for the industry. The chapter continues with a review of the nature of the industry and concludes with a consideration of the future of the tourism and hospitality professional.

For any organisation, the development, implementation and maintenance of HR policies, processes and practices can be costly as can the building of professional recognition of the workforce. For the tourism and hospitality industry, this is compounded by a mindset of economic determinism and a view that investment in people is not worthwhile and high risk. In the long term, such an attitude perpetuates the ongoing labour and skills shortage experienced by the industry worldwide and erodes an already tenuous reputation. Baum (2006: 308) rightly states that 'the human resource vision that will support the competitive position of tourism, hospitality and leisure is derived from the sustainable paradigm as the main tenets of the traditional model have increasingly been shown to be flawed'. In this light, the tourism and hospitality industry needs to take a visionary and holistic approach if it is to sustain a reputable and worthy presence in the global community.

This book concludes with a case study (Box 10.5) which considers absenteeism, a major issue that constantly challenges tourism and hospitality managers and organisations. The implications of absenteeism penetrate deep into the fabric of the organisation, affecting other workers, productivity and organisational performance. The case extends our thinking on the issue and prompts discussion on how absenteeism can be better understood and minimised. In so doing, it is envisaged that a holistic perspective will assist in creating healthy tourism and hospitality workplaces that set professional benchmarks for the future.

BOX 10.5 Case study – Understanding and managing absenteeism

A case study of St James's Club, Antigua

St James's Club (SJC) is part of Elite Island Group, an all-inclusive 279-room, 3-star resort located in the Caribbean island of Antigua. The owner of SJC is Rob Barrett, who can perhaps best be described as a self-made man, possessing acuity of mind on global financial and tourism-related issues. From personal interaction, and perhaps reflective of the 'mom and pop' type origin of the resort, Mr Barrett also shows (albeit not always overt) a genuine interest in staff beyond their work life. Over the last five to seven years, the resort has grown both in terms of room stock and specific

Figure 10.1 St James's Club, Antigua

human resource competencies, so that the organisation now has a corporate lawyer, financial controller and a human resources director. Other positions that are critical to the optimal and competitive functioning of the resort, are a Rooms Division Manager and a Front Office Manager, have not yet been filled. The last few years have also seen improvements with respect to the formalisation of a number of policy documents including Disaster/Hurricane Policy, Operations Procedure Manual and a Common Standards Employee Handbook, the latter of which is given to every employee on the first day of reporting for work. The changes are reflective of the owner's commitment to modernise his business practices so that the organization can remain a serious global competitor.

The management structure of SJC is implicitly hierarchical (top-down) with variations in decision-making and empowerment among the management and senior supervisory staff. Most of the team have been with the resort for over ten (10) years, and have been promoted from within, presumably based upon outstanding performance and organizational loyalty. Interestingly, the ascendency to a management or senior supervisory position has had a negligible effect upon confidence and autonomous decision-making. The daily management briefings revealed that with the exception of the General Manager, the Human Resources Director and to some extent, the Head of Security and the Food & Beverages Manager, other members of the management team did not or were unable to make decisions regarding guests' complaints independently. This variance in decision-making ability is likely to be related to educational levels and exposure to international and regional organisations.

The hotel has a staff complement of 340 full-time employees, most of whom are nationals of Antigua and Barbuda. The majority of the staff have not advanced beyond high school although the younger of them (18–35 age group), view SJC as a stepping stone to further professional development. Staff are provided with uniforms and meals and there is a daily scheduled shuttle service to and from the city of St John's for employees who do not live near the resort. Using the Antigua Hotel and Tourism Association classification, there are three (3) groups of accommodation plant in Antigua and Barbuda. Group A hotels are 4–5 star, Group B, 3 star and Group C, 2 star. In this official categorisation, St James's Club is classified as a 4 star resort, and the wages paid to staff are in most instances comparable to that paid in this hotel group. In other words, employees at SJC are paid the industry norm and above. Despite this, over half of the employees are dissatisfied with their pay package. The resort has also taken a formal policy to eliminate split shifts, although staff may choose to/have to perform one or two because of unscheduled absences by their colleagues.

Formal and informal discussions suggest that an 'open door' policy operates at SJC, with staff having direct access to the General Manager and/or the owner, Mr Barrett. Even though there is some version of an Employee Assistance Scheme, it appears that on a personal level Mr Barrett has been very generous to many employees and their families. Still, there appears to be a problem with the flow of information from management. This issue was raised in one of the daily management meetings and it was suggested that information asymmetries can have implications for trust and job performance among employees; however, no solution was put forward to deal with the problem In particular, the Kitchen, Watersports, F&B and Housekeeping Departments felt that management did not properly communicate its decisions, plans and policies.

Recruitment and selection are conducted on a 'needs' basis. Applications are filtered through the Personnel Department but prospective line staff is interviewed and selected by the requisite departmental manager. Supervisory and Management staff are interviewed by the Director of Human Resources, Mr Glen Young. On the first day of work, the new employee is given a name tag and a copy of the Common

Standards and Employee Handbook by Personnel (Human Resources). St James's Club does not utilise any scientific method of recruitment and selection (e.g. psychometric test, or the Talent Plus) to ensure that employees have an aptitude for customer care or that there is a proper 'job fit'. There is also no formal induction or orientation to the organisation for new staff.

Training of the line staff is the responsibility of the department head or supervisor, who must submit a training plan to Personnel detailing what training they intend to undertake for their staff. Again, this practice is not adhered to systematically. In addition, attendance at training sessions is not compulsory, so that staff sometimes choose not to show up at all sessions. Some members of staff have chosen to pursue professional/technical training outside the organisation, and upon successful completion, the organisation pays half of the tuition fee. However, continuous organisational training is *ad hoc* because of a lack of commitment by staff and supervisors.

There is a system of annual performance appraisal/evaluation for line and supervisory staff, where staff are evaluated on a scale of 1 to 4 on: job knowledge; quantity of work; quality of work; appearance; timekeeping; and personal skills. Line staff evaluation is done by supervisors and requires that the staff member signs off on the overall appraisal as well as lists their training and developments needs and any other comments. A similar evaluation exercise is done for supervisors by the Head of Department. It appears that the bi-annual performance evaluation is systematically done by supervisors even though sometimes it is tardy in being submitted. The Personnel Department is also quite strict in terms of ensuring that these evaluations are done. However, employees in the Food & Beverage Department felt that evaluations are not used to inform promotions, and another employee observed that evaluations can be sometimes biased, and need to be considered alongside previous evaluations.

Despite the improvements that have been made within the organisation, SJC continues to battle with high absenteeism which adversely impacts on direct and indirect costs, productivity, and service standards. St James's Club has a clear and transparent Absenteeism Policy with sanctions moving from verbal warnings to termination as absence behaviour increases. Organisational statistics indicate that the Food & Beverage Department has the highest absenteeism and uncertified sick rate. The commonly cited reasons for absence are illness of children, no baby-sitter, rain, transport, 'waking up late' and appointments running over time. While absent days (where staff neither phone in sick nor show up for work) and certified sick days have decreased by 16.8% and 20.8% respectively from 2004 to 2006, the number of uncertified sick days has remained relatively unchanged. Given the trend up to August 2007 (1172 uncertified days), it is likely that uncertified days would be similar to previous years' figures incurred by the Kitchen and Canteen. From January–July

2007, absenteeism (uncertified and certified) cost St James's Club EC$199,054 (approx US$73,723). This figure is quite alarming given the other operating costs with which resorts are faced.

In order to manage absence behaviour, management introduced positive incentives in the form of monetary remuneration for the employee(s) with the lowest absences. Some members of staff feel that this type of incentive works for the first quarter of the year but is forgotten thereafter, suggesting the need for other forms or a revised form of this incentive.

Case study questions and issues

You have been retained as a Human Resource Consultant by Mr Barrett to investigate and evaluate the factors that are most likely to be impacting upon absence behaviour at St James's Club. Part of your brief is to provide workable solutions and recommendations for the problems identified.

1. Provide an assessment of St James's Club organisational structure and management procedures.
2. Identify at least three factors that may be impacting upon employee absenteeism.
3. Craft recommendations that could be implemented in the short and medium term to help SJC minimise the number of uncertified absences.

Source: Dr Sherma Roberts, Lecturer in Tourism, Programme Coordinator, MSc Tourism & Hospitality Management, Department Of Management Studies, University of the West Indies, Cave Hill Campus, Barbados

CHAPTER QUESTIONS

1. Describe how you envisage tourism and hospitality work to be in twenty years' time.

2. List and discuss retentions strategies which can be used for talent management.

3. Identify and discuss the competencies required of a tourism and hospitality professional.

RECOMMENDED READINGS

Losey, M., Meisinger, S. and Ulrich, D. (eds) (2007) *The Future of Human Resource Management: 64 Thought Leaders Explore the Critical HR Issues of Today and Tomorrow.* Hoboken, New Jersey: John Wiley & Sons Inc.

A timely book showcasing the views of a panel of experts on contemporary thought on HR.

Lashley, C. and Morrison, N. (eds) (2001) *In Search of Hospitality*. Oxford: Butterworth-Heinemann.

> This book is a refreshing, engaging and illuminating treatise of what hospitality is, what it means to work in hospitality, and what the associated issues are.

Maister, D. (1997) *True Professionalism*. New York: The Free Press.

> This is a valuable book which highlights the importance of professionalism.

Riley, M., Ladkin, A. and Szivas, E. (2002) *Tourism Employment: Analysis and Planning*. Clevedon: Channel View Publications.

> This book attempts to recognise the importance of 'occupation' and its associated behaviour as key to the tourism and hospitality industry's gaining and maintaining hegemony.

Jayawardena, C. (2002) *Tourism and Hospitality Education and Training in the Caribbean*. Kingston 7, Jamaica: University of West Indies Press.

> This book presents unique insights into various people-related issues challenging the development of the industry.

RECOMMENDED WEBSITES

The Association for Tourism and Leisure Education (ATLAS) –
http://www.atlas-euro.org/

Cornell University School of Hotel Administration: The Center for hospitality research – Hospitality leadership through learning –
http://www.hotelschool.cornell.edu/research/chr/

Council for Australian University Tourism and Hospitality Education –
http://www.cauthe.com.au/index.html

School of Hotel & Tourism Management (The Hong Kong Polytechnic University) –
http://hotelschool.shtm.polyu.edu.hk/eng/index.jsp

The International Council on Hotel, Restaurant and Institutional Education (CHRIE): The hospitality & tourism educators –
http://chrie.org/i4a/pages/index.cfm?pageid=1

REFERENCES

ABS (2008) Australian Bureau of Statistics, *Population Projections. Australia, 2006 to 2101*, Cat. 3222.0.

ACAS (2009) http://www.acas.org.uk/index.aspx?articleid=1089. Accessed March 2009.

Aksu, A. and Köksal, C. (2005) Perceptions and attitudes of tourism students in Turkey. *International Journal of Contemporary Hospitality Management* 17(4/5), 436–447.

Amoah, V.A. and Baum, T. (1997) Tourism education: policy versus practice. *International Journal of Contemporary Hospitality Management* 9(1), 5–12.

Anon (2008) Recruitment goes into overdrive as InterContinental Hotels battles for talent. *Human Resource Management International Digest* 16(5), 5–8.

Anon (2009) TUC calls on tourism industry to audit supply-chain working conditions. http://www.ethicalcorp.com/content.asp?ContentID=2570. Accessed September 2009.

Armstrong, M. (1997) *A Handbook of Human Resource Management*. London: Kogan Page.

Arthur, M.B. and Rousseau, D. (1996) Introduction: The boundaryless career as a new employment principle. In M.B. Arthur and D. Rousseau (eds) *The Boundaryless Career: A New Employment Principle for a New Organizational Era* (pp. 3–20). Oxford: Oxford University Press.

Azjen, I. and Fishbein, M. (1980) *Understanding Attitudes and Predicting Social Behaviour*. New Jersey: Prentice Hall.

Bacall, R. (2008) *The Performance Management and Appraisal Help Center*. http://performance-appraisals.org/experts/whattosay.htm. Accessed May 2009.

Balnave, N., Brown, J., Maconachie, G. and Stone, R. (2007) *Employment Relations in Australia*. Milton, Qld: John Wiley & Sons.

Bardgett, L. (2000) *The Tourism Industry*. Economic Policy and Statistics, House of Commons Library.

Bardoel, E.A., DeCieri, H. and Santos, C. (2008) A review of work-life research in Australia and New Zealand. *Asia Pacific Journal of Human Resources* 46(3), 316–333.

Barlow, G. (1989) Deficiencies and the perpetuation of power: latent functions in management appraisal. *Journal of Management Studies* 25(5), 499–517.

Barrett, E. (1999) Justice in the workplace? Normative ethics and the critique of human resource management. *Personnel Review* 28(4), 307–318.

Barron, P. (2008) Education and talent management: Implications for the hospitality industry. *International Journal of Contemporary Hospitality Management* 20(70), 730–742.

Bartel, A. (1995) Training, wage growth, and job performance: Evidence from a company database. *Journal of Labor Economics* 13(3), 401–425.

Baum, T. (1989) Managing hotels in Ireland: Research and development for change. *International Journal of Hospitality Management* 8(2), 131–144.

Baum, T. (1995) *Managing Human Resources in the European Tourism and Hospitality Industry – A Strategic Approach*. London: Chapman & Hall.

Baum, T. (2006) *Human Resource Management for Tourism, Hospitality and Leisure: An International Perspective*. London: Thomson.

Baum, T. (2006) Reflections on the nature of skills in the experience economy: challenging traditional skills models in hospitality. *Journal of Hospitality and Tourism Management* 13(2), 124–135.

Baum, T. (2008) Implications of hospitality and tourism labour markets for talent management strategies. *International Journal of Contemporary Hospitality Management* 20(7), 720–729.

Bernhard, A., Dresser, L. and Hatton, E. (2003) The coffee pot wars: Unions and firm restructuring in the hotel industry. In E. Appelbaum, A. Bernhardt and R.J. Murnane (eds) *Low Wage America* (pp. 33–76). New York: Russell Sage Foundation.

Bianchi, R. (2000) Migrant tourist-workers: Exploring the 'contact zones' of post-industrial tourism. *Current Issues in Tourism* 3(2), 107–137.

Bignold, D. (2003) Hospitality sector reaches drink and drugs crisis point. *Caterer and Hotelkeeper* 9, 21–23.

Bishop, J.H. (1994) The impact of previous training on productivity and wages. In L.M. Lynch (ed.) *Training and the Private Sector: International Comparisons* (pp. 161–199). Chicago: Chicago University Press.

Blyth, A. (2006) Nando's spices up its leadership style. *Personnel Today*, October (10), 50–51.

Boella, M. and Goss-Turner, S. (2005) *Human Resource Management in the Hospitality Industry: An Introductory Guide*. Burlington (MA): Elsevier Butterworth-Heinemann.

Bohle, P. and Quinlan, M. (2000) *Managing Occupational Health and Safety* (2nd edn). Melbourne: Macmillan.

Boon, B. (2006) When leisure and work are allies: The case of skiers and tourist resort hotels. *Career Development International* 11(7), 594–608.

Booth, A. and Satchell, S. (1994) Apprenticeship and job tenure. *Oxford Economic Papers* 46, 676–695.

BPFRC (2009) http://work911.com/planningmaster/faq/hrdefinition.htm. Accessed March 2009.

Bratton, J. and Gold, J. (2003) *Human Resource Management Theory and Practice* (3rd edn). Basingstoke: Palgrave MacMillan.

Bray, M. and Waring, P. (2006) Theoretical Foundations. In P. Waring and M. Bray, *Evolving Employment Relations: Industry Studies from Australia* (pp. 3–16). North Ryde (NSW): McGraw-Hill.

Bray, M., Deery, S., Walsh, J. and Waring, P. (2005) *Industrial Relations: A Contemporary Approach* (3rd edn). Sydney: McGraw-Hill.

Bray, M., Waring, P. and Cooper, R. (2009) *Employment Relations: Theory and Practice*. North Ryde (NSW): McGraw-Hill.

Brotherton, R., Wolfenden, G. and Himmetoglu, B. (1994) Developing human resources for Turkey's tourism industry in the 1990s. *Tourism Management* 15(2), 109–116.

Brough, P., Holt, J., Bauld, R., Biggs, A. and Ryan, C. (2008) The ability of work-life policies to influence key social/organisational issues. *Asia Pacific Journal of Human Resources* 46(3), 261–274.

Brown, K. (2009) *Management Today*, March, 22–23.

Buckingham, M. and Vosburgh, R.M. (2001) The 21st century human resources function. It's the talent, stupid! *Human Resource Planning* 24(4), 17–23.

Buick, J. and Mathu, G. (1997) An investigation of the current practices of in-house employee training and development within hotels in Scotland. *Service Industries Journal* 17(4), 652–668.

Butler, J.E., Ferris, G.R. and Napier, N.K. (1991) *Strategy and Human Resource Management*. Cincinnati: South Western.

Cambridge Advanced Learner's Dictionary (2009) http://dictionary.cambridge.org/define.asp?key=22796&dict=CALD. Accessed April 2009.

Carmody, J. and Prideaux, B. (2008) Insights into the membership of the Savannah Guides Ltd. Report provided by Dr Julie Carmody, Postgraduate Researcher, JCU.

Casper, S. (2009) The Reno-Sparks Convention & Visitors Authority Makes Employee Appraisals Exciting and Fun, http://www.halogensoftware.com/customers/case-studies/education-government/study_renotahoe.php. Accessed September 2009.

Chand, M. and Katou, A.A. (2007) The impact of HRM practices on organizational performance in the Indian hotel industry. *Employee Relations* 29(6), 576–594.

Chappel, S. (2002) Hospitality and emotional labour in an international context. In N. D'Annunzio-Green, G. Maxwell and S. Watson, *Human Resource Management: International Perspectives in Hospitality and Tourism* (pp. 225–240). London: Thomson.

Cheng, A. and Brown, A. (1998) HRM strategies and labour turnover in the hotel industry: A comparative study of Australian and Singapore. *The International Journal of Human Resource Management* 9(1), 136–154.

Choi, J.G., Woods, R.H. and Murrmann, S.K. (2000) International labor markets and the migration of labor forces as an alternative solution for labor shortages in the hospitality industry. *International Journal of Contemporary Hospitality Management* 12(1), 61–66.

Choy, D. (1995) The quality of tourism employment. *Tourism Management* 16(2), 129–137.

CIPD (2008) Performance Management: An Overview, http://www.cipd.co.uk/subjects/perfmangmt/general/perfman.htm. Accessed May 2009.

Council of Europe Publishing, Directorate General III – Social Cohesion

Creighton, C. (1999) The rise and decline of the 'male breadwinner family' in Britain. *Cambridge Journal of Economics* 23, 519–541.

Crowell, C. (2009) Staff management is key for smaller budgets. *Hotel and Motel Management* February. http://www.hotelworldnetwork.com/training/staff-management-key-smaller-budgets. Retrieved March 2009.

D'Annunzio-Green, N., Maxwell, G. and Watson, S. (2008) Concluding commentary on the contemporary human resource issues for talent management in hospitality and tourism. *International Journal of Contemporary Hospitality Management* 20(7). Accessed 30.5.09.

Daft, R. (2005) *The Leadership Experience* (3rd edn). Australia: Thomson.

Dalglish, C. and Evans, P. (2000) Entrepreneurship vs Leadership, ICSB Conference, June 2000, Brisbane.

Dalton, M., Hoyle, D. and Watts, M. (2006) *Human Relations* (3rd Edn). Southbank, Vic.: Thomson Learning Australia.

Davies, D., Taylor, R. and Savery, L. (2001) The role of appraisal, remuneration and training in improving staff relations in the Western Australian accommodation industry: a comparative study. *Journal of European Industrial Training* 25(7), 366–373.

DeCieri, H. and Kramar, R. (2005) *Human Resource Management in Australia: Strategy, People, Performance* (2nd Edn). North Ryde, NSW: McGraw-Hill Australia Pty Ltd.

Deery, M. (2008) Talent management, work-life balance and retention strategies. *International Journal of Contemporary Hospitality Management* 20(7), 792–806.

Dell, D. and Hickey, J. (2002) *Sustaining the talent quest: getting and keeping the best people in volatile times* [Research Report]. New York: The Conference Board.

Dessler, G., Griffiths, J. and Lloyd-Walker, B. (2004) *Human Resource Management* (2nd edn). Frenchs Forest: Pearson.

Devine, F., Baum, T., Hearns, N. and Devine, A. (2007) Managing cultural diversity: Opportunities and challenges for Northern Ireland Hoteliers. *International Journal of Contemporary Hospitality Management* 19(2), 120–132.

Dewe, P. (1989) Developing stress management programs: What can we learn from recent research? *Journal of Occupational Health and Safety – Australian and New Zealand* 5(6), 493–499.

Dickens, L. (1992) Part-time employees: Workers whose time has come? *Employee Relations* 14(2), 3–12.

Drumm, H.J. (1994) Theoretical and ethical foundations of human resource management. *Employee Relations* 16(4), 35–47.

Dubrin, A.J. and Dalglish, C. (2003) *Leadership: An Australian Focus*. Australia: John Wiley and Sons.

Duce, C. (2007) Hospitality staff are sick of gloomy working conditions, http://www.caterersearch.com/Articles/2007/04/19/313216/hospitality-staff-are-sick-of-gloomy-working-conditions.html. Accessed September 2009.

Eldson, R. and Iyer, S. (1999) Creating value and enhancing retention through employee development: The Sun Microsystem experience. *Human Resource Planning* 22(2), 39–47.

Ely, R.J. and Thomas, D.A. (2001) Cultural diversity at work. *Administrative Science Quarterly* 46(2), 229–273.

Ethan, A. (1994) http://www.ewin.com/articles/hrlex.htm. Accessed February 2009.

Eurostat (1998) *Community Methodology on Tourism Statistics.*

Euzeby, A. (1988) Social security and part-time employment. *International Labour Review* 127(5), 545–557.

Evans, J. (2007) Talent strategy feeds growth at Nando's. *People Management* 13(9), 16.

Evans, J.R. (2008) *Quality & performance excellence: Management, organization, and strategy* (5th edn). Mason (OH): Thomson Higher Education.

Fáilte Ireland (2005) *Cultural Diversity Strategy and Implementation Plan*, Fáilte Ireland, Dublin.

Fennell, D. (2006) *Tourism Ethics.* Clevedon: Channel View Publications.

Foley, D (2003). An examination of Indigenous Australian Entrepreneurs. *Journal of Developmental Entrepreneurship* 8, 133–152.

Fowler, A. (1987) When chief executives discover HRM. *Personnel Management* 19(1), 3.

Fox, A. (1974) *Beyond contract: Work, power and trust relationships.* London: Faber and Faber.

Frabotta, D. (2000) Human resources director praises culture at Marriot. *Hotel and Motel Management* 215(19), 136.

Francis, H. and D'Annunzio-Green, N. (2004) HRM and the pursuit of a service culture. *Employee Relations* 27(1), 71–85.

Gale, D. (2009) War for talent placed on hold (company overview). *Hotels* 43(3), 26.

Garavan, T.N. (1995) Stakeholder analysis: The implications for the management of HRD. *Journal of European Industrial Training* 19(10), 45–46.

Gardner, H., Csikszentmihalyi, M. and Damon, W. (2001) *Good Work: When Excellence and Ethics Meet.* New York: Basic Books.

Getz, D. (1994) Students' work experiences, perceptions and attitudes towards careers in hospitality and tourism: a longitudinal case study in Spey Valley, Scotland. *International Journal of Hospitality Management* 13(1), 25–37.

Ghiselli, R., La Lopa, J. and Bai, B (2001) Job satisfaction, life satisfaction and turnover intent. *Cornell Hotel and Restaurant Administration Quarterly* 42(2), 28–37.

Giddens, A. (1998) *The Third Way: The Renewal of Social Democracy.* Cambridge: Polity Press.

Gilbert, D. and Guerrier, Y. (1997) UK hospitality managers past and present. *Service Industries Journal* 17, 115–132.

Gilbert, D., Guerrier, Y. and Guy, J. (1998) Sexual harassment issues in the hospitality industry. *International Journal of Contemporary Hospitality Management* 10(2), 48–53.

Goldsmith, A., Nickson, D., Sloan, D. and Wood, R.C. (1997) *Human Resource Management for Hospitality Services.* London: International Thomson Business Press.

Goldthorpe, J., Lockwood, D., Bechhofer, F. and Platt, J. (1968) *The Affluent Worker: Industrial Attitudes and Behaviour.* Cambridge: Cambridge University Press.

Gomez-Meija, L., Balkina, D. and Cardy, R. (2001) *Managing Human Resources* (3rd edn). Englewood Cliffs (NJ): Prentice Hall.

Graham, M. and Lennon, J. (2002) The dilemma of operating a strategic approach to human resource management in the Scottish visitor attraction sector. *International Journal of Contemporary Hospitality Management* 14(5), 213–220.

Grant, D. and Shields, J. (2002) In search of the subject: Researching, employee reactions to human resource management. *Journal of Industrial Relations* 44(3), 313–334.

Gratton, L. (2000) *Living Strategy.* London: Prentice Hall.

Greenblatt, E. (2002) Work/life balance: wisdom or whining? *Organizational Dynamics,* 31(2), 177–93.

Grönroos, C. (1994) From scientific management to service management: A management perspective for the age of service competition. *International Journal of Service Industry Management* 5(1), 5–20.

Gröschl, S. and Doherty, L. (1999) Diversity management in practice. *International Journal of Contemporary Hospitality Management* 11(6), 262–268.

Guerrier, Y. (1999) *Organizational Behaviour in Hotels and Restaurants: An International Perspective.* Chichester: Wiley.

Guest, D. (1995) Human resource management, trade unions and industrial relations. In J. Storey (ed.) *Human Resource Management: A Critical Text* (pp. 96–113). London: Routledge.

Guest, D.E. (1987) Human resource management and industrial relations. *Journal of Management Studies* 24(5), 503–521.

Haar, J. and Bardoel, A. (2008) Positive spillover from the work-family interface: A study of Australian employees. *Asia Pacific Journal of Human Resources* 46(3), 275–287.

Haar, J., Bardoel, A. and De Cieri, H. (2008) Work-life in Australia. *Asia Pacific Journal of Human Resources* 46(3), 258–260.

Hackman, J.R. and Oldham, G.R. *Work Redesign.* Reading (MA): Addison-Wesley.

Hall, D.T. (ed.) (1996) *The Career is Dead – Long Live the Career.* San Francisco: Jossey-Bass.

Handy, C. (2002) *The Elephant and the Flea.* Boston (MA): Harvard Business School Press.

Hannerz, U. (1996) *Transnational Connections: Culture, People, Places.* London: Routledge.

Hansard (1986) Debate 15 April 15 c734, http://hansard.millbanksystems.com/commons/1986/apr/15/libya#S6CV0095P0_19860415_HOC_178. Accessed April 2009.

Hanson, K.O. (2003) Confronting Unethical Conduct. http://www.scu.edu.au/ethics/publications/ethicalperspectives/confronting.html. Retrieved June 2009.

Harris, L. (2008) http://www.tourismforall.org.uk/10-good-reasons.html. Accessed April 2009.

Hart, T.J. (1993) Human resource management: time to exercise the militant tendency. *Employee Relations* 15(3), 29–36.

Härtel, C.E.J., Fujimoto, Y., Strybosch, V.E. and Fitzpatrick, K. (2007) *Human Resource Management: Transforming Theory into Innovative Practice*. Frenchs Forest: Pearson.

Haynes, P. (1999) A new agenda for researching hospitality HRM: comment on Lashley and Watson. *Tourism and Hospitality Research* 1(3), 199–204.

Haynes, P. and Fryer, G. (2000) Human resources, service quality and performance: a case study. *International Journal of Contemporary Management* 12(4), 240–248.

HCTC (1994) *Employment in the Catering and Hospitality Industry: Employee Attitudes and Career Expectations*. London: HCTC.

Herrbach, O. and Mignonac, K. (2004) How organizational image affects employee attitudes. *Human Resource Management Journal* 14(4), 76–88.

Herriot, P. (ed.) (1989) *Assessment and Selection in Organisations: Methods and Practice for Recruitment and Appraisal*. Chichester: Wiley.

Hillman, W. (2003) *Protectors and interpreters of the outback: A study of the emerging occupation of the Savannah Guides*, PhD Thesis, James Cook University. Accessed 20.4.09, from James Cook University Digital Theses, http://eprints.jcu.edu.au/79/.

Hjalager, A. and Andersen, S. (2001) Tourism employment: contingent work or professional career? *Employee Relations* 23(2), 115–129.

Hofstede, G. (2001) *Cultural Consequences: Comparing Values, Behaviors, Institutions and Organizations Across Nations* (2nd edn). London: Sage Publications.

Hofstede, G. (1980) *Culture's Consequences: International Differences in Work-Related Values*. Beverley Hills: Sage.

Hofstede, G. (1994) *Culture and Organizations: Intercultural Cooperation and its Importance for Survival – Software of the Mind*. London: Harper Collins.

Holden, L. (2004) Human resource development: The organization and the national framework. In I. Beardwell, L. Holden and T. Claydon (eds) *Human Resource Management: A Contemporary Approach* (4th edn) (pp.313–360). London: Prentice Hall.

Holden, N.J. (2002) *Cross-cultural Management: A Knowledge Management Perspective*. London: Prentice Hall.

Holland, P., Sheehan, C., Donohue, R. and Pyman, A. (2007) *Contemporary Issues and Challenges in HRM*. Prahran, Vic: Tilde University Press.

Hoque, K. (1999) Human resource management and performance in the UK hotel industry. *British Journal of Industrial Relations* 37(3), 419–443.

Hospitality Training Foundation (HtF, 2002) *Labour Market Review 2002 for the Hospitality Industry*, HtF.

Hotel and Motel Management, February, http://www.hotelworldnetwork.com/training/staff-management-key-smaller-budgets. Accessed March 2009.

http://wiki.answers.com/Q/What_is_the_Marriott_hotel_mission_statement. Accessed June 2009.

http://www.crctourism.com.au/Page/About+Us/Who+we+are.aspx, retrieved, December 2008.

http://www.crctourism.com.au/Page/Home.aspx. Accessed December 2008.

http://www.emeraldinsight.com.elibrary.jcu.edu.au/Insight/ViewContentServlet? contentType=NonArticle&Filename=Published/NonArticle/Articles/ 04120gaa.003.html

http://www.merriam-webster.com/dictionary/diversity. Accessed April 2009.

http://www.scu.edu/ethics/publications/ethicalperspectives/confronting.html. Accessed June 2009.

http://www.singaporeair.com/saa/en_UK/content/company_info/siastory/index.jsp. Accessed June 2009.

http://www.wotif.com/hotels/shangri-la-hotel-sydney.html. Accessed June 2009.

Hughes, J.C. and Rog, E. (2008) Talent management: A strategy for improving employee recruitment, retention and engagement within hospitality organizations. *International Journal of Contemporary Hospitality Management* 20(7), 743–757.

Hulin, C.L. and Blood, M R. (1968) Job enlargement, industrial differences and worker responses. *Psychological Bulletin* 69(1), 41–53.

Huselid, M., Jackson, S.E. and Schuler, R.S. (1997) Technical and strategic human resource management effectives as determinants of firm performance. *Academy of Management Journal* 40(1), 171–188.

Hussey, D. (1996) *Business Driven Human Resource Management.* Chichester: John Wiley & Sons.

Hyams, J. (2007) Grow your own. *Human Resources* April, 63–65.

ICF (2007) International Classification of Functioning, Disability and Health, http: //www.who.int/classifications/icf/site/onlinebrowser/icf.cfm. Accessed April 2009.

Iles, P. and Salaman, G. (1995) Recruitment, selection and assessment. In J. Storey (ed.) *Human Resource Management: A Critical Text.* London: Routledge.

Ivancevich, J.M. (2001) *Human Resource Management* (8th edn). Boston: McGraw-Hill.

Iveson, R.D. and Deery, M. (1997) Turnover culture in the hospitality industry. *Human Resource Management Journal* 7, 71–82.

Iwasaki, Y., MacKay, K. and Mactavish, J. (2005) Gender-based analyses of coping with stress among professional managers: leisure coping and non-leisure coping. *Journal of Leisure Research* 37(1), 1–28.

Jameson, S. (2000) Recruitment and training in small firms. *Journal of European Industrial Training* 24(1), 43–49.

Jarman, N. (2004) Migrant workers in Northern Ireland, http://www.ofmdfmni.gov.uk/ migrantworkers.pdf. Accessed April 2009.

Jones, P., Comfort, D. and Hillier, D. (2006) Reporting and reflecting on corporate social responsibility in the hospitality industry. *International Journal of Contemporary Hospitality Management* 18(4), 329–240.

Judy, R.W. and D'Amico, C. (1997) *Workforce 2020: Work and Workers in the 21st Century.* Indianapolis: Hudson Institute.

Kandampully, J. (2002) *Services Management: The New Paradigm in Hospitality.* Hospitality Press. Frenchs Forest: Pearson Education.

Kandola, R. and Fullerton, J. (1998) *Diversity in Action.* London: CIPID.

Kaplan, R.S. and Norton, D.P. (1996) Using the balanced scorecard as a strategic management system. *Harvard Business Review* January–February, 75–85.

Keenoy, T. and Kelly, D. (2000) *The Employment Relationship in Australia* (2nd edin). Sydney: Harcourt.

Kelley, H.H. (1973) The process of causal attribution, *American Psychologist* February, 107–128.

Kelliher, C. and Johnson, K. (1987) Personnel management in hotels – some empirical observations. *International Journal of Hospitality Management* 6(2), 103–108.

Knox, A. and Nickson, D. (2007) Regulation in Australian hotels: Is there a lesson for the UK? *Employee Relations* 29(1), 50–67.

Kusluvan, S. (2003) Characteristics of employment and human resource management in the tourism and hospitality industry. In S. Kusluvan (ed.) *Managing Employee Attitudes and Behaviours in the Tourism and Hospitality Industry* (pp. 3–24). New York: Nova Science.

Kusluvan, S. and Kusluvan, Z. (2000) Perceptions and attitudes of undergraduate tourism students toward working in the tourism industry in Turkey. *Tourism Management* 21(3), 251–269.

Lashley, C. (2002) A feeling for empowerment. In N. D'Annunzio-Green, G.A. Maxwell and S. Watson (eds) *Human Resource Management: International Perspectives in Hospitality and Tourism* (pp. 200–211). London: Thomson.

Lashley, C. (2002) The benefits of training for business performance. In N. D'Annunzio-Green, G.A. Maxwell and S. Watson (eds) *Human Resource Management: International Perspectives in Hospitality and Tourism*, pp. 104–117. London: Thomson.

Lashley, C. and Best, W. (2002) Employee induction in licensed retail organizations. *International Journal of Contemporary Hospitality Management* 14(1), pp. 6–13.

Lashley, C. and Lee-Ross, D. (2003) *Organization Behaviour for Leisure Services.* Sydney: Butterworth Heinemann.

Lashley, C. and Rowson, B. (2007) Trials and tribulations of hotel ownership in Blackpool: Highlighting the skills gaps of owner-managers. *Tourism and Hospitality Research* 7, 122–130.

Lashley, C. and Taylor, S. (1998) Hospitality retail operations types and styles in the management of human resources. *Journal of Retailing and Consumer Services* 5(3), 153–165.

Lawrie, J. (1990) Differentiate between training, education and development. *Personnel Journal* 69(10), 44–54.

Lee-Ross, D. (1996) *A Study of Attitudes and Work Motivation Amongst Seasonal Hotel Workers,* PhD Thesis. Cambridge: Anglia Polytechnic University.

Lee-Ross, D. (1995) Attitudes and work motivation of subgroups of seasonal hotel workers. *The Service Industries Journal* 15(3), 295–313.

Lee-Ross, D. (2000) Development of the service predisposition instrument. *Journal of Managerial Psychology* 15(2), 148–157.

Lee-Ross, D. and Pryce, J. (2004) A preliminary study of service predispositions amongst hospitality workers in Australia. *Journal of Management Development* 24(5), 410–420.

Legge, K. (1995) *Human Resource Management: Rhetorics and Reality.* London: Macmillan.

Leinster, C. (1985) Playing the tipping game. *Fortune Magazine*, 139–140.

Leiper, N. (1995) *Tourism Management.* Victoria: RMIT Press.

Lillard, L.A. and Tan, H.W. (1992) Private sector training: Who gets it and what are its effects? *Research in Labor Economics* 13, 1–62.

Lindsay, N.J. (2005) Towards a cultural model of Indigenous entrepreneurial attitude. *Academy of Marketing Science Review* [Online] 5: www.amsreview.org/articles/lindsay05–2005.pdf. Accessed 2007.

Lo, K. and Lamm, F. (2005) Occupational stress in the hospitality industry: An employment relations perspective. *New Zealand Journal of Employment Relations* 30(1), 23–47.

Lockyer, C. and Scholarios, D. (2004) Selecting hotel staff: Why best practice does not always work. *International Journal of Contemporary Hospitality Management* 16(2), 125–135.

Loden, M. (1996) *Implementing Diversity.* Homewood (IL): Irwin.

Lowry, D. (2001) The casual management of casual work: casual workers' perceptions of HRM practices in the highly specialised firm. *Asia Pacific Journal of Human Resource Management* 39(1), 42–62.

Lucas, R. (1995) *Managing Employee Relations in the Hotel and Catering Industry.* London: Cassell.

Lucas, R. (2004) *Employment Relations in the Hospitality and Tourism Industries.* London: Routledge.

Lynch, L.M. (1992) Private sector training and the earning of young workers. *American Economic Review* 82, 299–312.

Lynn, M., Zinkhan, G. and Harris, J. (1993) Consumer tipping: A cross country study. *Journal of Consumer Research* 20(3), 478–489.

Maclellan, N. (2008) Pick of the crop: New Zealand opens up to seasonal workers. *Pacific Magazine* March/April, 32–33.

Mahesh, V.S. (1988) Effective human resource management: key to excellence in service organizations. *Vikalpa* 13(4), 9–15.

Malpas, J. (2005) The dualities of work: self-consumption and self-creation. *Philosophy Today* 49(3), 256–63.

Mann, S. (1999) *Hiding What We Feel, Faking What We Don't: Understanding the Role of Emotions at Work.* Dorset: Element Books.

Mapunda, G. (2005) Traditional societies and entrepreneurship: an analysis of Australian and Tanzanian Businesses. *Journal of Asia Entrepreneurship and Sustainability* 1(2), 1–23.

Marhuenda, F., Martínez, I. and Navas, A. (2004) Conflicting vocational identities and careers in the sector of tourism. *Career Development International* 9(3), 222–244.

Marler, J., Barringer, M. and Milkovich, G. (2002) Boundaryless and traditional contingent employees: Worlds apart. *Journal of Organizational Behavior* 23, 425–453.

Mars, G. and Nicod, M. (1984) *The World of Waiters.* London: Allen and Unwin.

Mars, G., Bryant, P. and Mitchell, P. (1979) *Manpower Problems in the Hotel and Catering Industry.* Farnborough: Saxon House.

Martin, E. (2004) Who's kicking whom? Employees' orientations to work. *International Journal of Contemporary Hospitality Management* 16(2), 182–188.

Mason, A. (1997) Apprenticeships – do they work? *Hospitality* September/October, 26–27.

Maxwell, G. and MacLean, S. (2008) Talent management in hospitality and tourism in Scotland. *International Journal of Contemporary Hospitality Management* 20(7), 820–830.

Maxwell, G., Watson, S. and Quail, S. (2004) Quality service in the international hotel sector. *Journal of European Industrial Training* 28(2/3/4), 159–182.

McCrindle, M. (2007) *Understanding Generation Y,* The Australian Leadership Foundation. http://www.learningtolearn.sa.edu.au/colleagues/files/links/understandinggeny.pdf. Retrieved April 2009.

McGarrell, E.J. (1983) An orientation system that builds productivity. *Personnel Administrator* October, 75–85.

McGunnigle. P.J. and Jameson, S.M. (2000) HRM in UK hotels: A focus on commitment. *Employee Relations* 22(4), 403–422.

McKenna, E. and Beech, N. (2002) *Human Resource Management: A Concise Analysis.* Harlow, Essex: Pearson Education Ltd.

McKercher, B., Williams, A. and Coglan, I. (1995) Career progress of recent tourism graduates. *Tourism Management* 16(7), 541–519.

Mcleod, F. (2008) Glass ceiling still firmly in place. *The Australian*, June 27. http://www.theaustralian.news.com.au/story/0,25197,23926883–30537,00.html. Accessed April 2009.

Meadows, P. (1996) *Work Out – or Work In: Contributions to the Debate on the Future of Work.* London: Joseph Rowntree Foundation.

Medlik, S. (2003) *Dictionary of Travel, Tourism and Hospitality* (3rd edn). London: Butterworth Heinemann.

Merriam-Webster Online Dictionary (2009) http://www.merriam-webster.com/dictionary/diversity. Retrieved April 2009.

Michelson, G. and Kramar, R. (2003) The state of HRM in Australia: progress and prospects. *Asia Pacific Journal of Human Resources* 41(2), 133–148.

Miller, G.E. and Rowney, J.I.A. (1999) Workplace diversity in a multicultural society. *Women in Management Review* 14(8), 307–315.

Mincer, J. (1983) Union effects, wages, turnover and job training. *Research in Labor Economics* 5(5), 217–252.

Mistakes, World Federation of Productivity Science, http://www.wcps.info/academy/ thor.htm. Accessed May 2009.

Mohinder, C. (2004) Human resource strategies and global competitiveness: a study of Indian small and medium sized tourism enterprises. *International Conference on creating Global Competitive Advantage*. Shimla: Laxpara Foundation.

Mondy, R.W. (2008) *Human Resource Management*. Upper Saddle River: Pearson.

Morrison, A. (1998) Small firm cooperative marketing in a peripheral tourism region. *International Journal of Contemporary Hospitality Management* 10(5), 191–197.

Morton, L. (2004) *Integrated and Integrative Talent Management: A Strategic HR Framework* [Research Report, R-1360-04-RR]. New York: The Conference Board.

Morton, L. (2005) *Talent Management Value Imperatives: Strategies for Successful Execution* [Research Report, R-1360-05-RR]. New York: The Conference Board.

Mulcahy, J.D. (1999) Vocational work experience in the hospitality industry: characteristics and strategies. *Education and Training* 41(4), 164–174.

Mulvaney, R., O'Neill, J., Cleverland, J. and Crouter, A. (2006) A model of work-family dynamics of hotel managers, *Annals of Tourism Research* 34(1), 66–87.

Murray-Gibbons, R. and Gibbons, C. (2007) Occupational stress in the chef profession. *International Journal of Contemporary Hospitality Management* 19(1), 32–42.

Nankervis, A., Compton, R. and Baird, M. (2008) *Human Resource Management Strategies and Processes* (6th edn). Victoria: Thomson.

Nankervis, A., Compton, R. and Baird, M. (2005) *Human Resource Management: Strategies and Processes* (5th edn). Southbank, Victoria: Thomson.

Nelson, D.L. and Quick, J.C. (2009) *ORGB*. Mason: South-Western Cengage Learning.

Nickson, D. (2007) *Human resource management for the hospitality and tourism industries*. Burlington (MA): Butterworth-Heinemann (Elsevier).

Nolan, C. (2002) Human resource development in the Irish hotel industry: The case of the small firm. *Journal of European Industrial Training* 23 (2/3/4), 88–99.

O'Leary, S. and Deegan, J. (2005) Career progression of Irish tourism and hospitality management graduates. *International Journal of Contemporary Hospitality Management* 17(5), 421–432.

OECD (Organisation for Economic Co-operation and Development) (2002) *Implementing the OECD job strategy – Lessons from member countries*. Accessed on 22.05.09 at: http://www.oecd.org/dataoecd/42/52/1941687.pdf

Partington, C., Adam-Smith, D., Norris, G. and Williams, S. (2003) Continuity or change? The implications of the National Minimum Wage for work and employment in the hospitality industry. *Work, Employment and Society* 17(1), 29–48.

Peacock, M. (1995) A job well done: hospitality managers and success. *International Journal of Contemporary Hospitality Management* 7(2/3), 48–51.

People 1st. (2008) *Skills Needs Assessment: The Hospitality, Leisure, Travel and Tourism Sector in London*. UK: People 1st.

Peppas, S.C. (2002) Subcultural approaches to management: A comparative study of African and Euro-American Values. *Cross Cultural Management* 9(2), 45–64.

Pfläging, N. (2006) *Leading with Flexible Targets, Beyond Budgeting in Practice*. Germany: Campus Verlag, http://www.cognos.com/newsletter/finance/st_061129_01.html. Accessed May 2009.

Piore, M.J. (1795) Notes for a theory of labour market stratification. In R.C. Edwards, M. Reich and D.M. Gordon (eds) *Labor Market Segmentation* (pp. 125–150). Harvard University: D.C. Heath and Co.

Pitt, L. Foreman, S. and Bromfield, D. (1995) Organizational commitment and service delivery: Evidence from an industrial setting in the UK. *The International Journal of Human Resource Management* 6(1), 369–389.

Poppleton, S. (1989) Service occupations. In P. Herriot (ed) *Assessment and Selection in Organisations: Methods and Practice for Recruitment and Appraisal* (pp. 189–201). Chichester: Wiley.

Porter, M. (1985) *Competitive Advantage: Creating and Sustaining Superior Performance*. New York: Free Press.

Poulston, J. (2008) Hospitality workplace problems and poor training: a close relationship. *International Journal of Contemporary Hospitality Management* 20(4), 412–427.

Powell, S. and Wood, E. (1999) Is recruitment the millennium time bomb for the industry worldwide? *International Journal of Contemporary Hospitality Management* 11, 138–141.

Pratten, J.D. (2003) The training and retention of chefs. *International Journal of Contemporary Hospitality Management* 15(4), 237–242.

Price, L. (1994) Poor personnel practice in the hotel and catering industry: does it matter? *Human Resource Management Journal* 4(4), pp. 44–62.

Price, L. (1994) Poor personnel practice in the hotel and catering industry: does it matter? *Human Resource Management Journal* 4(4), 44–62.

Pryce, J. (2007) PhD Thesis. Cairns, Australia: James Cook University.

Purcell, K. and Quinn, J. (1996) Exploring the education-employment equation in hospitality management. *International Journal of Hospitality Management* 15(1), 51–68.

Ramos, V., Rey-Maquieira, J. and Tugores, M. (2004) The role of training in changing an economy specialising in tourism. *International Journal of Manpower* 25(1), 55–72.

Ready, D.A. (1995) Educating the survivors. *Journal of Business Strategy* 16(2), 28–37.

Redman, T. and Matthews, B. (1998) Service quality and human resource management: A review and research agenda. *Personnel Review* 27(1), 57–77.

Reece, B. and Brandt, R. (2008) *Effective Human Relations in Organizations* (10th edn). Boston (MA): Houghton Mifflin Company.

Riley, M. (1996) *Human Resource Management in the Hospitality and Tourism Industry*. Oxford: Butterworth-Heinemann.

Riley, M., Gore, J. and Kelliher, C. (2000) Economic determinism and human resource management practice in the hospitality and tourism industry. *Tourism and Hospitality Research* 2(2), 118–128.

Riley, M., Ladkin, A. and Szivas, E. (2002) *Tourism Employment: Analysis and Planning*. Clevedon: Channel View Publications.

Robinson, R. and Barron, P. (2007) Developing a framework for understanding the impact of deskilling and standardization on the turnover and attrition of chefs. *International Journal of Hospitality Management* 26, 913–926.

Rosenzweig-Fogel, R. and Therstrom, S. (1985) *Eight Hours for What we Will: Workers and Leisure in an Industrial City*. New York: Cambridge University Press.

Ross, G. (1997) Career stress responses among hospitality employees. *Annals of Tourism Research* 24(1), 41–51.

Ross, G.F. (1997) Career stress responses among hospitality employees. *Annals of Tourism Research* 24(1), 41–51.

Rousseau, D.M. (1995) *Psychological Contracts in Organizations: Understanding Written and Unwritten Agreements*. London: Sage Publications.

Rowley, G. and Purcell, K. (2001) 'As cooks go, she went': Is labour churn inevitable? *International Journal of Hospitality Management* 20, 163–85.

Rowley, G., Purcell, K., Richardson, M., Shackleton, R., Howe, S. and Whiteley, P. (2000) *Employers Skill Survey: Case Study – Hospitality Sector*. Nottingham, UK: Department for Education and Employment (DfEE).

Salaman, G. (1974) *Community and Occupation*. Cambridge: Cambridge University Press.

Salt, J., Clarke, J. and Wanner, P. (2004) *International Labour Migration*. Council of Europe Publishing, Directorate General III – Social Cohesion.

Sappey, R., Burgess, J., Lyons, M. and Buultjens, J. (2009) *Industrial Relations in Australia: Work and Workplaces* (2nd edn). Frenchs Forest, NSW: Pearson Australia.

Savannah Guides (2009) Handout provided by Ms Vicki Jones (Savannah Guides Manager).

Schlesinger, L. and Heskett, J. (1991) The service-driven company. *Harvard Business Review* September–October, 71–81.

Schneider, B. and Bowen, D.E. (1995) *Winning the Service Game*. Boston (MA): Harvard Business School Press.

Schneider, S. and Barsoux, J.L. (1997) *Managing Across Cultures*. London: Prentice Hall.

Schwartz, F. (1992) *Breaking with Tradition: Women and Work, the New Facts of Life*. New York: Warner.

Sheldon, P. (1993) Destination information systems. *Annals of Tourism Research* 20(4), 47–70.

Simons, R. (2005) Designing high performance jobs. *Harvard Business Review* July–August, 1–13.

Simons, T. and Hinkin, T. (2001) The effect of employee turnover on hotel profits: A test across multiple hotels. *Cornell Hotel and Restaurant Administration Quarterly* 42(4), 65–69.

Skinner, N. and Pocock, B. (2008) Work-life conflict: Is work time or work overload more important? *Asia Pacific Journal of Human Resources* 46(3), 303–315.

Smith, A. (2003) Recent trends in Australian training and development. *Asia Pacific Journal of Human Resources* 41(2), 231–244.

Source: TTNQ (2009) http://www.tropicalaustralia.com.au/_data/assets/pdf_file/0003/768072/TTNQ_Membership_prospectus_0910.pdf. Accessed June 2009.

Stone, R.J. (2008) *Managing human resources* (2nd Edition). Milton, Qld: John Wiley & Sons Australia Ltd.

Storey, J. (2007) *Human Resource Management: A Critical Text* (3rd edn). London: Thomson Learning.

Sullivan J. (2005) *Cost of Vacancy Formulas for Recruiting and Retention Managers.* http://www.ere.net/2005/07/25/cost-of-vacancy-formulas-for-recruiting-and-retention-managers. Accessed March 2009.

Szivas, E. (1999) The influence of human resources on tourism marketing. In F. Vellas and L. Becherel (eds) *The International Marketing of Travel and Tourism: A Strategic Approach.* London: Macmillan.

Taylor, R., Davies, D. and Savery, L. (2001) The role of appraisal and training in reducing staff turnover in the Western Australian accommodation industry. *Management Research News* 24(10/11), 56–57.

Teicher, J., Holland, P. and Gough, R. (2006) *Employee Relations Management: Australia in a Global Context.* Frenchs Forest, NSW: Pearson Education Australia.

Teo, S. (2002) Effectiveness as a corporate HR department in an Australian public sector entity during commercialization and corporatization. *International Journal of Human Resource Management* 13(1), 89–105.

Terkel, S. (1974) *Working: People Talk about What They Do All Day and How They Feel about What They Do.* New York: Pantheon Books.

Thachappilly, G. (2009) Personnel Management Expands into HR Management, *Human Resources Management. http://human-resources-management.suite101.com/article.cfm/personnel_management_expands_into_hr_management. Accessed February 2009.*

The Australian Leadership Foundation, http://www.learningtolearn.sa.edu.au/Colleagues/files/links/UnderstandingGenY.pdf. Accessed April 2009.

The World travel and Tourism Council (2006) Progress and Priorities 2005/06. http://www.wttc.org/bin/pdf/temp/progresspriorities05-06.html. Accessed February 2009.

Theibert, P.R. (1996) Train and degree them – anywhere. *Personnel Journal* 75(2), 28–32.

Thomas, D. (2006) Lawyers predict wave of whistleblowing once smoke ban comes in. *Personnel Today,* http://www.personneltoday.com/articles/2006/02/15/33948/lawyers-predict-wave-of-whistleblowing-once-smoke-ban-comes.html. Accessed September 2009.

Thomas, R.R. (1991) *Beyond Race and Gender: Unleashing the Power of Your Total Workforce by Managing Diversity.* New York: AMACOM.

Thompson, G. (2000) Where there's smoke. *HR Monthly* March, 31.

Thoms, P., Wolper, P., Scott, K. and Jones, D. (2001) The relationship between immediate turnover and employee theft in the restaurant industry. *Journal of Business and Psychology* 15(4), 561–577.

Thor, C.G. (2006) Performance Measurement: Models, Myths, Misuses, and Mistakes. World Federation of Productivity Science http://www.wcps.info/academy/thor.htm. Retrieved May 2009.

Timo, N. (1999) Contingent and retentive employment in the Australian hotel industry: reformulating the core-periphery model. *Australian Journal of Labour Economics* 21(4), 959–985.

Timo, N. and Davidson, M. (2005) A survey of employee relations practices and demographics of MNC chain and domestic luxury hotels in Australia. *Employee Relations* 27(2), 175–192.

Tong, C. (2009) http://www.ethnicmajority.com/glass_ceiling.htm. Accessed April, 2009.

Torrington, D. (1989) Human resource management and the personnel function. In J. Storey (ed.) *New Perspectives on Human Resource Management*. London: Routledge.

Towers Perrin. (2005) Winning strategies for a global workforce: Attracting, retaining, and engaging employee for competitive advantage. Towers Perrin Global Workforce Study, Executive Report TP449-05, Towers Perrin, Stamford, CT.

Townley, B. (1994) *Reframing HRM – Power Ethics and the Subject at Work*. London: Sage.

Trenberth, L., Dewe, P. and Walkey, F. (1999) Leisure and its role as a strategy for coping with work stress. *International Journal of Stress Management* 6(2), 89–103.

Trezise, E.K. (1996) An introduction to business ethics for human resource management teaching and research. *Personnel Review* 25(6), 87.

Ulrich, D., Halbrook, R., Meder, D., Stuchlik, M. and Thorpe, S. (1991) Employee and customer attachment: Synergies for competitive advantage. *Human Resource Planning* 14(2), 89–104.

Upchurch, R. (1998) Ethics in the hospitality industry: an applied model. *International Journal of Contemporary Hospitality Management* 10(6), 227–223.

Uren, L. (2007) From talent compliance to talent commitment. *Strategic HR Review* 6(3), 32–35.

van Barneveld, K. (2006) Hospitality. In P. Waring and M. Bray *Evolving Employment Relations: Industry Studies from Australia*, pp. 153–168. North Ryde, NSW: McGraw-Hill Australia.

VandenHeuvel, A. and Wooden, M. (2000) 'Immigrants' Labour Market Experiences in the Early Settlement Years. *Australian Bulletin of Labour* 26(1), 56–69.

VB (2007) www.tourismtrade.org.uk/MarketIntelligenceResearch/KeyTourismFacts.asp. Accessed February 2009.

Vinten, G. (1995) The whistleblower's charter. *Executive Development* 8(2), 25–28.

Von Bergen, C.W., Soper, B. and Foster, T. (2002), Unintended negative effects of diversity management. *Entrepreneur*, Summer 2002, http://www.entrepreneur.com/tradejournals/article/160542376_1.html. Accessed April 2009.

Walby, S. (2007) *Gender (in) Equality and the Future of Work*. Manchester: Equal Opportunities Commission.

Walenta, C. (2008) Diversity management discourse meets queer theory. *Gender in Management: An International Journal* 23(6), 382–394.

Watson, S. (1996) Productivity through people: The role of human resource management. In N. Johns (ed.) *Productivity Management in Hospitality and Tourism*. London: Cassell.

Weaver, A. (2009) Perceptions of job quality in the tourism industry: The views of recent graduates of a university's tourism management programme. *International Journal of Contemporary Hospitality Management* 5, 579–593.

Whatt, B. (2005) How to hire for cultural fit. *Human Resources* March, 14–15.

Wilcox, T. and Lowry, D. (2000) Beyond resourcefulness: casual workers and the human-centered organisation. *Business and Professional Ethics Journal* 19(3/4), 29–53.

Wildes, V. (2005) Stigma in foodservice work: How it affects restaurant servers' attention to stay in the business or recommend a job to another. *Tourism and Hospitality Research* 5(3), 213–233.

Witt, C.A. and Witt, S.F. (1989) Why productivity in the hotel sector is so low. *Journal Unknown* 1(2), 28–34.

Wood, J., Zeffane, R., Fromholtz, M. and Fitzgerald, A. (2006) *Organizational Behaviour: Core Concepts and Applications* (1st Australasian Edition). Australia: Wiley.

Woodd, M. (1997) Human resource specialists: Guardians of ethical conduct? *Journal of European Industrial Training* 21(3), 110–116.

World Bank (2004) Corporate society responsibility, www.worldbank.org/development communications/where1/environment/csr.htm

Worsfold, P. (1999) HRM, performance, commitment and service quality in the hotel industry. *International Journal of Contemporary Hospitality Management* 11(7), 340–348.

WTTC (2007) www.wttc.org/eng/Tourism_Research/Tourism_Satellite_Accounting. Accessed February 2009.

Yeung, A. (2006) Setting people up for success: How the Portman Ritz-Carlton Hotel gets the best from its people. *Human Resource Management* 45(2), 267–275.

INDEX